307. 42

Please return/renew this item
by the last date show.

To renew this item
call........ 01823 334344 (automated)
or.......... 0845 3459177
or visit........www.foursite.somerset.gov.uk

SOMERSET

County Council

I SO

1 3 0988843 2

ANOTHER COUNTRY

EDITED BY
MICHAEL MOSBACHER
AND
DIGBY ANDERSON

Published by The Social Affairs Unit

British Library Cataloguing in Publication Data
A catalogue record of this book is available from
the British Library

ISBN 0 907631 83 5

IN MEMORY OF EDGAR PALAMOUNTAIN

*The views expressed in this collection
represent the views of the individual authors,
not those of the Social Affairs Unit, its Trustees, Advisers or Director*

Book production and typesetting by Crowley Esmonde Ltd
Printed and bound in Great Britain by St Edmundsbury Press Ltd

Contents

The Authors

Dr Digby Anderson is founder Director of the Social Affairs Unit.

James Barrington was formerly the Executive Director of the League Against Cruel Sports and is now Director of the Wildlife Network.

Laurence Catlow is a teacher and the author of *Confessions of a Shooting and Fishing Man*.

Charles Clover is Environment Editor of the *Daily Telegraph*.

Dr Ian Crowe is an expert on Edmund Burke.

Professor Christie Davies is Professor of Sociology at the University of Reading.

David Edelsten is hunting correspondent for *Country Life*.

Professor Antony Flew is Emeritus Professor of Philosophy at the University of Reading.

Dr Frank Furedi is a lecturer in sociology at the University of Kent at Canterbury.

Dr Charles Goodson-Wickes is a barrister and physician. He was the MP for Wimbledon and the former Chairman of the Countryside Alliance.

Robin Hanbury-Tenison is an explorer and the former Chief Executive of the Countryside Alliance.

Professor Stuart Harrop is Professor of Wildlife Management Law at the Durrell Institute of Conservation and Ecology.

Dr Richard Howarth is a leading agricultural economist.

Jeremy Hunt is a writer and journalist specialising in livestock production and is an expert on hill farming.

Dr Jan Lester lectures in philosophy at the University of Middlesex.

Leanda de Lisle is country life columnist for *The Spectator* and a farmer's wife.

Leo McInstry is a writer and journalist.

Professor Keith Madelin is Professor of Civil Engineering at Birmingham University and is the former County Surveyor for Shropshire.

Robin Malim is a Fellow of the Royal Agricultural Society and Chairman of the Velcourt Group, a farming business.

Dr John Maloney is a lecturer in economics at the University of Exeter.

Michael Mosbacher is the Programme Manager of the Social Affairs Unit.

Dr Mark Neal is a lecturer in industrial sociology at the Aston Business School, Aston University.

Charles Nodder was Director of External Affairs at the Game Conservancy Trust and is a writer and public affairs consultant.

Richard North is an Environmental Health Officer, leading expert on food hygiene, a writer and a journalist.

Catherine Paice is a writer and journalist on land and agricultural issues.

Dr Mark Pennington is a lecturer in geography at the London School of Economics.

Elizabeth Peplow is features editor of *Horse and Hound*.

Dr Aidan Rankin was a press officer for Survival International and is a writer and researcher.

Anthony Rosen is an agricultural writer and lead columnist for *Farming News*.

Helen Searls was managing editor of *LM* magazine and is now a columnist for the magazine.

Professor Ian Swingland is founder of the leading Durrell Institute of Conservation and Ecology at the University of Kent at Canterbury.

Linda Whetstone is a Trustee of the Institute of Economic Affairs and is a leading dressage judge.

Diana Winsor is the author of several books on the British countryside.

Jane Wright is a business finance analyst working for a major institution in the City.

Country people as an oppressed minority: an introduction

Michael Mosbacher and Digby Anderson

Minorities

Say 'minority', and one thinks of blacks, homosexuals or even of 'minorities' which are, statistically, majorities, such as women. The term is no longer statistical. Today people are a minority if those in power are ignorant about them, prejudiced against them and discriminate against them. Minorities are, often, poor, though as the case of rich women shows, the presence among them of some rich people does nothing to invalidate the minority's right to be a minority. Minorities, we are told, deserve our sympathy, just as those who oppress them deserve our condemnation.

There is a minority in Britain today which is not on the usual lists. It is country people, those who live, work and enjoy themselves in the country. As with women, the country people include some very rich members. But they also include those with the lowest wages and the most arduous jobs. So miserable are some country people that they have some of the highest suicide rates in the population. Country people's jobs and livelihoods are currently threatened and so is their culture, including their traditional leisure pursuits. The threats come mostly from policy-makers and activists who live in large cities, especially London, but also from an urban population that no longer knows much of country ways. The reality of country life is quite different from the ideas about the country entertained by these politicians and city people. The true country is another country.

Until recently the country was ignored. It does not feature on any of the political agendas of the political parties during the last quarter century. Being ignored has its problems. But it was better than the new state of affairs in which the country is being interfered with by people whose long lack of interest in it has rendered them ignorant about it. Country issues are now on the political agenda and country people are being patronised and discriminated against. Those ignorantly interfering with them fall into four main groups. There are activists, sentimentalists, modernisers and regulators. They are the enemies of the countryside. They may not be witting enemies. They often believe that they are helping, improving or saving the countryside. They may even speak of their love for the English countryside. They are its enemies nonetheless.

Activists

The 1980s saw the demise of thorough-going socialism as a political cause. The vacuum has largely been filled by single issue politics. For the urban activist looking for a cause to employ his commitment, his spleen or just his busying, lobbying, restless, improving activism, the countryside offers an enticing menu. Road building can be denounced, hunters harried and the treatment of farm animals denounced. There are 'rights' to be discovered and pursued such as the right to roam. There are conspiracies against the public good to be exposed such as the contamination or the destruction of wilderness and the use of pesticides. To those whose political way of life is utopianising, exposing, denouncing, lobbying, issuing reports, campaigning and legislating, the countryside is a brave new world to be exploited. It is all the more enticing because there are old and familiar enemies there. The age-old hate objects of socialism, the employer, the owner and the rich are still there in the country to be hated. And there, with a little imagination, in stereotype: unscrupulous landowners raping the land and exploiting tenants; red-faced powerful men on horses threatening defenceless animals; and the multi-national corporation, despoiling the land with deadly pesticides and then deceiving urban mothers into poisoning their children with contaminated food.

Sentimentalists

Observers with very divergent political sympathies have noticed the rise of a new politics, a politics of gesture and spin, of sentiment rather than reason and commitment. In this politics, the goal is not a reasoned analysis and a coherent, realistic policy but a line which will play well on the media by mobilising sympathy and sentiment. Nowhere is it more the case than with country matters. The sentimentalist idealises the countryside. It is a park. She likes it to be as undisturbed as possible.

For her the requirements of those who earn their living there – roads, machines, houses – are a nuisance. She is agitated by modern artificial farming methods; indeed by anything which is not 'natural'. In so far as her idea of the natural means anything, it means not touched by man which rather rules out those who work in the country and tame it. It means also things as they were but she is not sure of when. In fact, of course, the countryside of parkland, rivers, trees, birds is very much the result of man's activity. Most of all the sentimentalist is exercised about animals. She has never seen a chicken coop scattered with 20 dead chickens killed by a fox or wondered what would become of animals if they lived naturally. Like 98 per cent of urban dwellers she eats meat while excoriating those who do what is necessary to provide it for her at the low prices she demands.

Modernisers

The common justification for contemporary political projects – such as reforming the House of Lords, dismantling the traditional Union of England and Scotland, introducing proportional representation or involving women and homosexuals in the front-line military – is not one of the usual ones such as equality or justice. It is that the project is 'modern'. Sometimes it is not clear just what 'modern' means. But, that apart, it is clear what it does not mean, what it is opposed to, and that is 'tradition'. Traditions can be justified but not in the language of modernity. At first glance they may look pointless. If they have a point it will usually be found slowly by taking part in them rather than in an argument. It is unfortunate for the countryside in these modernising times that it is rich in tradition. It is not only the home of the hereditary peerage, of shooting, hunting, fishing, of 'feudalistic' landlords but of old churches, traditional knowledge about animals and plants, and traditional village communities. The modernising project would sweep aside much of this. The countryside must become a part of the new country; it too must be a land of opportunity for all, governed for the many, not the few. Sporting estates must be replaced with leisure facilities for all the family; hunting must be replaced with rambling; and the hereditary peerage replaced with representatives of a youthful nation. Worst of all from the point of view of country traditions, this is to be done in the name of what is modern. There can be no answer to that once it is accepted as the sole criterion.

Regulators

Regulation is often the aim of activists, sentimentalists and modernisers. The activist wants the countryside put right. The sentimentalist does not care much about the effect of regulation but shows her commitment by publicly alarming for regulation. The moderniser sees regulation as a rational way of bringing the countryside and the traditional institutions it harbours up to date. But regulators are also guided by another motive. Modern society is risk-averse. The modern idea is that accidents should not happen and that safety should be guaranteed by regulation. The countryside needs regulating to stop threats to safety occurring and other hazards. According to the precautionary principle, now sanctioned by the European Union, every risk – however minute or unproven – should be avoided and can be, if the right rules are in place. If regulation is introduced to, say, counter food poisoning and people are still being poisoned, that just proves that more regulation is needed. If planning regulation is failing, it just needs to be tightened up. If agricultural subsidies do not achieve the called-for objective, they can be tinkered with to iron out a few problems. And if regulation has unforeseen consequences, then there is always another bit of regulation to sort them out.

Countryside under greater threat than ever before

Modern political culture then is characterized by these tendencies to activism, sentimentalism, modernising and regulation. As such it is a culture likely to find itself at odds with much of what happens in the country. Never before has there been such a confluence of forces whose aims and objectives are all so profoundly antithetical to the countryside. The new tendencies can, of course, be opposed to each other and those who support them. For instance the moderniser and sentimentalist may be different sorts of people. Yet their attitudes collectively amount to a massive attack upon the rural way of life.

This book has brought together a wide range of authors to examine the nature of these threats. They do not necessarily share each other's opinions, or those in this opening chapter but they do think the countryside is under threat and they do think that urban ignorance, the ignorance of those who make policy which affects the countryside, is a key problem. The country is not as many see it. There are myths about the countryside and the authors identify several of them.

Myth: country people especially farmers and hunters are cruel
Curiously many urban people *underestimate* the death and pain that
goes on in the country. Many animals experience pain and die before
their possible lifespan for a variety of causes which have nothing to do
with man. This suffering and death appears to be of no interest to the
urban sentimentalist. What he has latched onto is the idea that animals
have rights and these are being denied by cruel countrymen. In a
detailed analysis the philosopher, Antony Flew argues that the idea of
animal rights runs counter to any sustainable notion of rights. For, if
one accepts a notion of rights, what must these be based upon? The
only basis for such rights which draws on more than pure abstraction
can be reciprocity, ie, that I am entitled to be treated in a certain way,
or more accurately not to be treated in certain ways, because I am
obligated not to treat others in certain ways. Such mutual sentient
obligations clearly cannot be held between animals or between animals
and humans.

Yet the policy presumptions of animal rights are high on the political
agenda. This can be seen in the debates on hunting, the live transport
of animals and intensive farming. The animal rights view does not
come from being in the country and being close to animals. It comes
from human political philosophy transposed onto animals.

And even when town dwellers do go to the country they may not
see the truth. As Catherine Paice points out, children taken on visits to
city and suburban farms do not see the realities of living and working
in the countryside within sustainable, holistic systems that recognise
the circles of life and death, predators and pest control . Urban children
are given a sanitised view of the countryside at these places. They are
not confronted with the everyday reality of animal death. The situation
is made worse by our society's profound squeamishness about death.
The discussion of death and mortality has become taboo. The urban
populace does not connect its food with living and breathing animals.
For it, food is pre-packaged and comes from the supermarket. Nor
does the urban mother connect the intensive farming portrayed in a
30-second, edited television clip with her own desire for cheap food.

When the city is briefly faced with the reality of animal life and
animal death in the countryside, it uses the only tools it has at its
disposal – sentimentality and anthropomorphism. For many the only
contact with animals is a cat or a dog treated as a companion and
endowed with human emotions. The *kitsch* sold in pet shops goes to
show just how far this sentimentalisation has gone. Urban children

are far more likely to obtain their lasting mental image of pigs, sheep, and deer from the fantasy of the talking, singing dancing animals found in *Babe* or *Bambi* than from the farmyard or the moor. By these standards the farmer or the hunter will inevitably always appear to be a cruel, heartless killer.

Charles Goodson-Wickes describes how activists use the sensitivities and emotional responses of the sentimentalist for their own purposes. The sentimentalists' knee-jerk reaction to carefully selected images underpins much of the support for ill-thought out legislation. But the city dweller can soon forget the consequences of such legislation. It is the countryside which must live with, and suffer the consequences.

The urban attitude to animals must become more realistic if calls for such legislation are to recede. Only when suburban children realise that the purpose of 'My Little Pony' is to chase 'My Little Fox', say Christie Davies and Mark Neal, will the notion of the cruel countryside, and all the misguided policies flowing from that notion, be surmountable. Only this will cut the ground from under the activist. For myths about the cruel countryside are at the very core of the attack on the rural way of life.

Myth: the abolition of country sports would make us a more civilised nation

Britain has a land green and pleasant in parts and brown and barren in others. Field sportsmen and responsible farmers, argues Charles Nodder, should show the urban decision-makers why it is that the boundaries between the two fall where they do. Country sports are the cornerstone of the management of wildlife, and its habitats. Much of the current appearance of the countryside is owed to country sports. Banning country sports would make our countryside less diverse.

It is country sports which give an economic value to wildlife, explains Ian Swingland . It is this value which accounts for the efforts put into preserving wildlife. The animals which flourish are those which are of value to man; restricting country sports would reduce the value of the fox, the deer, the pheasant and the grouse. This would have inevitable consequences. Why expend effort in preserving habitats and the species themselves if they are no longer of any benefit and in many instances of detriment? The methods, patterns and practices used in the countryside – in the valuing of wildlife, but also the management of land, the grazing of animals – have evolved over many hundreds of years. Stuart Harrop shows that it is not possible to tinker with just one facet of a complex eco-system without affecting many others. Tampering with delicate interrelationships between species (including the human species) is invariably perilous. Yet politicians are contemplating, or rather assuming postures, about the banning of hunting, and possibly shooting and fishing – the arguments are similar – without taking any account of the wider effects these will have. This is an illustration of the modern politician's desire to do something, anything for gestural effect without consideration of the consequences.

Image is, in several ways, what counts. The realities of the welfare of foxes is not the issue. James Barrington, the former head of the League Against Cruel Sports, shows the only way a ban on hunting may lead to a utopia for foxes is in the literal meaning of 'utopia', nowhere. Elizabeth Peplow argues that New Labour truly reflects the values of middle-class suburban Britain – its disregard for dress codes, table manners, school uniforms. The coincidence of anti-ritualism and political correctness in the burgeoning middle classes, and its reflection in its elected representatives and institutions, has meant trouble for the red-coated hunter. The fact that the red-coated hunter is more myth than reality matters little. That is the image and it is image which counts. Just pointing out its falseness will not save hunting. Hunting is identified with ritual. If the moderniser hates one thing above all, it is ritual. The inherent worth of the rituals of hunting must be defended for the tradition, decency and form they give to what would otherwise be just another pastime. The true value of hunting lies in these rituals. This becomes even more important since hunting is one of the last bastions of ritual.

What is being attacked is not cruelty, or even hunting itself. The activists' aim is to outlaw those who hunt – not simply by the legal banning of hunting but also by turning hunt supporters into moral outcasts, argues Helen Searls. Here modern Britain shows its true colours. It cannot accept values and lifestyles other than its own. Hunting does not fit into the new urban homogeneity. The consequences of banning hunting cannot be known for sure – but one thing is certain. It would make Britain a less civilised country.

Myth: there is a right to roam

We have seen that one attraction of the anti-hunting cause is that it provides an opportunity to re-open the class war. This is even more the case with the pursuit of the right to roam. On one side is the greedy rich landowner wanting to keep the countryside to himself and, no doubt, to exploit it for profit. On the other hand are the distinctly unwealthy urban masses being barred from a little innocent ramble. As the right-to-roam activist, and leading figure in The Land is Ours, George Monbiot once put it: our exclusion from rural Britain is the most manifest of class barriers.

If emotive calls for the right to roam are class-fuelled, they are also unrealistic. As Robin Hanbury-Tenison shows, they take no account of the realities on the ground. Such calls ignore the vast amount of work done by landowners, to preserve the rural environment, the 2.5 million acres already open to the public due to landowners' permission, and the damage a presumption of access would do to farming and conservation efforts.

What those calling for a right to roam are attacking is the very notion of private property. They are revelling in the age-old hatred of wealth and privilege. They are, in fact, calling for the expropriation of land. For in what way does one still meaningfully own land if one cannot decide who may or may not use it? The activists of old were merely more honest. When they wanted to expropriate land they said so openly. Today's activist seeks to expropriate land, offer no compensation, and then call it the right to roam. The debate, points out Jan Lester, is not really about forbidden Britain versus the right to roam; it is about the licence to trespass versus the right to own.

Myth: the countryside has been contaminated by greedy farmers and the agrochemical industry

We have already encountered the view that Nature is pure, clean, undefiled until sullied by man. This is particularly advanced against modern man, and modern corporate man. Modern agriculture is bad because it uses scientific methods; organic farming is good because it is natural. Simplistic dualisms such as this play an important part in the attack upon the countryside. They have been prominent in food scares. Greedy farmers and producers using unnatural methods have been blamed for BSE, salmonella in eggs, food poisoning, and alleged cancer risks from agrochemicals. Regulators, as Richard North shows, have used these scares to push for ever more regulation. After all, they argue, no costs are too high when human life is concerned. But what is forgotten is that these unnatural methods have, without doubt, made food safer today than ever before. Food poisoning, for example, only accounts for about 50 deaths per year out of an annual UK death rate of around 500,000. CJD, whatever its cause may be, has been responsible for considerably fewer. There is no proven link between modern agrochemicals and cancer, and most respectable scientists would argue that such a link is extremely unlikely. And the costs of such regulation – in the destruction of time honoured practices, human misery and the closure of otherwise viable businesses – is simply ignored. The ever-increasing regulation of food production amounts to a swingeing tax upon the countryside. It has meant that regulation appears to be the only rural growth industry. And the regulation has, in instances, made food less safe. For example one of the primary causes of food poisoning from meat is contamination caused by meat inspectors handling freshly killed carcasses.

Unnatural practices are feared in much the same way today as they were in the Victorian era. It is just the nature of what is deemed unnatural that has changed. Witness the current debate about genetically-modified crops. Many scientifically questionable arguments are peddled against them, but what the activist and the sentimentalist alike really object to about them is that they are unnatural, that they were developed in laboratories. The same, however, is true – as Robin Malim points out – of all the advances in agriculture which mean that a fraction of those once employed on the land can now produce more varied, better quality, cheaper food to cater for the ever fussier demands of a growing urban populace. The attacks upon GMOs are in fact an attack upon modern agriculture itself.

Taking this to its obvious conclusion such illustrious champions of organic farming as Prince Charles ask, would it not be nicer if farmers could go back to the natural methods of their forebears? But, as Leanda De Lisle shows, organic farming – currently accounting for a mere 0.3 per cent of land use in Britain and 0.06 per cent of agricultural output – can never be the future of mainstream agriculture. Suggesting otherwise is like believing that Jermyn Street shirts can be the future of British menswear. Most urban consumers are simply not prepared to pay extra for organic produce. They may pay lip service to organic food in surveys, but they do not buy it. As Alastair Leake of CWS Agriculture put it, 'all the surveys done show that people think organic farming is wonderful and if they were faced with the choice of buying organic food, then they would buy it. But when faced with the reality, which is that the product is sometimes inferior to look at and always more expensive, then people start to shift.' The urban supermarket shopper may be right in her decision, for the environmental arguments for organic farming over conventional methods are far from clear –

modern chemicals are considerably less harmful than natural copper sulphate and sulphur used by organic farmers. But even if modern agriculture were despoiling the countryside, who would really be to blame for this – the farmer simply meeting the demand for ever cheaper food or the urban consumer creating that demand? It is no good urban sentimentalists bewailing the methods of modern agriculture if they are not willing to pay the extra for less intensively produced food.

The agrochemical industry and farmers are not the only sources of pollution which the activists see in the countryside. There is also that ever handy villain, alcohol. The activist is, rightly, concerned by fatalities caused through drink driving and demands that further action be taken. But this action does not involve cracking down on the small number of hardened habitual drink drivers who are the real menace. That would be too difficult. Instead the regulator has come up with the proposal of reducing the legal level of blood alcohol from 80mg per 100ml (about 2 pints) to 50mg per 100ml (about 1¼ pints). But will such a change save lives? John Maloney shows that such claims are based upon one highly dubious American survey and another which shows no basis for lowering drink-drive limits. New, tighter regulations are thus being considered without any valid basis. The impact such regulation might have upon country pubs – many of whom have too few customers within walking distance to be viable – and the livelihood of publicans is simply ignored. Politicians are keen to talk of community, but are considering imposing a regulation which is not needed and is not shown to have any benefits but which could destroy many rural livelihoods and the focal point of many rural communities.

Myth: the countryside is being choked through road building and development

Roads themselves are, of course, a central concern of activists. The road protester has become the symbol of activism in the 1990s. These protesters claim they are defending the countryside. But defending the countryside for whom? Certainly not the people living in the countryside. Keith Madelin shows that an improved road system is essential if rural life is to be sustained. Rural roads are facing the fastest growth in traffic volumes. This will continue as more women acquire driving licenses and the proportion of elderly drivers increases. If rural roads are not improved, the road system will simply be unable to cope. Apart from the environmental impact of this, it will drastically reduce the standard of living in rural communities. For the country person a car is not a luxury, but essential just to carry out the mundane tasks of everyday life from doing the weekly shopping to picking children up from school.

Activists talk of improving public transport. This may well be a sensible policy for the cities. But public transport can never adequately cater for rural communities. Less densely populated, more dispersed communities simply cannot adequately be catered for by public transport. Only private cars can provide the flexibility needed for country life to function. When the road protesters call for an end to road building, they are threatening the freedom of country dwellers in a very tangible sense. Road protesters are largely urban, middle-class, disaffected youths who have swallowed an ideological mantra whole. They cannot see that, far from protecting the countryside, they are doing their best to destroy it.

Are roads necessarily eyesores? This is the question addressed by Charles Clover. There are all sorts of societies to protect this part of our heritage or that kind of hedge, but no-one stands up for England's historic roads. Some modern roads, though necessary, are undoubtedly aesthetically displeasing. But many roads are masterpieces of engineering, spectacularly cutting through magnificent countryside. They can be objects of real beauty. Others are at least as historically significant as many of Britain's great houses. Perhaps it is time not just to defend roads on utilitarian grounds, but to actively embrace them as an integral part of our heritage.

When the regulators talk of protecting the countryside, they usually mean greenbelts and land-use planning more generally. But these very policies have harmed rural communities and damaged the environment. As both Mark Pennington and Linda Whetstone argue, land-use planning has forced up the price of property in the countryside by restricting supply, meaning that fewer rural dwellers can afford to buy homes. Organic communities of those living and working in the countryside are thus undermined in favour of the weekend cottage owners. This is now widely acknowledged.

What they also show is that the very kind of low grade, monotonous, poorly designed housing the preservation lobby is – justifiably – most hostile to, is encouraged by land-use planning. For the high cost of land and the limited occasions when developers do get planning permission has meant that developers try to cram as much housing as possible into an area when planning consent is granted. This can be contrasted to the more piecemeal, scattered and sensitive modern housing found in rural France, Italy and Spain where planning controls are less draconian. Land-use planning and greenbelts are thus not the friends of the countryside many erroneously believe them to be. The rural developments which are most hated date from after the introduction of wholesale planning controls in 1948; the ones which the preservationists most admire are virtually without exception pre-1948.

Myth: the charming countryside can serve as the city's playground

The sentimentalist often sees the countryside merely as a quaint place to be visited when town life becomes oppressive It is a relaxing place in which to unwind and forget the worries of everyday life. She can even daydream of moving to the countryside, downshifting, getting out of the rat race. Using the example of the hill farmer, Jeremy Hunt shows how very different the reality of rural life is to this. Instead of leading the contemplative good life, the hill farmer must work far longer hours, far more arduously than the vast majority of city dwellers. He must contend with the vagaries of the weather and the changing – these days inevitably falling – price of sheep. And for this his rewards may be as little as £8,000 per year. The image and reality of the hill farmer's life may be wider apart than that of most country occupations, yet it is symptomatic of the wider picture.

Sentimentalists do not understand that such genuine country people cannot afford to romanticise the countryside as a charming quiet rural backwater. They cannot afford to preserve the countryside as the picture-book idyll of a 1930s *Miss Marple* television set. The city must be made to realise that the countryside has its own concerns, that it plays a central part in the economy, and that development is a necessity – argues Jane Wright .

How modern Britain's values are threatening the countryside

What underpins the various conflicts between the countryside and the city is a profound lack of understanding in the city of the rural way of life. But it is more than this. It is a clash of cultures. Modern Britain simply cannot accept the rural way of life. The countryside is threatened by modern Britain in two ways. The first of these is subtle. It is the threat that the modern ethos is adopted by the countryside. Leo McInstry warns against this. There is a danger that the countryside, instead of defending and extolling its way of life, will play the modern game. That is the game of special pleading and the subsidy culture. The countryside will not have won if all it gains is subsidies for post offices and village shops. It will merely have joined the modern hand-out culture of believing it has been hard done by and needs a hand-out in recompense.

The modern subsidy culture is not a salvation for anything. Its disastrous effects can be seen in what it has done to farmers' incomes. The general ills of the Common Agricultural Policy have been widely discussed elsewhere and are not our concern here. But one would have thought that a vast, highly expensive regime of subsidies would at the very least boost farmers' incomes. Richard Howarth demonstrates that the CAP has not even achieved this. In fact farming must be the only area where real incomes fell by over 50 per cent between 1970 and 1990. The modern subsidy culture offers no future to the countryside. All that subsidies have achieved is the fostering of misplaced resentment against farmers and the countryside's voice being lost on other issues.

The second is more direct. As Aidan Rankin, Frank Furedi, and Laurence Catlow all argue, the moderniser's problem with the countryside is that he cannot understand its values – they are so different from his own. Not only does he know little about it, he is intolerant when its values diverge from his. This is one minority he will not support. Indeed, he is doing his best to destroy it.

So, although education, the education of urban policy-makers and their supporters in the realities of country life, is part of the answer, it is not enough. The countryside 'debate' is not a debate. It is a clash of cultures. The countryside has no wish to impose its culture on the city. But the city – or rather those in it who subscribe to a culture of sentimentality and activism, of modernising and regulating – does wish to impose its culture on the country. Perhaps the realisation of the sheer arrogance and intolerance of this project might do something to defeat it.

1

Cruelty: urban sentimentality versus the realities of rural life

Catherine Paice

Pets are sentimentalised and anthropomorphised as never before. Two billion pounds are spent on them per year in the UK. When urban sentimentalists think of animals, they think of pets. They are ignorant of the cycles of animal life and animal death found in the countryside. The cheap meat found in supermarkets is simply not associated with living and breathing animals. Sentimentalists complain about the treatment of farm animals. Yet they do not connect this to their own desire for cheap food. The urban consumer proclaims her support for less intensive farming, but is simply unwilling to pay the price for it. If consumers see images of the treatment of farm animals they do not like, then they are as much to blame as the farmers. But it is the farmers who are blamed.

A gruesome picture landed on my desk. It shows what appears to be, by its reddish hue, a skinned cattle head, damp and shiny, the eye rolled down in its socket. The head is being sprayed with an azure blue paint. Behind it is a stockpile of azure blue cattle heads, their eyes staring straight out of the page.

This photograph adorns the front cover of a report entitled *BSE: The Cost of a Crisis*, published by the National Audit Office. Inside, the picture caption explains that it shows the application of Patent Blue V dye to the head of a cow, one of the controls to ensure specified risk material does not enter the food chain.

BSE, British farming, and animal welfare

Well over six million cows and calves have been slaughtered under the various Government schemes introduced since March 20th, 1996.

That was the day when the Secretary of State for Health announced the possibility of a link between Bovine Spongiform Encephalopathy (BSE) in cattle and a new variant of Creutzfeldt-Jakob Disease (CJD) in humans. The events leading up to and stemming from his statement have resulted in the summary destruction of a third of our national cattle herd.

It could take many more years to establish, or disprove, that link scientifically. No-one close to the livestock industry could dispute that the drive to intensify the production of cheap meat was leading to practices that could not be condoned – whether or not farmers understood their implications. As farmers are among those who have lost touch with the food chain beyond the price of the product they are eating or producing, it seems fair to assume that the vast majority did not. Ten years ago, as BSE began to rear its ugly head, it was something of a joke among *bon vivant* members of the farming press that some of the worst food you could be offered – of the tinned meat and limp lettuce variety – was on farms.

The enormity of what MAFF and the farming end of the food industry had allowed to happen required draconian measures. The ongoing Government inquiry into BSE continues to reveal the complacency, cost cutbacks, communication problems and failure to address early signals evident more than ten years ago. We have now spent three years seeing lorry load upon lorry load of apparently healthy cows and heifers driven off to be incinerated because a political decision had to be made to avert what could have been an infinitely greater crisis. In the interests of public health, the fate of these animals has gone virtually unnoticed. That this should slip past the animal welfare flag-wavers presents an irony. Not a word has been breathed by the Royal Society for the Prevention of Cruelty to Animals, or by anyone else outside the farming press.

The sentimentalisation of animal life contrasts with reality of animal deaths

We are a nation which is in danger of elevating the status of animals – both domestic and wild – to heights unknown outside the United States of America, and we are threatening to follow US citizens into a state of split personality with regard to animals.

While we croon over pet cemeteries and celebrate the advent of pet supermarts, mushrooming as the latest local convenience to supply and fuel our love of domesticated creatures, there is not one farmer in the country who has not felt the impact of seeing those millions of living creatures led off to the slaughterhouses of hell. It is overtly manifest by the sharp increase in farmer suicides, but such is the knock-on effect of this crisis that it is implicit in farmyard conversations every day, everywhere.

A great many farmers will never recover from the devastation of seeing animal upon animal carted off to meet an untimely death as scheme upon scheme is introduced in a bid to convince our European partners that we are rid of this pestilence. It has been an undignified, unmitigated horror of shame and disaster, unparalleled in the history of agriculture.

Farmers bear the consequences of townies' healthist *angst*
Farmers are men and women who face life and death with equal equanimity, as a fact of life. The cost to them has been far more than financial. The BSE crisis will have cost some £3.5 billion by the year 2000. The vast majority do not look at their animals only as a cash crop. They are genuinely fond of them in the way that the animal sentimentalists can hardly understand.

If you journey from the Welsh borders down into the south west, you will now find whole tracts of the countryside bereft of cows. Its landscapes, its management by those who derive their living from it, and the natural maintenance of soil fertility and quality is dependent on grazing stock that is no longer there to do its job. For those farmers whose drive towards profitability was jeopardising their common sense towards animal husbandry, this will have brought them up short.

Does this animal genocide reach the hearts and minds of the very people it is designed to protect? Not a bit of it. The billions of pounds being spent on quality assurance and welfare schemes to monitor what goes from the farm into the food chain – most of the cost of which is being borne by farmers – has scarcely begun to make an impact on consumer purchasing patterns.

When BSE broke, the sales of pork and chicken – which are the most intensively produced meat products in this country – soared. Over 80 per cent of total meat sales is through the multiples, who are using their massive buying power while beef exports are banned to dictate stringent terms of production and price. One moment they pay lip service to buying British, and to trumpeting the high welfare standards of British meat, and then they drop British products in favour of buying more cheaply from countries which do not have the same welfare standards.

Consumers unwilling to pay extra for non-intensive, quality-assured meat...

Rules are being imposed on farmers which insult those who pride themselves on good husbandry. If that is the way to impose stringency in welfare and standards, so be it. But we as consumers must accept that we cannot impose rules without following them through. We are forcing farmers to pay for welfare-friendly systems and then turning round and buying cheaper meat from unspecified sources.

If Richard and Louise still insist on loading the Discovery with supplies of prepacked supermarket meat before each visit to their rural retreat in Dorset, buying predominantly on price, what hope is there for those whose purse strings are more tightly drawn. How will Keith and Julie be persuaded about the principles of good, healthy food?

It is disheartening to see so many families on the weekly shop, calculator in hand, spending three times the amount they need to on packaged and processed food, and paying least for staple food products whose origins and means of production will soon be traceable from shop to farm gate.

As we lurch from health crisis to health crisis, it must be time to take stock of ourselves and our motives. The bottom line is that the desire for cheap food promotes intensive farming. We can blame the Common Agricultural Policy, but most of all we have ourselves to blame. Higher production is leading to metabolic and physiological stresses on animals. For the sake, at least, of all those murdered cows, BSE must teach us a fundamental lesson. The basic premise of life is that you are what you eat.

...But spending £1.4 billion to feed pets

Against this we have a population with at least one pet in more than half of every household in the country. We own 6.6 million dogs, 7.7 million cats, eight million caged birds and three million small mammals. From the mouths of our children we direct £1.4 billion annually to feed animals alternately fawned over and ignored, that pollute areas of public enjoyment and are kept cooped up for hours on end in unsuitable environments and confined spaces. The cost of food, treats, accessories, grooming, boarding and vets' fees runs to two billion pounds a year.

Urban cruelty to animals

The number of people prosecuted by the Royal Society for the Prevention of Cruelty to Animals rose by almost a quarter in 1977, with calls to the society averaging one every 22 seconds. The number of people convicted of cruelty rose from 971 in 1996 to 1,195 in 1997, with cats and dogs the most common victims.

We are a nation of animal lovers. Looking after an animal involves care, cost and commitment – a premise which good farmers have recognised for centuries. We are also a nation of people who like to keep alligators in our back gardens for fun, who subscribe to a fashion for keeping wildcats as accessories, who have to be reminded not to keep dogs shut up in cars on a warm day.

Among the convictions was a student who admitted cooking a live hedgehog in a microwave oven. One chap bit his girlfriend's gerbil to death, a revenge attack after she killed his goldfish. A man who had a collection of 170 exotic creatures was jailed after admitting causing unnecessary suffering to reptiles, birds and snakes kept in 49 tanks and cages in Swindon. An 11-year-old girl found her rabbits stabbed to death with a screwdriver after she appeared on the *Barrymore* show to sing a song about them. A man killed three rabbits with a hammer because his children would not look after them.

Sentimentalists perceive rural cruelty, yet know nothing of rural realities

This catalogue of cruelty does not mitigate wrongful care and attention of farm animals and wildlife. But children taken on visits to city and suburban farms are lied to. This is not the reality of living and working in the countryside within sustainable, holistic systems that recognise the circles of life and death, predators and pest control.

The sentimental motives of people who drag thousands of pets through their miserable lives are a manifestation of the elevation of feelings above reason. While the money they are taxed is being spent on promoting farming systems that allow farm animals the freedom to move and relate to each other as nature intended, their pets are imprisoned.

Pets have become a status symbol, a symbol of a consumer society that is more concerned with what it owns than what it eats, a society that perceives cruelty by farmers towards livestock, but fails to respond to the fate of those millions of fine cows that have been killed to ensure that British meat is safe.

For many, the self-indulgent obsession with animals will substitute for the affections and responsibilities due to their nearest and dearest. This is something with which farmers' spouses will sympathise – but the farmers' motive is livelihood. Few who devote their work to animals will consciously abuse them.

If animals are treated badly, the nation as a whole responsible, not just farmers

The myth is that farmers preside over the killing fields of the countryside, sacrificing an appreciation of animals to greed. The reality is that it is the sentimentality and greed of the nation as a whole that is leading to a distortion of values.

Consider the Jungian concept: sentimentality is a superstructure covering brutality. There is an inherent paradox in a people which trumpets animal welfare and rights, yet rears its young on violent videos and computer games, endorses the brutality of cheap food production, and fosters the keeping of pets in unsuitable environments.

While we pay lip service to animal welfare in our own homes, farmers are paying for it with their lives and livelihoods. Unless Britain's much-vaunted love of animals is translated to our pets and our plates, that love will be held up as the real myth.

2

Cruelty: the activist's rhetorical device

Charles Goodson-Wickes

In the current debate on the treatment of animals, the word 'cruelty' is frequently flung about. Farmers need to be further regulated because they are 'cruel' to their animals; hunting must be banned because it is 'cruel'. But what is rarely asked is what cruelty actually means. Charles Goodson-Wickes shows that the bandying about of the term merely obfuscates complex issues. It conflates the time-honoured traditions of the hunter with the brutish, mindless cruelty of the urban thug. The activist has used the image of cruelty as a device to whip up resentment against faceless country people.

The myths of cruelty in the countryside can be illustrated with this story. Two shooters were on their way to a morning's rough shooting with their shotguns broken over their shoulders, when from across the canal, an angler shouted: 'You cruel bastards! Shooting harmless birds!' As the shooters retreated, a fish took bait, and he began to play in the hooked fish, with great delight. What could be more subjective than the concept of animal cruelty? We all understand and condemn sadism, where an animal is captured and tortured for the sole and explicit purpose of enjoying its suffering. Yet whenever we are talking about an acknowledged and legitimate use of animals, such as for food, companionship or sport, there is a wide spectrum of opinion over what constitutes cruelty and what does not.

The word 'cruelty' widely misused

To John Bryant, leading light of the League Against Cruel Sports, owning a pet dog is cruel. As he says in his book, *Fettered Kingdoms*: 'Let us allow the dog to disappear from our brick and concrete jungles

– from our firesides, from the leather nooses and chains by which we enslave it'. Rural people themselves are sometimes guilty of using the word 'cruelty' carelessly. For example, you sometimes hear country people describing foxes as cruel predators, although no animals can truly be cruel, because animals lack the capacity to be cruel, to be kind, or think inside the terms of human culture. Anthropomorphism has clouded thinking on animal welfare for generations. *Aesop's Fables* put human thoughts and emotions into the heads of animals, and the literary device has always been popular through Beatrix Potter and the politically-correct mammals of *Farthing Wood*. But today, anthropomorphism has left the nursery, and there are adults among us who truly believe that animals have human-like thought processes, with consequent civil rights. Nevertheless, it is not rural people, it is the political activists, the issue-impresarios, who have degraded the word 'cruelty', and exploited anthropomorphism.

It is alleged that cruelty is a feature of agriculture and country life. Since the Industrial Revolution, the countryside has seemed an alien and almost sinister place to the townie mind, as well as being at the same time an ideal of beauty and tranquillity. Conan Doyle made Sherlock Holmes say: 'It is my belief that the lowest and vilest alley in London does not present a more dreadful record of sin than the smiling and beautiful countryside.' The press eagerly reports isolated cases of farm cruelty in technicolour detail, and Channel 4 commissioned a series called *Undercover Countryside* to probe by means of hidden cameras into the treatment of livestock. Why is there a market for this myth? Perhaps some urban people are willing to believe that the countryside is a cruel place because it helps them to displace the heavily suppressed guilt that they feel about the abattoirs that they never see and never want to see, and their guilt arising from their sense of alienation from nature. Guilt has to go somewhere. The commonest destination is to other people.

Video evidence is always very convincing. Indeed, the programme's cameras revealed some instances of genuine, repulsive maltreatment of animals. Yet the programme makers generalised their findings. They claimed that, if their undercover camera operators could just walk into jobs and film maltreatment, it must be going on everywhere. Not at all. A process of selection was taking place that led them to that false conclusion. Only farms and businesses that are careless about their livestock would hire such people as the undercover camera operators. The infiltrators would not naturally have appealed to prospective employers, and they would have been unable to demonstrate any relevant experience or sincere interest in the job. Good employers would quite likely have been suspicious, so the shoddy, fake employees naturally found themselves shoddy employers. The series is largely forgotten, but the same kind of myth-generating film will surely be commissioned again and do the same damage. The camera doesn't lie, but the documentary editor can be creative.

Mindless accusations of cruelty stir up hatred

Anti-field sports campaigners are responsible for debasing the meaning of cruelty by using the word as a verbal harpoon to throw at field sports enthusiasts. They reach for every possible epithet without much discrimination, and frequently associate hunt supporters with perverts and child-molesters. These jibes work when the victims of the verbal abuse are hidden and unknown to the public. That is how orchestrated hatred works best – when the scapegoat has no face and no voice to reply to the allegations. The countryside lobby, in the form of the Countryside Alliance, has rolled back some of the years of defamation by organising the hugely successful Countryside Rally and Countryside March in London. Media interviews and pictures of the people who are involved in field sports began to overcome the cultivated stereotype of cruel rural ogres on horseback. That is the most potent refutation of any charge of cruelty levelled against hunting or shooting people: the activities cannot be cruel, because the people are manifestly not cruel people. Talk to those people. Find out how they look at life in general. See how well and how naturally they relate to other people. See if you would rather have a drink with them, or with the emotionally brittle personalities on the other side of the hunting debate.

Let us examine the character and humanity of the people accused of cruelty. That is the best way to make philosophical sense of it. Cruelty cannot just mean inflicting pain. Veterinary surgeons inflict pain and slaughtermen inflict pain, and we do not call them cruel. What we are looking for to establish cruelty is a guilty frame of mind. Cruelty is a word that is laden with moral connotations. If a definition of cruelty does not address human motives and state of mind, it is pretty valueless. However, there is, surprisingly, a group of people who think that animal welfare is more important than human welfare. For a physician, this is a difficult concept.

What is 'unnecessary suffering'?

The RSPCA and allied organisations rely on a legalistic definition of cruelty derived from the 1911 Protection of Animals Act, which defines cruelty as the 'infliction of unnecessary suffering'. The notion of unnecessary suffering works very well as a test for any cruelty that is alleged to have happened in the course of some legal activity such as pig keeping or horse training. Did the defendant keep those pigs in conditions that were unnecessarily miserable for the purposes of rearing pigs? If so, he's guilty; case closed. The question of whether it was necessary to rear pigs in the first place is a completely different one. In fact, the unnecessary suffering test is useless when applied outside the existing framework of law, as a test for what should or should not be legal. To some people, meat and dairy farming are unnecessary, therefore the whole process causes unnecessary suffering; therefore such farming is cruel. To others with a different set of values, livestock farming is a legitimate use of animals, and is not cruel as long as any suffering is minimised.

Trying to apply the 'unnecessary suffering' test to decide what should be legal and what should be banned has got the RSPCA into a pickle over angling. Say what you will, angling is not necessary. Say what you will, it does involve suffering, unless fish are much less sentient than anyone currently believes. The RSPCA is a formidable force that takes the long view, and it has been opposed to angling since 1968. In the 'bloodsports' section of its policy documents, the RSPCA says: 'The report of the Panel of Enquiry into Shooting and Angling has proved to the satisfaction of the RSPCA that fish are capable of experiencing pain and suffering. The RSPCA is opposed to the infliction of pain and suffering on any animal in the name of sport'. It is hard to see how the RSPCA can resist such a clear, logical mandate to campaign against fishing. Fearing entryism by pro-hunters, the RSPCA is currently considering making members pledge that they oppose 'avoidable suffering', a pledge that would logically purge the Society of angling members.

The political campaign to abolish hunting in 1998 by means of a Private Member's Bill also foundered on a sloppy definition of cruelty as 'unnecessary suffering'. A document entitled *The principles of the Bill* published by MP Michael Foster in July 1997 says: 'the hunting and killing of wild animals by dogs inflicts unnecessary suffering'. Yet the Bill specifically exempted the hunting of rabbits and rats with dogs. The Bill seemed to be saying that unnecessary suffering only happens to political animals like foxes, and not to pariah animals like rats. The RSPCA, the League Against Cruel Sports and the International Fund for Animal Welfare lavishly bankrolled the Bill, and named themselves jointly The Campaign for the Protection of Hunted Animals. In reality, they were a Campaign for the Protection of Certain Hunted Animals. If the animal activists can't even apply a definition of cruelty consistently across two species as similar as hares (cruel and wicked to hunt them) and rabbits (not cruel and wicked to hunt them) then it's clear that the activists are not fit to be left in charge of an ethical debate. The moral difference that they try to erect between rabbits and hares would be more credible if they could tell them apart. An anti-hunting MP was famously caught out on *Newsnight* when he was given pictures of a rabbit and a hare, and challenged to distinguish which was which.

Genuine cruelty to animals more common in cities than in countryside

Whenever there is an ethical debate about hunting or horseracing, abolitionists reach for the examples of bear-baiting and cockfighting, like a clumsy DIY enthusiast reaches for his heavy hammer. Those banned activities could not be more different from genuine field sports where no animal is held captive and no animal suffers a deliberately prolonged death or injury. The animals that are killed are liable to be killed in any case for food, for culling or for pest control. In the case of fox hunting, the participants rarely witness the death at close quarters, much less relish it. No, the really interesting myth of cruelty is that the banned activities of dog-fighting, cockfighting and bear-baiting were rural. They were urban vices, and where they continue illegally today, they often still are. Take a look at Mayhew's classic study of the Victorian London Underworld, and you will see how enamoured nineteenth-century, urban villains were of sadistic animal fights. There was even a cock-pit within Whitehall Palace. When dog-fighting rings are exposed today, the offenders are invariably urban criminals, not the sort of people you will find walking puppies or following hounds. It is people who are inexperienced with animals and detached from nature who have the greatest capacity for cruelty. Is it really 'crueller' to shoot a stag that has lived free on a mountain all its life than to keep a dog confined to a small flat, as many urban people do? Rural people are accused by animal rights activists of being steeped in the depraved culture of animal abuse. It is my observation that familiarity breeds

11

respect, not contempt, for animals, and that country dwellers know a good deal more about animal welfare than their urban and suburban counterparts.

The RSPCA announced a 25 per cent rise in animal cruelty cases in 1998. Judging by the Society's press release, its concern is primarily for domestic pets, rather than for livestock. Today's animal cruelty has an urban flavour. It is a shame that the RSPCA has been spending a lot of money, up to a million pounds in the last year, on campaigning against hunting, while the caseload for their inspectors piles up in every town. It is not as if no progress in welfare would be made without their campaigns. Field sports people are actively involved in promoting genuine animal welfare legislation, such as the 1996 Wild Mammals (Protection) Act. For the RSPCA and their peers, the difference between the laudable practice of spending money on casework, and the dubious practice of spending money on campaigning is that casework eats up money, while campaigning has a return in the form of new legacies and donations.

Be sceptical about 'caring' organisations that capitalise on myths of cruelty. It's time that we replaced emotion with informed opinion.

Why are opponents of different targets – seal culling, fox hunting, nuclear weapons – the same people?

Christie Davies and Mark Neal

Activists need issues to get het up about. Nuclear weapons were the issue from the 1970s to the mid 1980s. But there have always been many others, including seal culling in the 1970s and fox hunting perennially. As the Bomb has receded as an issue, activists find more time to concentrate on these other issues. Professor Christie Davies and Dr Mark Neal ask what these issues have in common? The activist cannot abide, however justified, the use of force by social elites. He has no problem with the 'dispossessed' using the force. The burglar and the mugger are not his concern. The violent protester is his hero. He glorifies force in the name of 'progress'. It is just when the bourgeoisie, the state or the Neanderthal throwback uses force that the activist gets agitated.

Violence more prevalent in cities

In almost every advanced industrial country, rates of violent crime are lower in rural than in urban areas, with the highest rates being found in large cities. An individual is much less likely to be mugged or seriously assaulted in rural Cornwall or Pembrokeshire than in Manchester or Birmingham. Despite this, an obsession with rural cruelty prevails among many suburban dwellers who are much more concerned about the hunting and killing of animals than with the high levels of violence against people to be found only a few miles from their doorsteps. Those who think the countryside is cruel have a strange order of priorities in which human beings do not rank as high as they might.

For town-dwellers, the death of an animal is a distant, hidden event. Their meat comes wrapped up in plastic, and they have little understanding or sympathy for those who raise and kill the animals. Their own direct contacts with animals are usually limited to the pets who live in their houses, who have names and share their food. Such animals have little in common with the sheep on a Welsh hillside or the pigs on a Berkshire farm who are people's breakfast, lunch and dinner. Accordingly a false dichotomy exists between 'animal life' in the suburbs, which means the cherishing of doggies and pussycats, and 'animal death' in the countryside which means the killing of livestock and pests. The suburbs thus have a sentimentalised understanding of animals which is not shared by those in the countryside who work with animals on a daily basis.

In recent years, the number of middle-class suburbanites who work in the 'caring and creative professions' has multiplied, while the number of people employed in agriculture has declined markedly. The suburban majority with its numbers and power thus feels able and morally justified to challenge the rural minority who actually have to work with livestock and control the pests that threaten their businesses. Urban and suburban middle-class radicals commonly have strong links and access to various mass media. People who work in the countryside have thus found themselves labelled 'cruel', 'ignorant' and 'violent', with no institutionalised means with which to defend themselves.

Yet the activist concentrates on rural cruelty and violence – the case of Newfoundland

This suburban demonisation of country-folk is not just a British phenomenon, but is striking for being on an international scale. One of the best documented examples of people with a rural way of life being labelled cruel and violent, and subjected to suburban persecution comes from Canada. For centuries the people of Newfoundland survived through hunting and fishing. In many ways their outlook on life was very traditional. Indeed, had they been a non-European indigenous people, they might have been revered by modern environmentalists. However, most Newfoundlanders had their roots either in the south west of England or the south east of Ireland, and as such they were suitable objects for hostile middle-class campaigning.

The attack came from outside protesters and was directed against the annual seal hunt, an event that in the past had been central to the

local economy and way of life, and which was still a revered tradition.[1]
Tellingly, the protestors directed their attack not just against those
directly involved in the hunt, but against the entire people of this
predominantly rural province, who were thus collectively stigmatised
as being 'violent', 'cruel' and 'primitive'. During the 1970s, the
protesters sent hate mail to individual Newfoundlanders, and made
anonymous and even random phone calls to respectable and law-
abiding citizens. The rhetoric used was to the effect that the people
who lived in the province were backward, violent rustics and inferior
in civilisation to the enlightened people of the (sub)urban world. The
values that underpin these views can be clearly be seen in the following
quotations from the protesters' hate-mail:

> Newfoundlanders from North to South are ignorant, primitive,
> stupid, cold-blooded people. I have many questions of the people
> of your town [St Antony, Newfoundland]. Do you know that
> airplanes have been invented? Do you live in caves and eat raw
> meat...Do you ride around in dog sleds? [unsigned].[2]

> Don't you know that this is the twentieth century? The whole
> world is aware that on this earth there are still savages in
> Newfoundland who go around with their clubs, killing baby
> seals...I thank God that we live far away from you in a civilised
> world. [Letter from Illinois, USA][3]

> I guess it's true. Newfoundland is backward, ignorant and pre-
> historic. [From Milwaukee, USA][4]

> Savages wear skins. I take it you pander to savages...[From South
> Africa to the Premier of Newfoundland][5]

Such accusations consistently combined two themes: the theme of
violence and cruelty, and a theme of backward, out-of-date savagery.
Such is the urban view of the rural periphery. It is a curious
combination of themes given that violence and cruelty have been
strikingly twentieth-century phenomena, practiced in massive,
deliberate, rational, modern and systematically organised ways by such
great torturers as the governments and agents of German National
Socialism, and of Communism throughout the world.

It is also worth pointing out that far more violence and cruelty was

15

practised in Millwaukee and the cities of Illinois and South Africa than among the peaceful and gentle folk of Newfoundland. It was however the urban dwellers who were in control of the megaphone, and they were able to use their access to the media to heap further abuse on the tiny rural population in a way that would be called racist were the Newfoundlanders not paler than is politically fashionable.

Seal hunting in Greenland – a personal experience

Animal rights issues often become confused when ethnicity is involved, especially when the anthropomorphic notion of animal rights conflicts directly with the sentimentalised worship of 'traditional cultures'.

This was brought home when, in the 1980s, one of the authors (Christie Davies) went seal hunting with the Inuit. The episode began when the author met an Inuit official of the Danish post office in the harbour of a small town in Greenland. The official asked him whether, for a small consideration, he would like to travel down the coast with them in the official mail boat. The opportunity was too good to be missed. An hour later the author, together with half a dozen Inuit (at that time known as Eskimos) sailed out of the harbour and into the open sea. The Greenlanders at this stage behaved as if they were middle-class Danish officials. Indeed, the senior member of the party wore a uniform with shining metal buttons, and would not have looked out of place in Copenhagen, Odense or Aarhus.

Soon the little boat was out of sight of the Danish bureaucracy in the town and close to a dangerous mass of icebergs emerging from a nearby glacier. At this point the officials took off their jackets of bureaucracy and retrieved hidden guns from underneath the lifeboats and from within various lockers. The captain then steered the boat straight for the icebergs and weaved around them through open patches of sea. A moment later there was enormous excitement when a seal was spotted, and everyone opened fire. Within five minutes the seal had been shot and retrieved from the water. One of the party cut it open with a sharp knife and the Greenlanders proceeded to eat it while it was still warm. For the first time in his life, the author understood the meaning of the term 'the scuppers run with blood'.

The crew eventually went on to deliver the mail to various isolated villages up and down the coast, leaving the seal behind at the chief official's ancestral village. Finally, the boat turned back towards headquarters. During the return journey every last trace of blood was removed from the deck by a thorough use of hosepipes, and by the time the boat was back in harbour, the guns had been hidden away and there was no evidence that the crew were anything other than tame and obedient Danish postal workers.

It was quite apparent that the crew knew perfectly well that their behaviour was against the rules, and that the Danish colonial officials would have been horrified at this misuse of the government's boat. However, if something had gone wrong and the Danes had found out, the author, as a third party, could have played the ethnic card to get them out of trouble. This would easily have been achieved by representing the Danish post office as a colonial oppressor and the Greenlandic hunters as an indigenous people following their traditional and natural way of life.

Hunting is fine...so long as you are a 'noble savage'

Unfortunately, this particular rhetorical trick was not available to the Newfoundlanders. They had lived and hunted in their barren and threatening island for centuries and were as entitled to claim a traditional way of life as any indigenous people. What was missing was that, together with the Faroese and the Norwegians, they did not enjoy the sentimental esteem of a middle class that revered 'noble savages' almost as much as it did animals. Accordingly, they could be subjected to any kind of derogatory stereotype involving violence.

The Norwegians have had to put up with similar stereotyping. For instance, they have had to suffer the indignity of having their national flag dipped in a bucket of blood by urban middle-class radicals in Stockholm, anxious to insult the peripheral maritime country that chose to secede earlier this century. When asked about this image of them as being violent rustics and frontiersmen, Norwegians are apt to shrug their shoulders and observe that the use of violence is not necessarily wrong. Certainly, most Norwegians would say that the use of violence to oppose evil during World War II was justified.

The moral of this is not that Norwegians, even rural Norwegians, are violent, but merely that they are on the whole more in touch with reality than some other industrialised countries. They know that the world is a potentially dangerous place and they are ready to resist danger. This unsentimentalised realism is another facet of rural life that so infuriates the urban middle classes.

The activist always needs an issue

Essentially the same pattern has characterised the current attack on country sports in Britain. In recent years, middle-class radicals who were preoccupied with banning the Bomb or planning a socialist utopia have seen their ideologies fall apart. There will always be a certain number of middle-class people with radical dispositions and these will filter through into whatever 'causes' are available at a particular time in history.[6] With the decline of other channels of radicalism, and with the rise of environmentalism as an ideology, recent years have witnessed a sustained and increasingly violent campaign to ban hunting.

The hunting issue is particularly interesting in the light of other moral debates and controversies. Moral arguments in Britain are nearly always 'causalist', ie, about harm minimisation.[7] Abortion was legalised because it was argued that operations carried out by doctors caused less harm than back street abortionists. Homosexuality was decriminalised because of the fear, suffering and blackmail that the old law inflicted upon homosexuals.[8] In such ways the British State has generally retreated from imposing morality upon its citizens, thus creating a more libertarian society.

Hunting fits the bill
We are now, however, faced with a glaring return to authoritarianism – the attempt by a group of Labour MPs and their urban middle-class supporters to ban hunting with dogs. Worryingly, such a ban is not only an affront to individual liberty, but it will inevitably increase the level of harm experienced by the people, dogs, horses and foxes presently involved in the hunt. As has been well documented, farmers would be forced to find other and more unpleasant ways of culling the fox population; there would no longer be any reason for maintaining the fox's attractive natural habitat. A ban would also inevitably mean the slaughter of redundant dogs and horses, and unemployment for thousands of country folk whose livelihoods are presently bound up with the sport. The anti-hunt brigadiers are thus the advocates of harm.

How then have these activists been able to sell the prospect of legislation that both restricts liberty and increases harm? This surely is a double cost without any compensatory benefits. The answer to this is that the activists have concealed their real motives. The anti-hunt campaign is not about balancing harm, but is motivated by moral absolutes. Hunting is morally evil. Its critics are morally right. There can be no compromise, no surrender.

When it comes to public debate however, these same activists are forced to argue their case in 'causalist' terms, ie, to argue that they are

18

primarily concerned with harm reduction. They have to do so, because this is the preferred mode of moral discourse in British politics. Their 'causalist' rhetoric, however, is bogus. One common trick is to concentrate upon the last five minutes of the fox's life during a hunt, displaying or describing carefully chosen scenes which are designed to shock and draw the public gaze away from the wider environmental context.

They thus push the message of harm reduction for a small number of individual foxes, whilst ignoring the wider picture of the well-being of the fox as a species. The anti-huntists deliberately restrict their message in this way because they cannot win the wider environmental case. Hunting with dogs has long been understood to be the most balanced and most enjoyable way of controlling pests like foxes and deer. The hunted species benefit through the weeding out of older and weaker animals who are more likely to fall prey to the dogs than younger and fitter rivals. Also, the continuation of hunting as an activity ensures that the copses, bridleways and hedgerows that so enhance the British countryside are well cared for, and balanced stocks of the hunted species are maintained.

Envy and opposition to elite force – the real motives of the anti-huntists

The anti-huntists know this. Their arguments are thus put forward in bad faith. They use misleading and restricted 'causalist' arguments but they are driven by a moral indignation of the same kind that leads other extremists to bomb abortion clinics or to beat up homosexuals. This disjunction between the real sentiments that drive people and the arguments they use in public has long been noticed by sociologists, notably Vilfredo Pareto in his theory of 'residues' (basic prejudices) and 'derivations' (the acceptable public arguments).[9]

Underlying the basic prejudices of the anti-hunt movement are two social forces. First, there is the politics of envy, so well described by the German sociologist Helmut Schoeck.[10] Many lower-middle-class people simply dislike the expensive ritual which is so central to fox and stag hunting. They themselves cannot afford the required horses, clothing and training and so they resent other people enjoying them. In addition to this, they hate the social prestige that goes with the symbols of hunting because it is a reminder of the persistence of the old social order in England. To them the rituals of hunting embody and sustain traditional class differences within British society. It simply

19

isn't 'modern'.

Curiously such people do not resent vulgar displays of wealth by leading entertainers, footballers and supermodels – in their Brave New England gross inequality is acceptable, but only if it is 'modern'. In contrast, it never crosses the minds of the anti-hunt agitators that, numerically speaking, most hunt followers are country people of modest means who happen to keep horses.

The second 'residue', or deep prejudice, is their pathological fear and dislike of the use of force by members of a social elite. They are nothing like as perturbed as they should be about the use of force by muggers, burglars and vandals, but any use of force by people of high status, or on behalf of their country, is anathema.

The Anti-Force Movement – from opposing the Bomb to opposing hunting

The anti-huntists are only the latest in a long line of movements against the elite use of force. Often seen in isolation from previous movements, they are actually the moral descendants of the pavement squatters who joined CND in the 1960s, the other rather different folk who infiltrated CND in the 1980s,[11] and of the inane pacifists who prevented Britain from rearming in the 1930s when we were threatened by Hitler; they call to mind Orwell's fruit-juice-drinking, sandal-wearing, vegetarian pacifists crawling towards the smell of 'progress'[12], 'progress' being the achievement of a world from which the use of elite force is banished.

One common thread running through these movements against force is that the negative consequences of their campaigns were completely overlooked. For example in the 1930s, the Labour Party tried to abolish the RAF at a time when Hitler was building up the *Luftwaffe*. Had we been willing to use force against Germany at the time, World War II might have been avoided, and the overall level of harm experienced by everyone would have been reduced. There is thus a direct link between the Peace Pledge Union of the 1930s and the London Blitz. It is no accident that these people wore sandals and ate only vegetables; it was not just to prolong their miserable lives, as Orwell suggests,[13] but also to avoid using force against animals. They rejected both the bomber and the abattoir.

The sociologist Frank Parkin has shown that the supporters of CND in the 1960s were 'middle-class radicals',[14] people in service occupations whose sense of their own status greatly exceeded that afforded by their incomes. They didn't like force, and they didn't like commerce – they were the herbivores of the caring professions. In other words, they had the same social profile as the much of the anti-hunt movement of today.

By the 1980s CND had some members who appeared to be dedicated to the undermining of Britain's defences while largely ignoring the aggressions of the Soviet Union.[15] The consequences of their policies may well have been to sell us into slavery under Soviet rule, much as their moral ancestors would have allowed the Nazis to take over Britain. Although the motives of the two groups were somewhat different, they were both driven by an obsessional fear and hatred of the use of force by what they saw as the British Establishment. The Soviet Union is now thankfully dead, and there is no longer any real need for Britain to target a Trident missile on St Petersburg or Kiev. What, then, is left for the indignant middle-class radicals to do?

Hunting for an easy target

Hunting was always vulnerable to attack, but for a long while it had to compete for the attentions of middle-class radicals with Nuclear Weapons and the Arms Race. These channels for radicalism were better at attracting campaigners because they were more often in the news. Such developments were of grave political consequence for people throughout the world, and as such the media gave them high priority.

With the demise of these big issues, middle-class radicals young and old had to search around for other examples of the use of establishment force. They found one in hunting, which was quickly promoted to the Premiership of middle-class evils.

Banning hunting is an easy target. It is a relatively safe option for the Labour Party, to which many middle-class radicals belong. Certainly, it is a lot safer than banning the Bomb. The strength of support for CND within its ranks kept Labour out of office throughout the 1980s. By contrast, a total ban on hunting would mean the loss of only a few rural seats.

Anti-huntists the real source of violence

Paradoxically, many pacifist, vegetarian, anti-hunt fanatics are great believers in violence. Their very obsession with the evil of violence against animals is easily turned round so that they have no conscience to restrain them from committing some outrage in the name of animal liberation. Most sensible people weigh up carefully the consequences of when violence should be used, but these individuals are prepared to use indiscriminate violence in order to create their utopia, a violence-free world. The activists thus see themselves in a holy war to end all war; in a sacred hunt to end all hunts. They are people of a naturally extreme disposition for whom moral absolutes are an excuse for violent amorality.

For this reason, those involved in hunting can expect a great deal of violent sabotage in the future, much as has been the experience of vivisectionists or those producing genetically-modified organisms.

Ironically, such violent behaviour may well encourage the preservation of hunting. Anti-huntists often claim that opinion polls show that a majority of the British people are against hunting. This may be the case at the moment. The truth of the matter however is that most ordinary people do not care about hunting one way or the other. If you live in Hackney or Sparkbrook, or the Gorbals, or on the Shankhill Road, hunting simply does not impinge on your life very much. It is for this reason that middle-class Labour MPs voted into office to look after the economic interests of their working-class constituents can afford to prance around in Parliament getting up anti-hunting legislation without fear of political damage. However, if violence against persons and property by hunt saboteurs should continue, public opinion will move very rapidly against the anti-hunting thugs.

How hunting can be defended

What then is to be done to defend the countryside from those who would press the myth of cruelty? First, those who support hunting must get it across to the British people that the real and threatening violence in our society comes from the animal liberationists, and not from the hunters. It is important to record and to inform the public about any escalation in thuggery, and for rural hunters to make common cause with people who shoot, the meat industry, animal experimenters and anglers, for they all face the same threat.

Secondly, hunting must be made to look more democratic. In some British rural areas and in most of France, this is not a problem. Rather, what it needed is to get the horse-obsessed children of suburban families involved in hunting. They should be brought to see that there is more glory in catching a fox than in winning a rosette. It is time that suburban children realised that the purpose of 'My Little Pony' is to chase 'My Little Fox'.

Thirdly, the continuities between popular mass sporting events such as the Grand National and the Cheltenham Festival, and the more *recherché* activity of fox hunting should be stressed. Urban fans of steeplechasing often do not realise that the sport that gives them so much pleasure and excitement is firmly rooted in hunting. Even now, it is not generally known that much loved racehorses such as Sir Peter Lely, Old Applejack and Master Oats were all products of the hunting scene. Urban racing fans should be left in little doubt as to the effect of a ban on their favourite pastime.[16]

In the long run we need not be too pessimistic about the strength of the anti-hunting lobby, for its base of support is ephemeral. Indeed, the situation we face is parallel to the one that Britons faced when CND was in the ascendent. CND were defeated. Likewise, with our allies, we defeated the Soviet Union. With a sustained effort we can expose the anti-huntists for what they are, and dispel for ever the myth of rural cruelty.

4

Animal rights: nonsense on stilts

Antony Flew

The notion of 'animal rights' is increasingly paraded to justify attacks upon the rural way of life. Professor Antony Flew analyses the case for 'animal rights'. He shows that the notion of animal rights runs counter to any sustainable notion of rights. For, if one accepts that there is such a thing as 'rights', what must these be based upon? The only basis for such rights which draws on more than pure abstraction can be reciprocity, ie, that I am entitled to be treated in a certain way – or more accurately not treated in certain ways – because I am obligated not to treat others in certain ways. Such mutual sentient obligations clearly cannot be held between animals or between animals and humans.

Animal welfare concerns 1776-1970 – a brief outline

It was in 1776 that Dr Johnson remarked that he was hearing 'much talk of the misery which we cause the brute creation'. Certainly there were at about that time several relevant publications. Today it perhaps needs to be explained that in catholic Christianity, both Roman and Anglo, the brutes are all non-human animals: that is to say, those of which the material bodies are not supposed to be distinctly occupied and managed by immaterial and immortal souls. The first Act of Parliament directed to reducing the miseries of any of these brutes was passed in 1822. The RSPCA, the Royal Society for the Prevention of Cruelty to Animals, was founded two years later, in 1824. A further growth of such concern, focusing initially on anti-vivisection, began in the early 1870s and lasted roughly 40 years. Its first legislative achievement was the passage of the Cruelty to Animals Act in 1876. Its last was the passage of the Protection of Animals Act in 1911.

During and between the wars the work of the RSPCA of course continued. But it seems that legislative changes were neither achieved nor very strenuously attempted. During the first 25 years after World War II there were four official enquiries – into blood sports, live exports, modern farming and animal experimentation – and the National Anti-Vivisection Society (NAVS) and the League Against Cruel Sports (LACS) persuaded backbench MPs to introduce various always aborted Private Members' Bills. But from then on what had traditionally been called the animal welfare movement began to grow, and to change very substantially. From being middle-class, non-political, and predominantly female and elderly, it became classless, youthful and politically activist. It grew to be a substantial element in what Peter Simple used to call the protest industry. As a movement it now concentrates on the institutionalised evils of factory farming, animal experimentation, and wildlife exploitation rather than the mistreatment of domestic pets.

What is meant by a 'right'? A definition of conflicting notions

For us what is most relevant in this transformation was the introduction of claims that the brutes have rights. The development of these claims is to be attributed to a group of philosophers working in Oxford in 1970 – Andrew Linzey, Stephen Clark and, a little later, Peter Singer. But the original identification and labelling of the new sin of speciesism was the achievement of Richard Ryder, a social scientist. He published this finding first in a pamphlet in Oxford during that year.

Any philosophical inquiry into rights has to begin by making three crucial distinctions. The first is that between moral rights and legal rights. Since legal rights are created by and maintained under some particular system of law it is possible for some individual or set of individuals to have, under that system, either a legal right to something to which they have no moral right or a moral right to something to which they have no legal right. (By Cantor's *Axiom for Sets*, the sole essential feature of a set is that its members have at least one common characteristic, any kind of characteristic). The second distinction is that between option and welfare rights. Option rights are rights to be left free to choose. Welfare rights are rights to be supplied with some good, presumably either by some other person or persons or by some organisation. The third distinction is between artificial and natural rights. Legal rights are all as such and necessarily artificial, since they 'are created and maintained under some particular system of law'. But it is also possible for individuals artificially to create moral rights.

For instance: by promising to give someone some specific sum of money if they fulfil certain specified conditions I thereby endow them with a moral right to receive that sum of money from me if they satisfy those conditions.

The classic proclamation of option rights was made in the American Declaration of Independence: 'We hold these truths to be self-evident, that all men are created equal, that they are endowed by their Creator with certain unalienable Rights, that among these are Life, Liberty and the pursuit of Happiness.' Welfare rights were prominent among the rights proclaimed by the General Assembly of the United Nations in December 1948. Consider, for instance, Article 22: that 'everyone, as a member of society, has the right to social security'; or Article 24 that 'everyone has the right to...periodic holidays with pay'. (The members of the Committee drafting this Declaration appear to have been hard-line socialists, in whose ideal world everyone would be a state employee and no-one would be self-employed).

'Animal rights' advocates argue animals possess moral rights

No doubt all those who maintain that some or all of the brutes possess rights also want these rights to become rights proclaimed and defended by the state. But it is by insisting upon their being, in the first instance, moral that they hope to achieve that objective. So, since these moral rights are supposedly possessed by all the members either of the set of all brutes or of some of its subsets, the protagonists of animal rights are in effect issuing a declaration of the universal moral rights of all the members of another, non-human, kind of individuals.

How are human 'moral rights' justified?

But how is this declaration to be itself justified? To the Signers of the American Declaration of Independence it was apparently self-evident that the Creator had endowed all men with certain unalienable rights. It would have been hard enough to persuade them that the expression 'all men' has to be construed as embracing all mature and sane human beings of either sex without proceeding to insist that it should also include members of some species of brutes. There are in any case difficulties with the rationale provided in the Declaration of Independence for the more limited rights claims which it actually makes. Here it will be sufficient to say no more than that the rights prescribed by the positive law of the Creator or of any other individual

26

or institution would, necessarily and as such, be legal rather than moral. The heart of this particular matter of logic was first laid bare in Plato's *Euthyphro*: if you define the moral in terms of the will of God you thereby disclaim all possibility of rendering substantial and non-tautological praise to God for the Divine goodness.

So what is to be done? The first step must be to insist that the rights proclaimed in that great Declaration, rights to the validity of which the supporters of liberalising legal reforms in the UK often appealed during the 1960s, should not be construed, as critics nowadays often pretend that they were then construed, as being rights for everyone to do whatever they might choose to do regardless of the harm they would inflict on others by so doing.

Since everyone is, according to that Declaration, endowed with equal rights, the rights of every individual are necessarily restricted by the corresponding and equivalent rights of everyone else. It is this essential restriction which provides a basis for the contention that these equal rights of all men or, better, all human persons – could there be non-human or non-physical persons? – I am at one and the same time asserting both my own rights and my corresponding duties to others.

Beings can only possess rights if they can recognise the rights of others

At this point I propose to maintain that no class of beings can properly be said themselves to have rights unless it is a class of which members are not only able to claim those rights for themselves simply as members of that class but also to recognise corresponding and consequential duties to the other members of that same class. For I can think of no other way of justifying the contention that the option rights proclaimed in the American Declaration of Independence are indeed moral rights. For better or for worse this justification – and what other is available? – rules out all possibility of moral rights for any of the brutes.

This rationale for the possession of moral option rights has the very great merit of exposing the outrageousness of claims to possess supposedly moral welfare rights – rights which apparently impose no corresponding duties upon their possessors. This suggestion is of its greatest practical importance in the context of consideration of the reform of a welfare state. For, as is stated in Murray's *Law of Unintended Rewards*, 'Any social transfer increases the net value of being in the condition that prompted the transfer.' Where the condition prompting some set of transfers is one to which those suffering from that condition

27

could not by their own efforts avoid becoming and/or remaining subject, there is no need to take account of this law. Many of the conditions unintendedly rewarded by existing state welfare provisions are, however, conditions into which at least some of their victims could and perhaps ought to have avoided falling and/or which they could and perhaps ought to escape partly or wholly by their own efforts.

No programme for welfare state reform which aspires to deserve the diploma description 'radical' can, therefore, continue to insist that all those falling into and/or failing to escape such conditions must continue to be 'non-judgementally' provided with such transfers as their (it is said 'socially') just entitlements. It is, therefore, an occasion to retell a story told of Confucius – a sage, it seems, now once again honoured in his own country. A pupil once asked him whether his rule of conduct might not perhaps be epitomised in a single word: 'the master replied, "Is not 'reciprocity' the word?"' (*Analects* XV, Section 23).

All this might perhaps seem to be, if not formally and strictly, at least in some way inconsistent with my own eagerness – which would surely not have been shared by Confucius – to insist that we do have duties to at least some of the brutes. But it is not. For to insist that we can and do have duties to some of the brutes is perfectly consistent with maintaining that, because they do not and cannot have duties either to other members of their own species or to members of ours, they do not and cannot have rights to our execution of any of our duties to them.

Might some 'higher' brutes be close enough to humans to possess rights?

One understandably popular line of argument for the conclusion that at least some of the brutes have rights begins by pointing out that the members of the set of this favoured some are endowed with characteristics in embryonic form which are in more developed forms considered to be peculiarly and distinctively human. From this observation the argument proceeds, by way of the suggestion that the difference between human beings and the brutes is a mere difference of degree, to the desired conclusion that it is simply not possible to draw a sharp, clear line between one category and the other.

That it should be possible to find most of what have been taken to be defining characteristics of humanity among the brutes – at least in some embryonic form – is of course implied by general evolutionary theory. But before dismissing all differences of degree as mere differences of degree we should consider what is meant by a 'difference of degree' and look at one or two other examples of such differences.

Let us say that a difference of degree between two extremes is one such that there is a series of actual or theoretically possible cases stretching between one of these extremes and the other, and with the amount of difference between each member of the series and the next vanishingly small. It now becomes obvious that differences which are both large and in this understanding also differences of degree can be of the most enormous human importance. For the differences, for instance, between age and youth, between sanity and insanity, between a free society and one in which everything which is not forbidden is compulsory, are all both of enormous human importance and yet at the same time differences of degree in the sense just explicated.

In the present case it really is, although the differences between the embryonic and the developed forms of the defining characteristics of humanity are all differences of degree, unusually easy to draw a sharp, clear line between the distinctively human and the distinctively non-human.

No brutes possess sufficient human qualities to claim or recognise rights

There are three reasons for this. The first is that there are several characteristics which have been suggested as defining, and all of these need to be present if a being is to be accepted as unequivocally human. The second is that the surviving species most similar to ours must surely be very much less similar than were other species which have not survived. The third is that some of the relevant differences of degree are very large indeed. Thus, for instance, there is a huge difference between the most sophisticated communication systems employed by any non-human species and the most primitive of human natural languages. Certainly no such non-human communication system is equipped with the concepts which would make it possible for those who employ it to use it either to claim rights as members of their own species or to recognise their corresponding and consequential duties to their fellow members.

Real issue is animal welfare, not fantastical 'animal rights'

I have so far been arguing, however inadequately, both that all human beings are by our natures as such endowed with moral rights and that the brutes are as such disqualified from enjoying a similar endowment, I nevertheless wholeheartedly agree with Jeremy Bentham – who had no time for any notion of rights – about what it is which makes them proper objects of moral concern: 'The question is not can they reason or can they talk, but can they suffer?'

Indeed they can. And certainly it is a possibility which has been, and despite all the efforts of animal welfare movements, continues to be, far too abundantly realised. The prime motive of all animal welfare movements has always been, and surely still remains, compassion rather than a concern to secure and promote the putative rights of non-human animals.

5

Country sports: their contribution to the landscape

Charles Nodder

The British countryside has been eulogised by countless poets and writers. Politicians extol its beauty. Yet what is not sufficiently understood is the contribution country sports play in maintaining this beauty. Charles Nodder shows that sporting estates contribute more to conservation, and are more environmentally friendly, than other uses of the countryside. 'Britain has a land green and pleasant in parts and brown and barren in others. Field sportsman and responsible farmers have to show the urban decision-makers why it is that the boundaries between the two fall where they do.'

Problems of countryside too subtle for the urban policy-maker

It must be hard for the urban bureaucrat to understand the arguments surrounding the future of our countryside. He knows from what he reads in his newspaper that his country cousins are upset about housing, farming policy and, most immediately, the threat to field sports. Yet, as he passes through rural England on an Intercity 125 to his next business appointment, he looks out on a substantially green and pleasant land. Seen from the comfort of a franchised railway carriage, the countryside still appears a pleasant enough place to live and hardly to be on the brink of social and economic collapse.

But, as those who understand the countryside know, the devil is in the detail. Country men and women have seen enough change even in the span of their own lifetimes to understand the catastrophe of urban encroachment, and the devastating impact that fluctuating farm incomes can have on the way the countryside looks. Furthermore, they know that the real quality of our environment has to be measured

31

not just by appearances but in minute detail. It is no good our bureaucrat assuming that the birds are doing fine just because when he drives his family down to Windsor Great Park for a day out he sees more magpies, kestrels and cormorants than he used to. Unlike the urban visitor, the countryman will remark today not upon the prevalence of these common predatory species, but on the disappearance of the songbirds he remembers from his youth, and the butterflies which used to bring life to so many green lanes and woodland glades.

Remaining rural idylls threatened by opponents of field sports

Yet there are still many places where wildlife thrives in the countryside. There are the great estates where wild gamebirds abound or where the jealously guarded salmon rivers teem with otters, dippers and myriad insects. There are the great hunting shires where well turned-out riders glide timelessly over beautifully laid hedges in classic hunting country. There are humble shoots and small coarse fishing clubs whose woods and waters are loved and cared for as much as ever a piece of land or water could be. In these places, where field sports are alive and well, the social cohesion which has held country life together for generations continues to bind and, in consequence, the very fabric of the countryside, its variety and its nature, stays healthy.

What the urban decision-maker so urgently needs to understand, however, is that these remaining rural idylls hang by a gossamer thread. Break it, and the complex web of countryside and country ways which we all value, and which are often regarded overseas as the true identity of Britain, will be blown away and irretrievably lost.

Sporting estates conserve wildlife and the environment

It is easy to assert that field sports help to conserve the countryside. Every one of the 250,000 Countryside Marchers who assembled in London on 1st March, 1998, would have been prepared to swear blind that it was true. But in this age of public scepticism, proof – no less – is what the decision-maker will require. That proof exists in two forms.

First, there is proof by example. Past winners of accolades such as the Laurent Perrier Award for Wild Game Conservation come immediately to mind. Lord Barnard's Raby Castle Estate in County Durham is a grand example of an estate teeming with wildlife on account of the good gamekeeping and careful farming which take place there. Manydown Farm in Hampshire, where Hugh Oliver-Bellasis has restored wildlife in defiance of his proximity to Basingstoke is another well-documented case. Less well-known, but no less valuable as an example, would be the River Piddle in Dorset, where careful management for fishing by Richard Slocock has led to six-fold increases in wild trout as well as helping rare species like the freshwater crayfish.

Some of these showpieces are now the subject of scientific monitoring and here the telling weight of statistics can be added to the story. At Muirkirk in Ayrshire, for example, the revival of grouse moor management in 1992 has led to a 30-fold increase in the numbers of red grouse on the estate. Other species have benefited too, in particular from the reduction of overgrazing by sheep. Insects have more than doubled and black grouse have established several new breeding sites. The same sorts of wildlife increases are now being monitored scientifically on Invercauld and other nearby upland estates where management for shooting is taking place

Further south, on the Allerton Trust farm at Loddington in Leicestershire, profitable farming and game and wildlife conservation are being carefully combined. This has led to six times as many wild pheasants, three times as many wild partridges and a seven-fold increase in the fledging success of song thrushes, making it practically the only place in the country where this species is known to be in recovery. The Game Conservancy Trust, which runs the project, is now able to use the estate as a showpiece for convincing sceptics of the general benefits of game management for the countryside.

Study finds 70 per cent of gamekeepers look after Sites of Special Scientific Interest

But demonstrations by example have their limitations. Increasingly the public seem to suspect that whenever such flagships are being deployed they are being used in order to disguise weakness in the rearguard. While this in no way lessens the validity of the examples, it does explain the additional value of more widespread proof that field sports help to conserve the countryside. In the past, it has been in this area of wider proof that campaigners for the country way of life have been inclined to be lacking. Recently, however, some fascinating national statistics have started to come to light.

In July 1997, Lord Carnarvon's Standing Conference on Countryside Sports launched an updated edition of its report, *Countryside Sports, Their Economic, Social and Conservation Significance.*

Sadly, the report's valuable contents were missed by most commentators. Collating figures supplied by a whole range of countryside bodies which are represented on the Conference, it showed that professional gamekeepers alone have a responsibility for six million acres of wildlife habitat. Even more significantly, 70 per cent of them are looking after at least one Site of Special Scientific Interest. The report went on to detail the 1,000-plus miles of conservation headlands around cereal fields in Britain, almost all of them on sporting estates, and demonstrated a direct positive correlation between the number of hares and the habitat diversity of the farms on which they live. The Standing Conference also found that 60 per cent of lowland hunts carry out covert management, usually by laying the shrub layer to provide warmth and cover at ground level, a technique invaluable not just for the fox but for woodland wildlife as a whole.

Quango study shows shooting estates are more environmentally friendly

Even more compelling are the findings of the 1996 report, *Game Management in England*, compiled by Graham Cox, Charles Watkins and Michael Winter, all working at the Centre for Rural Studies under a contract from the Countryside Commission. Their national questionnaire survey of landowners showed that not only did the shooting estates have far more woodland, but that they were planting three times as many new woods and that they were five times as likely to be managing them properly. In the case of coppicing for example – a practice known to be of great benefit to songbirds, butterflies and woodland flora – estates releasing pheasants were eight times as likely to be undertaking it as those without a sporting interest.

Further recent work by Nicholle Howard and Dr John Carroll, shows that in Essex, lowland driven game shooting is a crucial influence in persuading farmers in the county to adopt less intensive land management practices. It is the sporting estates in the county which have the best record in hedge retention and maintenance, the most careful spraying regimes and the most woodland planting. Howard and Carroll found that recreation, primarily through field sports, and not conservation, was the main motivation governing such management.

Whilst today's urban-based politicians, with their almost puritan tendencies, seem inclined to believe that enjoyment is a politically incorrect reason for doing anything, the wildlife on these farms and, just as importantly, the 'Essex' men and women who wander through them at weekends, will thank these far-sighted landowners for what they have done.

Britain has a land green and pleasant in parts and brown and barren in others. Field sportsmen and responsible farmers have to show the urban decision-makers why it is that the boundaries between the two fall where they do.

6

Country sports:
adding value to wildlife

Ian Swingland

It is man's exploitation of wildlife which gives wildlife value. Humans conserve species because they gain benefits from them, be they in the form of food, sport, profit or any combination of these. When humans can gain no benefit from a species – when they have no value – extinction often follows. Thus the hunting of wild animals gives an economic value to British wildlife. The total value of country sports in the UK is estimated at £6.2 billion per annum. The consequences of removing value from wildlife can be seen throughout the world. In Britain it can be seen in what has happened to the deer population of the Quantocks since the National Trust's ban on deer hunting.

How much would you pay to stop a species from extinction? Do you view wildlife as valuable because they provide a service, a pleasure, an excitement or indeed you believe they have a right to life which humans have no right to destroy? Although economists attempt to put values on wildlife species to clarify planning and management options, it is neither practicable nor reliable to apply such approaches in biodiversity conservation programmes. We cannot equate a plant or animal to a sum of money.

Humans place a value on wildlife according to its use to them – and act accordingly

It is the *context* in which species are regarded that is the key to a perceived value. A species in some particular interaction with humans prescribes some sense of what it is worth. A fox is worth very little to a city dweller but (s)he might still want them conserved as beautiful animals. A countryman might agree but place an additional value on them as a pest or for hunting. To an African villager, dispossessed of access to wildlife by being ejected from his home by the establishment of a new national park, the value of an antelope is food for a month. To the foreign hunter who pays to shoot it, the prey is merely a trophy – and the villager will not get the meat unless he pays. So poaching is invented which leads to wildlife extinctions. The 'executioner' (ie, villager) no longer has control over his wildlife. The value of the wildlife has changed for him as he no longer 'owns' the wild animals and therefore cannot husband the populations to provide sustainable subsistence.

Humans place a value on wildlife depending on what it is worth to them and act accordingly. Plants in the wrong place are often defined as weeds, and so animals in the wrong place, doing the wrong thing, from a human viewpoint, are pests.

Idea that wildlife can be preserved without human exploitation simply false

So what is the most substantial myth in the countryside? That wildlife should not be used; that they should be preserved rather than conserved. Species should be protected with no interference by humans.

Nearly all landscapes are man-made and this gross interference over the centuries has left an inheritance that has to be managed. This is conservation. Once an ecosystem has been changed it has to be managed thereafter if it is not to deteriorate. For a system with humans either living within the habitat or, like the example above, living outside the conservation area, the management imperative is even more critical. In these situations a wildlife population can often become unbalanced either exploding or shrinking, and this can have a knock-on effect on other species.

In the British and European countryside, a melange of humans and wildlife, people have always found that they have used and relied on wildlife for sustenance. In some instances this evolved into rituals where the process of finding and killing wild animals, or the cropping of plant material, was associated with various practices and ceremonies. This evolved in parallel all over the world. Hunting, one particular aspect of wildlife usage, has become a ceremony in its own right valued to such an extent that even if the hunt is after artificial prey (eg, drag hunting) the process, although not the associated employment, will continue. This constant wildlife management or conservation through these various practices has to be maintained to conserve the rural areas even though today Europeans no longer need to rely on wildlife to survive but only for income or pleasure.

Exploitation of wildlife vast industry globally

So how are wildlife valued today when they are mainly used for leisure or recreationally (ie, non-essential) and only occasionally have a real financial importance, as in the case of estates that rely on wildlife income? It is this modern-day relationship between humans and wildlife that has set the scene for the current conflict between the users and the carers. The latter accusing the former that since they do not need to use wildlife to survive it is morally and ethically reprehensible to use wildlife for such frivolous reasons.

Of course trade in wildlife services and products is one of the largest industries in the world (US$410,610,000,000 per annum[1]). But, like much of the use of wildlife in Europe, it is merely profiteering. A very small percentage is that which local people depend on and is inculcated in their culture.

Field sports most profitable use of the British countryside

So what is the value of wildlife to country sports? It is estimated that the total expenditure on countryside sport including wildlife hunting in the UK is £6,249,000,000 per annum.[2] This income when balanced against costs is more profitable than any other country practice such as agriculture. Overheads are lower, wildlife can use marginal areas better than livestock, the resistance of wild animals to parasites and diseases is much higher than livestock (bringing lower management costs), and many other advantages. The wildlife industry produces a higher return on uplands and other marginal habitats than with livestock or crops.

Would country sports continue without wild animals even though the practice is largely traditional and ceremonial? I have said earlier many practices would continue using drag hunting practices but the value of the practice to the countryside would diminish as many of the support systems would vanish – jobs, skills, etc. In many instances where control of pests is needed (such as foxes) until better practices, both in preventing pest damage and in their control, are invented, hunting is still the best option as well as retaining skills and livelihoods which would otherwise be lost.

If country sports were prohibited wildlife would lose its value

The value of wildlife to sport is such that without it sport would disappear. If hunting disappeared no one would continue to manage it and in the absence of anyone taking care of the wildlife it would be neglected. It would cease to have value. There would be no husbandry or conservation. (Does English Nature spend less than the sports brigade on conservation?) Wild animals, which eat trees or crops, would turn from being an asset that could be hunted into a pest and shot. When the National Trust banned the hunting of deer with hounds on its land recently as a result of an incomplete piece of research they commissioned, it was predictable that with no alternative management plan in place the deer would be decimated. Within three months only a proportion were left alive and all the stags had been shot – sometimes badly.

Where wildlife has no value extinction often follows

Across the planet it has been obvious for decades that where people do not have a shareholding in local wildlife, a right to benefit, and can together conserve the wild stocks, extinction is prevalent. With the power of management people can control the resource for sustainable use – almost reinventing the wheel of two centuries ago where their reliance on wildlife to survive meant they naturally husbanded the populations their tribe or village relied on.

The countryside's treatment of wildlife – both animals and plants – will determine whether it survives or not. Countryside sport involving wild animals, providing it is pursued humanely, is one of the many ways species are used that give value to wildlife. And it is this lateral viewpoint where I believe the true value of wildlife lies.

Welfare and conservation legislation: its unintended consequences

Stuart Harrop

Ecosystems have complex interrelationships, many of which are not fully understood. It is not possible to tinker with just one facet of an ecosystem without affecting many others. Yet Stuart Harrop argues that most conservation laws and regulation seek to tackle a particular perceived problem without considering the wider implications. For example the protection offered to cormorants has had detrimental affects on aquatic life. In the debate on hunting the potentially very wide implications both for other species and for the look of the countryside itself have quite simply not been considered.

Most systems – whether mechanical, biological or social – possess a 'keystone'
I never cease to be amazed when I see an old stone bridge, its structure intact through the operation of one small component: the keystone. Remove this often innocuous, unassuming component and the whole interrelated structure will inevitably lose its cohesion, its beauty, its utilitarian function and become an amorphous mass of rubble. The keystone is often difficult to detect, it may not be the largest, best cut stone within the bridge, it may not have the testimony of the builders carved into it; nevertheless, it retains its unique and crucial function.

Keystones or their equivalents are found in most systems be they structural, mechanical, biological or social and, unless we take steps to appreciate which items are key in a system, we tamper with its components at our peril. Although our interference may not directly affect the keystone, because of the interlinking between all or most of the elements within the system, we can disturb the equilibrium which ultimately forces the keystone to detach.

Keystone species central to ecosystems

In the world of ecological systems where many and diverse species live together in apparent symbiosis there are also keystone species; species which are essential to the continuance of the ecological community and which are, themselves, dependent on others. Instigate changes which destabilise the keystone species and the ecological repercussions will be immense. Species may disappear altogether, others will increase their numbers dramatically, invaders will appear and the structural nature of the habitat itself may even be transformed. Sometimes the transformation can be so extensive that the entire ecological system breaks down, the geology of the habitat changes and even the local climate alters. Systems such as those flourishing in the Amazon rainforest are so finely balanced that removal of key species can create an inevitable and irreversible decline to near-desertification in sharp contrast to the natural state of affairs.

But often difficult to identify

Discovering and documenting the keynote species and the essential relationships between species is often an almost insurmountable task and those who study the dynamics of ecosystems would be the first to admit that their field of study is still in its infancy. Of course some key species and principles are very obvious and easy to detect: we are all aware of the massive impact which the African elephant has on the African savannah and the changes which occur when it is removed. However, in other ecological niches the keystone species and the key interrelationships may be superficially innocuous: perhaps a species of ant, fungi or micro-organisms in the soil and detritus of a rainforest, the removal of which can have far-reaching, even catastrophic consequences.

In the context of biodiversity preservation, keystone species and the delicate interrelations between species in ecosystems, Edward Wilson, in the book *The Diversity of Life* said:

> There comes a time, in all science, when it is profitable to move away from the bold and obvious and circle around a bit, inventing more and subtle approaches to search for concealed phenomena.

In the study of communities, this strategy requires greater attention to context, history and chance.[1]

UK ecosystems are as they are because of centuries of man's activity

This throws a further gloss on the challenge of finding the key to the structure of ecosystems. We must think laterally, think widely – not merely sequentially with only a narrow focus. When we examine, with this attitude in mind, the context, history and chance of biodiversity preservation in the countryside closer to home – in the United Kingdom – we note immediately that there are very few truly wild places (if we define 'wild' by excluding human intervention). Our 'natural' habitats often depend upon long-standing, tried and tested human practices, and social structures for their existence. In addition, therefore, to finding the key species and key relationships in a habitat we must also discover the human practices which sustain the habitat. The beautiful Adonis Blue butterfly, common only in a few isolated colonies, has a complex and dependent relationship with ants and with its foodplants. However, if it were not for the patterns of grazing instituted, carried out and carefully organised by man over the centuries, the conditions for its co-dependents would not be quite right and the butterfly would probably not be found on the South Downs of England. If it were not for man's long-evolved practices of agriculture, the vast proportion of the Scottish, Welsh and English mountains, hills and fells would be very different habitats today. If it were not for the Norman Conquerors' desire to hunt, as a form of recreation, they would not have planted that extensive 'natural' habitat, and beautiful part of the English countryside, we still call the New Forest.

In the United Kingdom, therefore, to find the key principle that holds together, sustains and creates integrity within our country habitats, more often than not we have to look to the diverse and evolved idiosyncrasies of our culture. We may not, thereby, find a keynote species, principle or activity but we should be able to establish where the balance of power lies and thus be empowered to make a choice. Would we choose endless, hedgeless fields populated by a monoculture and a sparse collection of crows, woodpigeons and rats? Or would we prefer to see in arable lands: woods, hedgerows and ponds in between the cultivated fields and a wide diversity of birds, mammals, amphibians and insects in addition to trees and wild flowers?

Nature conservation legislation protects minor pockets of 'wild habitat', but inevitably ignores extensive habitats found on cultivated land

The decision often rests on either the maintenance of long-standing practices or some very carefully considered alternatives implemented with extreme caution. Do the prevalent regulatory regimes promote this approach? New nature conservation regimes, both in Europe and in this country (in the Habitats Directive and the Wildlife and Countryside Act 1981[2]), are among those legislative instruments that promote the protected area; a separate haven for wildlife. This is all to the good: we must reserve, at the very least, pockets of land which represent the remnants of our wild habitats; we must retain specially protected areas that provide the unique conditions for species to survive. But does this regulatory system preserve biodiversity on land that is largely given over to agriculture – land that is shared between a rich diversity of wildlife and human users? Many of our native bird, mammal and insect species depend upon hedgerows and coppices interspersed liberally on arable land managed in a 'traditional' manner. These areas are not transient, weed-ridden 'set-aside' but areas of land that have sustained the bushes, trees and ponds for many years to the point that the species are utterly dependent upon them. However, these areas of land cannot just be given over to public ownership or to a trust who will manage them in the unique way required. We cannot, by a system of protected area management preserve the British hedgerows. And yet we need to do something: many species of birds, common 20 years ago, are rushing to the list of endangered species precisely because the hedgerow, once a typical incident of our farming practices, is under attack since it is in the way of easy agriculture. In the meantime and perhaps crucially, the conservation legislator has not acknowledged the importance and tradition of the hedgerow or catered for it in the modern legislation.

Blanket protection for birds has had detrimental consequences

Beyond the regulation of habitats the modern approach to the conservation of animals also appears to deal somewhat haphazardly with the interrelationship of species. Birds receive almost comprehensive protection in the UK. This is no bad thing but to what extent does this all-round protection take account of the interrelationship of birds with their habitats and with other species. Why is it that many mammals, reptiles and amphibians receive little or no protection at all?

Fishery owners are concerned that the incredible influx of cormorants to their rivers and lakes will disturb not just the fishing but the entirety of the aquatic environments. But there's little that can be done because of the comprehensive protection received by birds. We can perhaps sit back and glibly say we are not concerned with the profit from fisheries but that need not be relevant. What about the other birds frequenting the area, the small mammals, and the amphibians that may disappear, in the face of the new and dominant arrivals and the sudden and unusual imbalance? The imbalance is probably triggered by man's downstream activities but he has, as yet, prepared no rectification plans and his law designed to preserve biodiversity is working against its prime objective.[3]

Consequences upon biodiversity of banning fox hunting ignored

Where recreation and biodiversity meet we often find even more confusion. The regulation and administration of recreational fishing is geared to some continuance of the status quo. Tried and tested systems of close seasons and the regulation of fishing methods coupled with the topping up of fish populations by man and the control of the introduction of alien species all contribute to maintain the aquatic biodiversity. But what of other, equally ancient recreational pursuits, in particular fox hunting? This sport is hardly regulated at all and until very recently the wild fox had no legal protection whatsoever and it certainly has a lot of catching up to do if it is to receive the same protection extended to common bird species in the United Kingdom. By the very nature of the fox hunting debates in parliament we could be forgiven for believing that the issue is entirely polarised around one question: is hunting cruel or not? Assuming that the answer to this question is an emphatic yes! we must still exercise caution, however, before banning hunting with hounds overnight. First we must take steps to analyse the consequences to the biodiversity of some parts of the British countryside.

Countryside shaped by fox hunting also offers habitats to other species

In some areas where fox hunting is maintained the interest of the participants in their sport is so great that the countryside is shaped by their desire to create haunts for their prey. The result can be aesthetically beautiful agricultural land with many woods, coppices, lakes, ponds and thick hedgerows. Not only do these areas support healthy populations of well-dispersed foxes they also support, encourage and nurture countless other animal, insect, reptile, amphibian and plant inhabitants.[4] Compare this with some of the areas where fox hunting does not take place and the picture is often quite different. There may be an area of agricultural monoculture or there may be an area, almost like the fox hunting country in appearance where, because of the gamekeeper activity (often much more efficient than fox hunting in terms of fox eradication), there are no or few foxes with, often, a somewhat more sterile environment. Of course there may be other explanations for these geographical differences or other social factors, which also assist in supporting the stability of the biodiversity-rich areas. Nevertheless, the necessary analysis, if it has been carried out at all, does not seem to be available to enable the legislators to debate hunting and make a properly informed decision about the matter with all due precaution. Thus if hunting is to be banned all well and good if we are satisfied both that biodiversity will not be affected by the disappearance of this activity and that hunting is cruel. However, if fox hunting as a cultural and social factor, rather than other factors actually plays a significant part in holding together some of our familiar ecosystems, through whatever accident or idiosyncrasy of British history, what incentives, or regulatory system will be put in place to ensure that the environmental status quo remains in the old hunting country? This is by no means a global issue, but the countryside is in our trust. Therefore, there is no reason why grand principles like the precautionary principle,[5] embodied in international conservation agreements and now in the constitution of the European Community, should not apply at home. Don't we owe it to ourselves to ask the right questions and take all preliminary action that reasonable precaution requires before tampering with the long-established and familiar country, in the interests of the welfare of the fox, biodiversity and also those who will inherit our responsibilities?

Ultimately conservation legislation must take careful note of the whole environment and all relevant interests – it should not be side-tracked by the single issue. Tampering with delicate interrelationships between species (including the human species) is invariably perilous and should only be done after a thorough and dispassionate examination of the consequences.

8

An end to hunting: utopia for foxes?

James Barrington

Opponents of hunting usually claim their aim is solely to protect foxes from unnecessary suffering. Yet they do not ask themselves if the lot of the fox would be improved if hunting were banned. James Barrington shows that foxes might well fare worse if fox hunting were to be banned. He argues that true animal welfarists should seek to reform fox hunting, not ban it. A ban on hunting may well lead foxes to a utopia only in the literal sense of that word, nowhere.

For an activity which hardly touches upon the lives of the vast majority of people in the UK, the issue of fox hunting can arouse passions few other subjects are able to manage. We all think we know about it and whether that knowledge comes from first-hand experience or the propaganda of organisations which have a vested interest in the issue, our minds seem to be firmly set one way or the other.

The concept of taking pleasure in the suffering of others, whether they be humans or animals, is felt by most people to be fundamentally wrong. There are, of course, exceptions – a good example might be boxing, though the casual observer can at least see that the sport involves willing participants. 'Killing for fun' is not, so the argument goes, something society should be countenancing as we move into the twenty-first century. It is morally wrong and that is all one needs to know about it to consign fox hunting to the history books and presumably let foxes live out their lives peacefully.

Simplistic questions lead to simplistic answers
If it were that simple, I would be supportive of any legal measure to

bring a ban into effect, but, as ever, life is rarely that straightforward and for the genuinely open minded even the most cursory glance at the various factors involved indicates a much more complex activity than we are at first led to believe. Organisations opposing fox hunting draw upon support from various quarters, claiming that they speak for the majority of people in Britain and usually rely on public opinion poll figures of something like 70 per cent of the population stating disapproval. The problem with many opinion polls is that the answers given can reflect the simplicity of the questions asked. Most people do not hunt, know very little about it other than what they see on television or in newspapers and leaflets and are quite naturally turned off by some of its images. In a straight 'for or against' poll, of course they fall into the against category – they have nowhere else to go. Would they, however, make that choice with such alacrity if they were shown the other forms of control, some of which are likely to increase and which can cause more suffering to the fox? Occasionally, a poll might even contradict itself, which was the case in August 1997. A Gallup poll for the *Daily Telegraph* showed 63 per cent of all respondents wanting Parliament to ban fox hunting, yet in a following question 59 per cent of those asked felt that landowners should have the right to allow hunting on their land!

Opponents of hunting an uneasy coalition of sentimentalists, animal rightists, class warriors and vested interests

When one analyses the support for a ban, it appears that those who focus their attention on fox hunting, for whatever reason, do not sit comfortably together. So often one will hear from ordinary members of the public that they accept foxes are a pest, but that they should be dealt with 'some other way'. A second category will be individuals or groups, perhaps gamekeepers, who can control foxes much more efficiently (that is in greater numbers) by snaring or shooting. I recently heard one gamekeeper claim that he had killed almost 300 foxes in one year and yet, because he was anti-hunt, his support for prohibition was welcomed in a television debate. A third category will be those ardent animal rightists, whose principles appear to be more important than any progress and who will not accept any healthy animal being killed. These three positions are not compatible and whilst it is a fact that hunting with hounds has been scrutinised time and time again, the case of the 'coalition of antis' has not been analysed nearly enough.

Perhaps, in the minds of some people in a fourth category, this does not really matter. The perception is that those who ride to hounds are the landed gentry, the 'toffs', the old Tories and now, with a new Labour Government moving towards the turn of the millennium, such activities do not have a place in 'Cool Britannia'. To them, fox hunting appears to typify a certain kind of person and attitude. A ban would be an opportunity to get rid of these people and if the general perception is that animal suffering will be relieved, this only strengthens the argument.

Cruelty not the real issue for opponents of hunting

More and more, however, it appears that the issue of suffering is becoming irrelevant, though it is often quoted as being the main reason for the abolition of hunting. In reality, the battle has now become a political struggle. Certain conversations during the Parliamentary debates on Michael Foster's failed Wild Mammals (Hunting with Dogs) Bill, indicated that some MPs would like to consider the issue more fully, but cannot because they do not wish to be seen to be 'breaking ranks'. The campaign to outlaw fox hunting has such a head of steam that now it appears there is no time to even consider where it is going. The Bill, though backed, reportedly, to the sum of five million pounds by various organisations, was so badly drafted that it provided opponents in the House of Commons numerous opportunities to put down amendments and thus failed to become law.

Whilst constantly referring to the welfare of animals, the proponents of the Bill seemed to overlook the fact that hunting with hounds is simply one method in a spectrum of fox killing activities. Foxes can be legally shot, either with a rifle or a shotgun, they can be snared or they can be live cage trapped (where they can be either shot or released elsewhere) though generally this is not a serious method of control. They can be gassed or poisoned, both of which are illegal, but nevertheless remain an option for some people. They will no doubt continue to be set upon by other types of dog, for example lurchers or terriers, as it is the case that some people will not adhere to any ban on hunting with dogs, just in the same way that badger diggers now ignore the Badgers Act. That situation will only get worse if many pro-hunting landowners lose interest in the fox.

Only ten per cent of the 250,000 foxes deliberately killed by man per year killed by organised hunts

The number of foxes killed deliberately each year amounts to approximately 250,000 or more, whereas the total killed by organised hunts is something less than ten per cent of that figure. The sceptic would say that those other methods of killing foxes would in the main be undertaken for control reasons rather than entertainment. This is simply not true. To one degree or another, human enjoyment is a factor in most of these activities or the reason for them being undertaken. The fox, however, is not interested in your morals, it is not interested in whether you are wearing a red coat, nor is it interested in your mode of transport. It is simply interested in what you are doing to it.

If hunting is banned, other methods of control will take its place

So it is clear, that if fox hunting with hounds as we know it is proscribed, other forms of fox hunting would continue, though very little appears to be heard about these methods from the organisations which are campaigning for a ban, other than perhaps the phrase 'humane shooting'. So what would happen after a hunt ban? Quite frankly, no-one knows for sure. It is a little odd that a university report designed specifically to answer this question, found no evidence that foxes would suffer in greater numbers in a post-ban period. This should be obvious; there is no evidence because we are not yet in that position. What we do have, however, is anecdotal evidence from a variety of sources and our own common sense. If foxes are perceived as pests, even in the light of numerous scientific reports which may indicate otherwise, is it not reasonable to assume that they will continue to be killed by one method or another? Is it not also reasonable to assume that, as unpalatable as it may be to many people, the fox is given some sort of status as a quarry species and perhaps tolerated in many areas where, in the absence of a hunt, it would not. If this is so, it therefore follows that by removing the hunt, as an albeit fairly inefficient means of controlling the fox, other methods will be substituted which are more efficient, though not necessarily humane.

If foxes no longer offer sport landowners and farmers will no longer tolerate them

In the light of a hunt ban, some pro-hunt landowners would view the fox in a very different light. Shooting estates, for example, generally do not want foxes in high numbers. Look at the difference between East Anglia, a mainly shooting area, where the fox is ruthlessly controlled, and the shires of the Midlands, where numerous foxhound packs exist and the fox population is higher.

It may also be the case that more foxes will be killed for another reason in that hunts tend to be bring many rural people together and if they know that a certain number of foxes have been killed, they will be quite satisfied. The alternative would be for each landowner to deal with foxes as he or she finds them, with the likely result being that many more in total are killed.

Other methods of control often less humane

The fox killing methods adopted will differ from area to area and will be the preference of the landowner involved. Currently, it is quite legal to shoot a fox with totally inappropriate birdshot, knowing that you are going to wound the animal and that it will crawl away and die at some later stage. Yet, 'shooting' (as if that is only one activity and always humane) is often hailed as the alternative to fox hunting. In some areas where expert marksmen, usually gamekeepers, are operating shooting probably is, more often than not, humane. However, such people do not exist in every area and rifles could not be used in all parts of the UK, nor indeed would their use be desirable in every area such as those which are heavily wooded and across which numerous rights of way exist.

In Wales, different kinds of hunts operate, ranging from the commonly known mounted packs through to gun packs which use fox hounds to flush foxes from cover into lines of shotguns. Once again, the latter is efficient, though not every fox is killed outright by the first blast of shot and clearly there are 'good' packs as well as bad ones. In a post-ban period it is likely that such groups would increase in number. To some other landowners who are troubled by foxes or feel that they pose a potential problem, more direct methods may be used such as gassing or poisoning. Though illegal, they would be very difficult to detect.

For ban on hunting to be effective country people would have to acquiesce

This is a key point often overlooked in the hunting debate. It is the landowner or farmer who can make the law work or not. Countryside law is notoriously difficult in any case to police and if those landowners who are at present in favour of hunting with hounds wish to turn their back on the fox, the welfare benefit of any law that may be passed by Parliament would be non-existent.

Very little consideration has been given by anti-hunting organisations as to how such a law would be policed. When one considers that some hunts operate over large tracts of private land, detection of a breach of the law would be almost impossible. Even if a hunt was witnessed, who, for example, would be arrested? The Master, the Huntsman, the Whippers-in or the whole field? What about observers? Are they guilty too? At least one animal rights activist holds the view that each hunt would be assigned a mounted police officer, with the possible use of a police helicopter over large estates. With approximately 22,000 hunting days a year, I wonder if the police forces around Britain will have a sudden injection of cash to meet their extra needs; I think not. Yet, this is a practical difficulty which the police would face on day one after a hunt ban.

Reform of hunting, not a ban, is correct way forward for animal welfarists

Surely there is a better way forward – indeed any way forward out of this seemingly intractable stalemate would be novel. Wildlife Network, a body created by former senior officials of the League Against Cruel Sports, was formed to seek benefits for wildlife and a reduction in suffering, but believes that a simple removal of fox hunting will cause more suffering to the fox. Consequently, reform of hunting is the answer. This is a view held by a number of politicians who have recently formed the new Parliamentary Middle Way Group. Lembit Öpik MP, one of the founding members, outlined the aims perfectly: 'We are not seeking victory here, we are seeking solutions.' In an atmosphere which is less antagonistic, hunters would, I believe, be willing to change some of their practices to reduce the suffering of the quarry. Those people seeking an all-out ban have, ironically, caused the hunting world to unite and fight, in some cases around undesirable practices. How much more productive it would be to discuss areas of concern with those involved in hunting, and indeed shooting as well, in order that changes could be made. The potential for reduction of suffering is enormous, yet the activities of hunting and shooting would still be retained, enabling governing bodies to concentrate on weeding out those individuals who break rules. Such moves would certainly be workable and sustainable, as those involved in the activities would be part of the process of change.

Foxes will pay the price of the intransigence of animal rightists

It is time that the main animal welfare bodies looked at the greater picture, rather than concentrating on reaching the 'animal rights' milestone of banning hunting with dogs. In the mad rush to ban something, the danger is that the repercussions of such a measure will have been overlooked and the people who helped the law onto the statute book, many of whom have the best of intentions, will then turn their attention to other issues, leaving what they feel to be some kind of utopia for foxes in the countryside. They should understand the true meaning of 'utopia'.

It is highly likely that Parliament will again have to address the issue of hunting with dogs. Caught between the powerful and wealthy animal groups and an equally strong countryside lobby, a third option might appear attractive. If those advocating the 'Middle Way' view are wrong, it may lead to the opportunity to achieve a total ban being lost, but at the very least some suffering will have been reduced by way of reforms. If, however, they are correct and fox hunting is prohibited, the price will be high, though it will be foxes who pay it, not those 'principled' individuals calling for an all-out ban.

9

Country sports: putting man in his proper place

Laurence Catlow

Country sports should be defended, argues Laurence Catlow, not because they are rural activities, but because they are morally right. Increasingly, animals are being anthropomorphised and humans are being down-graded to the level of animals. Country sports put men – and foxes, and pheasant, and trout – in their proper place. They underline the absolute difference between men and animals, and should be defended for that reason alone. Yet politicians who know nothing of country sports are contemplating banning them for no other reason than 'feel-good' gesture politics. Such a ban would be the statutory triumph of ignorant popular sentiment over reason and reflection.

I was unable to take part in the Countryside March, otherwise I should have walked through the middle of London, peacefully waving a placard that would have proclaimed my solidarity with hunting folk; but I confess that it would have been waved with some misgivings: not, of course, about the rightness of the cause, for it is my unwavering belief that field sports, blood sports, country sports (I do not care too much what people call them) are morally wholesome and enriching activities; not, I repeat, about the rightness of the cause, but rather about my own right to participate in a march that belonged to the countryside. I should have asked myself how far a man who earns a meagre living teaching Latin and Greek, even one who lives in a small Cumbrian town and spends as much time as possible killing pheasants and fish, ought to think of himself as a countryman. I am not so regarded by the real countrymen it is my privilege to count among my friends.

Country sports appeal to many only tangentially connected to the countryside

As a participant in the Countryside March, I should have thought myself a partial fraud, aware that my roots in the countryside are roots of affection: spiritual roots rather than those that grow from continual association and essential need. Looking round I should have seen, as well as many indisputable countrymen, many others like me: schoolmasters, lawyers, stockbrokers, builders, bakers, even accountants, men with a passionate love of the sports that belong to the British countryside, but men who only get earth on their boots and mud on their faces when out in pursuit of foxes, pheasants and fish, men who make their living by sitting indoors and longing for the weekend.

There is a widespread misconception about those who take part in and support our traditional field sports: that most of them practise such sports because they never knew any better, that, born and bred in backward shires or remote valleys, they began to kill rabbits and hunt rats just as soon as they could walk, that, surrounded by the hard facts of nature, they have never asked themselves whether it is civilised behaviour to hunt and kill. They are, it is believed, men with blunted sensibilities and primitive attachments; they have been left behind by the development of ever-more refined and caring attitudes. They deserve some pity and much disapproval and, like all anachronisms – hereditary peers, for example – their days are numbered.

Debate about country sports not merely an urban versus rural issue

But the widely-held assumption that the debate about field sports is a debate between urban and rural man, is quite simply false. Isaac Walton called fishing the contemplative man's recreation; fly fishing might more properly be called the professional man's recreation. At a typical pheasant shoot I guess that most of the guns, and many of the beaters, have driven to the coverts in flight from urban occupations. Perhaps hunting derives more of its support from those who spend a good portion of their lives under the open sky, but it inspires men who sweat in offices and factories to climb onto horses and risk their necks, while not all those who hunt with the foot packs of the North live out their lives in the shadows of the fells over which they follow hounds.

It is also true that many countrymen have little interest in field sports. Field sports do not reflect the universally-shared values of the rural community. Some farmers hunt; others loathe the local hunt as passionately as they loathe VAT forms. Some shoot; others rent out their shooting to syndicates; many do neither. Very few farmers go fishing for trout.

I see now what I should have done if I had been able to join the Countryside March. I should have left my flat cap at home and hung my Barbour beneath it; I should have polished my only pair of black shoes and worn (someone else's) pin-striped suit. I should have tried to group around me those thousands of marchers who worked in towns and went hunting, fishing or shooting in the countryside. My placard would have read something like: 'Give the semi-urban the right to enjoy themselves'. And I should not have been surprised if the thousands marching under this banner had proved to be the majority of the great gathering.

Case for country sports is that they are morally right, not that they are country activities

My only quarrel with the Countryside March is that it came close to promoting a distortion: the view that country sports are exclusively practised by country people, whereas it seems to me that we make a better case for field sports when we point out how many participants come from non-rural walks of life, resorting to the countryside for delight and consolation rather as ramblers do.

On the whole I think town-bred shooters, hunters and fishermen are less arrogant and destructive than ramblers. They do not wear away mountains with their boots, their dogs rarely maul sheep and they do not claim the right to wander wherever the fancy takes them over land that does not belong to them. But that is not the point. My point is that the argument in favour of field sports is in danger of taking a false turn: with a vision of a homogeneous countryside, united in its approval and practice of field sports, clinging to these pursuits as the expression of traditional and unchanging rural values. Now this is dangerous because it is not true; it is also dangerous because, if the field sports lobby sets itself up as the voice of the countryside, speaking against the louder roar of the town, it is likely to make that roar louder still and its voice is almost certain to be drowned.

The Countryside Alliance, formed with the admirable purpose of defending field sports and, as far as I can tell, a wholly admirable institution, should have been called something else. Its present name suggests that support for these sports is confined to the countryside and almost universal in the countryside. It encourages those who regard them as primitive rural practices to persist both in their belief and their disapproval. It would be better if arguments in favour of field sports spoke less about rural values and more about the sports themselves; it would be better if men from towns, who have proclaimed their origins and the enrichment they have found from their precious and unsentimental contact with the life of nature. The case for hunting, shooting and fishing can be best made by insisting on the essential rightness of the activities themselves.

Country sportsmen tend to identify themselves as country people even when they are not

Some myths express profound truths. Others promote falsehood. The myth that country sports are the preserve of country people is of the second sort. It is unfortunate that the myth appeals to many who follow country sports without themselves being of the countryside. Field sports are wrongly associated by most people with the rural upper class; some of us, who do not ourselves belong to that enviable group, are nevertheless partial to the association and inclined to go along with it. But it is not all snobbery, for the followers of field sports come to love the countryside so passionately that they begin to think of themselves as countrymen in spirit. In their worn breeches and torn Barbours they thus perpetuate the myth and, it seems to me (though I am as guilty as the next man in this respect), they thus endanger the future of the things they love.

Country sports put men – and foxes, and pheasant and trout – in their proper place

The present controversy about hunting in particular and field sports in general is not, except in unimportant ways, a confrontation between urban and rural values. It is a controversy about our treatment of animals other than ourselves; it is here that the war should be waged. Supporters of field sports should argue that to hunt the fox is just to show a very proper respect for what is admirable about foxes, just as to catch and kill trout, or to shoot and kill pheasants shows a very proper regard for their place in the economy of nature. They should insist that, if such attitudes are wrong, then the town dweller will sooner or later be as profoundly affected as his bloodstained cousins in the countryside.

The abolition of hunting would not drastically change the rural way of living and it would change the rural landscape much less than is often claimed. It would deprive those who presently hunt of an activity they love, making of it their art, their freedom, their fulfilment. But, and this is the important bit, if the arguments currently developed against fox hunting are successful and if at some time in the future they are applied less selectively to our involvement with animals (which they certainly should be if they are thought to be convincing in the particular context of hunting), then it is not just rural practices that will be changed; the habits of the whole nation will be transformed by the upheaval.

The supporters of field sports should not, if they hope to win the argument, defend hunting as part of a traditional feature of country life. They should rather insist that, with religion lost as the moral guide of our actions, man's place in the order of creation needs redefinition, that his relations with the creatures around him need urgent re-examination. They should then expose the current hostility towards hunting as intellectually dishonest sentimentality proceeding from that dangerous tendency of the age: to lavish emotions upon things of which we have no knowledge or experience, to wallow in sentiment rather than to struggle to understand. It is easy to feel pity for foxes; it is very difficult to establish a reasoned philosophy for our treatment of animals. It is clearly irrational and fraudulent to single out fox hunting as a moral abomination, while refusing to acknowledge that the demands of contemporary society presently subject animals to treatment at least as questionable as pursuit by a pack of hounds.

If for no other reason, fox hunting should be preserved because it underlines the absolute superiority of men over animals

And there is another feature of the age that demands attention, a feature at once disturbing and subversive, a feature grimly illustrated by the present outcry against the monstrous suffering of foxes; this is that, as we come more and more to look upon ourselves as mere animals, so we are tending more and more to regard animals as something like human beings. There is, I suppose, a chilling logic to this, in spite of the irrational selectivity with which it is currently applied, and I dread to think where it might end. Fox hunting should be preserved: if only as a means of insisting upon the absolute difference between men and animals.

It is, I suppose, barely conceivable that considerations such as these might encourage one or two members of Parliament to attempt a few moments of disinterested reflection, before they come to their senses and reach the inevitable conclusion that, whatever the rights and wrongs of the matter, the prudent course will be to humour their constituents and assume an appropriately outraged posture in defence of the rights of foxes. When hunting is banned, it will be seen as the triumph of civilised values over barbarism. But its real significance will be this: that popular sentiment unsupported by knowledge, reflection and reason has at last been plainly acknowledged as an appropriate basis for legislation. It will be proclaimed a victory for morality; it will, in truth, be an act of moral surrender, conceding to the majority the right to limit the freedom of minorities in areas about which it knows almost nothing but is inclined to disapprove. It will be seen as a triumph and it will stink to high heaven.

10

Red coats and rituals: what modern Britons hate about hunting

Elizabeth Peplow

The red-coated, red-faced, middle-aged, overweight hunter is the dominant urban image of hunting. It is a useful stereotype for the anti-hunting activists, because it represents all that modern Britons despise most – tradition, privilege, and ritual. Elizabeth Peplow finds that much of the opposition to hunting is motivated by modern Britons' contempt for what they regard as outmoded and for what they do not understand. It is a far stronger motivation than concern for the welfare of foxes. Anti-hunting activists are happy to play upon these prejudices against the red-coated hunter. Never mind that it gives a totally false image of the sport and those who enjoy it.

'I have found it exciting this morning: there has been a whiff of class struggle in the air', Ian Gibson MP (Norwich, North). From the Wild Mammals (Hunting With Dogs) Bill, standing committee, *Hansard*.

'Hunting is not all about toffs in red coats', William Hague.

Red spells danger, anger, bloodshed, burning, violence and revolution. And increasingly, the splash of red, as the hunt streams through the British countryside, has brought all these things together, igniting them into what has been turned into one of the last great moral and political debates of the century.

'There is a war going on in the countryside, and it is going on largely unreported', trumpeted the Hunt Saboteurs' Association (HSA) last year, listing a catalogue of violence taking place at hunt meets, in which it said its members had come off badly at the hands of a justice system intent on 'doffing its cap' to the hunters.

Anti-hunting activists' attempt to lose class war image rings hollow

While the politicians who packed the House of Commons to give resounding support to the second reading of Michael Foster's Wild Mammals (Hunting With Dogs) Bill, may have – perhaps in the spirit of premature triumphalism – scented a whiff of class struggle, activists more attuned to the negative PR of such a link, reject claims that they are inspired by 'nothing more than anarchist class war'.

The HSA claims in an article headed: 'Lies, Damn Lies And Green Wellies' that: 'In the past three years the hunting community has realised it has a serious image problem and has put substantial effort and millions of pounds into trying to make themselves more acceptable. Much of this effort has consisted of a smear campaign…exposing saboteurs as class war militants bent on violence and destruction.'

However, repeated references by anti-hunting spokesman to a way of life 'outdated in modern Britain', to 'red-faced, red-coated huntsmen', to the mocking 'time for the last tally-ho' reveal a motivation that is not just class-based but broadly anti-tradition – a tradition symbolised by the scarlet-clad hunt follower. The image of the red-coated huntsman has become contentious. Ludicrously, hunting modernisers last year made tabloid headlines when they dared to suggest scrapping the red coat. In Ireland, where hunting is a national obsession it was pointed out that anything goes in the hunting field including pink anoraks and red wellingtons. The antis responded swiftly by saying that the issue was about cruelty in the countryside not dress sense, knowing all too well, in the multi-million pound industry that is the animal rights movement, the powerful weapon on their side of the symbolic red coat in raising both funds and recruiting new members.

The red coat an inspiration to artists and a symbol of rural England

For generations, the red-coated hunter has been used by countless artists and writers for another purpose, to symbolise the thrill of the chase within the beauty of rural England. Captured by sporting artists from Stubbs to Lionel Edwards and by authors such as Fielding, Surtees, Trollope, Kipling, Masefield and Sassoon, he is often the master of the hunt or the huntsman who organises the hunt and directs it while the chase is on.

Others, however, may wear red if they have earned a coveted hunting button, which is awarded by the master of the hunt for contributions to the hunt. The red coat is shrouded in myth and is commonly misunderstood not just by anti-hunt campaigners, but by those who support or are indifferent to hunting with hounds. Indeed, confusion surrounds the very colour of the coat, which is commonly but mistakenly referred to as a 'pink'. Whatever its origins, students of either art history or contemporary photographs that capture the visual splendour of the hunting field, printed in magazines such as *Horse & Hound, The Field* and *Country Life*, cannot deny its important visual impact. Michael Clayton, former editor of *Horse & Hound*, contends: 'Increasingly the pressures stem from urban values, yet there is strong evidence that the traditions and customs of rural life continue to be highly prized as part of the nation's cultural heritage. Consequently, they form one of the many attractions for both domestic and overseas tourists.'

Even the anti-hunt Conservative MP Ann Widdecombe alluded to the colour of the hunting field as having been an integral and positive part of rural Britain. But in the debate on the Bill to outlaw hunting, she said that she would rather see the scene played out on her living room curtains than in real life, to a roar of laughter from fellow MPs. This showed just how effectively the image of the red coat has been more used by the anti-hunt lobby than its supporters.

Red coat used as propaganda tool by anti-hunting activists

Advertising campaigns by the League Against Cruel Sports, the International Fund for Animal Welfare and the RSPCA in daily newspapers invariably depict photographs of red-coated huntsman or hunt masters engaged in either allegedly cruel or laughable pursuits. The stereotype is a useful one and crops up repeatedly to the extent that suburban Britain increasingly sees the red-coated hunter as a politicised symbol of all that is wrong with rural England. He has become a multi-purpose bogey man, a soft target for those who would whip up indignation against traditional country ways.

Hunting represents what is most despised by modern Britons – privilege, ritual and tradition

The hunter has thus become multi-symbolic. For suburbanites he symbolises aristocracy, the old discredited order of master and serf, of have and have-not. In other sectors he symbolises man's hubris in his dealings with the natural world. The colour red is the colour of blood. It symbolises danger and in its putrefied form, ultimately death. For the anti-hunt movement, the red-faced, red-coated huntsman is the privileged agent of death and destruction.

Problems have arisen for the hunting community as symbolised by the red coat with the development of a culture that is increasingly anti-ritual and politically correct. This is particularly so as we now have a government which has modernist rationality as a core belief system. New Labour has turned its attentions to all kinds of rituals that it has perceived as being irrational and un-modern: the proposed changes to the House of Lords; the Chancellor of the Exchequer's refusal to follow traditional dress codes; the Prime Minister's insistence on being called 'Tony' at Cabinet Meetings. In this sense, New Labour truly reflects the values of middle-class suburban Britain – its disregard for dress codes, table manners, school uniforms and its preference for no religion or ritual-free folk services.

The coincidence of anti-ritualism and political correctness in the burgeoning middle classes, and its reflection in its elected representatives and institutions, has meant trouble for the red-coated hunter, for he fails on three Cool Britannia counts. Firstly, he is the very essence of ritual. The wearing of red is ritual, it signifies a great deal about the wearer and his activity. Secondly, the redcoat is politically incorrect, his prime activity sees to that. Finally, and perhaps most damning, he is perceived to be 'unmodern'.

Hunting, its rituals and the red coat under attack because they are anti-modern

Indeed, the fox hunter on his charger seems anti-modern in essence. Every aspect of his appearance, his mode of transport and his chosen sport is an affront to cool modernity. This is a message opponents of hunting have been united in voicing. Kate Parminter, director of the Council for the Protection of Rural England, speaking in 1997 in a previous incarnation as spokesman for the Campaign for the Protection of the Hunted Animal said hunting was 'outdated and not part of modern Britain. MPs believe it is time for the last tally-ho'. Michael Foster MP, when launching his ill-fated anti-hunt Bill in the House of Commons, echoed her words and urged MPs to stand proud and 'make a modern Britain'. Using the same script a month later, John Cooper of the League Against Cruel Sports condemning the tradition of Boxing Day meets said: 'Bloodsports are out-foxed, out-dated and out-voted. It's time for the last tally-ho.'

Press statements by the Hunt Saboteurs' Association are keen to promote the image as badly out of step, referring to a world of red-coated riders and forelock-tugging by police. In one incident of alleged violence by a huntsman on a saboteur, the HSA, seemingly obsessed by the poor old red coat, remarks: 'He had thoughtfully removed his red coat, possibly not wanting to get the blood of a hunt saboteur on it.' Elsewhere the HSA accuses the police of 'rolling out the red carpet for the hunts', and of unfair bias against its members simply because they are 'blowing a horn [to distract hounds] in the wrong clothes'.

But the red coat actually a relative newcomer to the hunting scene

The fact that the red coat has come to symbolise the *ancien regime* is bizarre, because it is actually a relative newcomer to the hunting scene. As Mark Hedges, deputy editor of *Horse & Hound,* points out: 'Old hunting prints show riders wearing a variety of clothing. Most people wore pretty much what they wanted. The wearing of the red coat throughout the hunting field has grown during [this] century and stemmed from the awarding of hunt buttons to those who had contributed to the hunt in some way. It was usual that once a hunt button had been awarded, the recipient could then wear a red coat.'

Rituals not just under attack on the hunting field

Thus the red coat is in hunting's terms as much a modern development as the automobile, rocket science, glam rock and the anti-runway protester. However, it does display in an exaggerated way the ritual that has become such an integral part of the chase. Whereas in previous generations such ritual may have been advantageous in terms of public relations it has now undoubtedly become a liability. As any social institution that previously thrived on ritual has discovered to its cost, ritual is out. The high churches have modernised (with disastrous results). The dress codes at Oxford and Cambridge have gone. The wigs of office are heading for the museum cabinets of tomorrow.

This is not the first time that ritual has fallen out of fashion. The Reformation was hard on many rituals and the vested interests that relied upon them. So was the cultural revolution that was the 1960s. As a social movement, hunting has not escaped these exigencies of fashion, indeed the rituals surrounding hunting have always been influenced by the prevailing moods of the day. Linda Colley, writing in *Britons* points to the roots of the surge in popularity of fox hunting in Britain as being a direct reaction to the French revolution.

Importantly, she cites a cultural reaction which saw the abandonment of foppish wigs and frills in favour of practical riding clothes and the increase in popularity of fox hunting as a need to do something useful in the countryside.

Rituals inculcated aristocratic values in newly moneyed and lower classes

Slowly, however, the *laissez faire* social attitudes of the late eighteenth century and early nineteenth century gave way to the Victorian culture of 'respectability' with its core concerns about social propriety, social climbing and status. The etiquette of hunting attire thus became an issue in the later era of the Industrial Revolution. But while the farmers stuck to the discreet black coat, it was the newly moneyed fox hunter and industrialist who sought social acceptance. Many thus attributed the development of a uniform in the hunting field, not to exclusive privilege, but to an openness of class.

Writing in *Peculiar Privilege*, David Itzkowiz says: 'While hunting people boasted of the openness of the hunting field, there is no question that the values the field fostered were conservative and aristocratic, and it was considered to be one of the great benefits of the openness that even the lower classes could be thus imbued with gentlemanly ideals.'

Modernists within hunting keen to abandon red coats for the sake of 'image'

Today, modernists in the hunting world concede that the red coat is one of the fancy dress aspects of hunting. Mark Hedges says: 'This is regrettable because the only people who really need to wear red coats are the officials who need to stand out from the rest of the field in times of emergency or when visibility is poor. From our point of view, if the red coat causes so much offence, and is seen as symbolising an almost feudal system, then it would be better to abandon it.' Michael Clayton concedes that, in the 1980s when *Class War* emerged, far from being seen as a social advantage, the top hat, and by implication, the red coat, the image conveyed 'was sometimes directly harmful'.

Support for hunting crosses all classes

A recent survey in *Horse & Hound* indicates, as ever, a wide range of socio-economic groupings in support of hunting. A return of approximately 12,000 readers listed a diverse and unexpected range of careers and occupations with beekeepers and watercress growers lining up alongside road sweepers, nurses, policemen, actuaries, long-distance lorry drivers, actresses and artists. Such a survey would find no dissenters at the organisation Cambridge Animal Rights, who say: 'Bloodsports are not the prerogative of the wealthy. Hare coursing still exists and is to a large extent, a working class sport. Even a fox hunt consists of a wide spectrum of people. You have to be rich to be able to afford to ride with the hunt, but not to be a terrierman, a foot follower or a supporter. These people are not just the puppets of the aristocrats, they are the enthusiastic participants in the hunts.' And it is here, that the ultimate myth of the red-coated hunter as a focus of evil for the anti-hunt lobby must be laid to rest. While the politicians were happy to 'rake over the ashes of class politics', according to Janet George of the Countryside Alliance, with bizarre allegations such as that surrounding the Countryside March of 280,000 people through London, which it was claimed most working people were forced to attend by their employers, analysis of the anti-hunt movement's own literature shows that the 'battle lines' are broader than the politicians would care to admit.

Anti-hunting activists aware of the cross-class support for hunting – but happy to use handy and effective stereotypes

The Hunt Saboteurs' Association claiming the issue of class is irrelevant says: 'Saboteurs come from all backgrounds, age groups, professions and political points of view. On the other side of the coin, the worst perpetrators of cruelty and violence at hunts are terriermen who are solidly working class.' While its own members more commonly don the uniform of combat gear and balaclava, it claims supporters include a 'brave, granny group of saboteurs in Surrey, all over 60 and with not a mohican among them'.

Kate Parminter, saying that anti-hunt legislation would attempt to outlaw more than organised hunting, noted: 'many people seem to associate this Bill [the failed Wild Mammals Protection (Hunting With Dogs)] solely with people in red coats. Hunting with dogs sadly has many other guises.'

Animal rights web sites on the Internet speak of night club bouncers and soldiers working for hunt security and make allegations of 'shady terriermen and lurchermen' from inner cities as being involved in a campaign of violence against sabs. To the image makers and breakers, such a picture is a world away from the men and women in red, but, just as 'nature is red in tooth and claw', so is the society formed around it.

The anti-hunt movement has conveniently given suburbia a neat, painless solution to the so-called moral issue of hunting that so sticks in its gullet, with an enemy it can so easily identify. To strip away the stereotype is to move into a more murky territory, away from the black and white dogma that has both fuelled the anti-hunt campaign for decades and its quarry for centuries.

11

Anti-hunt legislation: an attack on hunters, not a defence of foxes

Helen Searls

Why has hunting become such an issue in this Parliament? It is not because the banning of hunting would be especially popular; there may be opinion poll majorities in favour of a ban, but it is very peripheral to most urban voters' concerns. Nor is it because our MPs are terribly concerned about the welfare of foxes. For some on the left it is a 'safe' way of having a go at 'toffs'. But this is not the main reason. Hunt supporters' values are at odds with 'modern Britain'. Helen Searls argues that modern Britons are intolerant of all values other than their own. They may speak of a tolerant society, but by this they mean tolerance of their own ways. They cannot abide the pleasures of others.

Why has banning fox hunting become such a *cause célèbre*? And why is it that New Labour and the left in particular are so excited by the prospect of banning the hunt?

Parliamentary opposition to hunting not simply a reflection of public opinion

To listen to the new anti-hunting lobby you could be forgiven for thinking that support for the ban was driven by unprecedented public pressure. This is, after all, what opponents of hunting continually try to claim. Time and again they tell us that 70 or even 80 per cent of the British public favour a ban on hunting with hounds. They ask us 'what democratically-elected politician can fail to respond to such overwhelming public pressure?'

But while opinion polls show that many people do not care for hunting and would not object to banning the hunt, it would be wrong to assume that support for this Bill was the result of a ground-swell of public opinion. The idea that there is a genuinely popular demand for the ban is a fantasy. Fox hunting was not a major issue in the 1997 General Election and it has never been a major political issue in British politics. The public are not banging on the doors of Parliament demanding the outlawing of this practice. And anyway, as we all know, if what Parliament debated was ever to be decided by opinion polls, issues like capital punishment would beat the banning of fox hunting every time.

Nor due to concern for the welfare of foxes

So what is driving this force for the banning of fox hunting? The first point to note is that the desire to ban hunting today is not driven by the same kind of sentiment that has surrounded the issue in the past. There have always been those who have an old fashioned love of animals and have sought to protect bushy-tailed foxes. Undoubtedly such people still exist but it is not their concerns that ignited the passions of the new intake of Labour MPs. Today the fox is a relatively minor player in the campaign to outlaw hunting. All sides accept that farmers will continue to kill foxes long after the hunt is banned.

But an attempt to demonize and criminalise hunt supporters

Rather than focusing on the fox or any other wild mammal, the new campaign against hunting is a campaign against people. It is in essence a campaign about what is and what is not morally acceptable in New Labour's Britain. Only once it is seen in this light do the sentiments aroused by the issue begin to make sense.

The goal of those who want to ban hunting is to demonize and criminalise those who hunt. It is this objective which drives the new anti-hunt lobby. Their aim is to outlaw those who hunt – not simply by the legal banning of hunting but also by turning hunt supporters into moral outcasts. The fox was never meant to be the beneficiary of this campaign. Whatever legislation is eventually passed, foxes will be killed and maimed by other means. Rather, the main players to benefit from the anti-hunting campaign are the campaigners themselves. By seeking to demonize hunt supporters as morally bankrupt, the campaigners know that their own authority in New Labour's Britain has already been boosted substantially.

For the old left it is proxy class war

The campaign's focus on people rather than foxes is evident in all the debates and discussions that Michael Foster's failed anti-hunting Bill provoked. For much of the old left the campaign against hunting is a means of fighting the old class struggle by proxy. *Socialist Worker* was explicit on this point. In a series of articles in Spring 1998 *Socialist Worker* writers, while ignoring completely the fate of the fox, described hunt supporters as 'a right-wing rabble' and 'racist filth' and explained to its readers that 'fox hunting is about class privilege'.[1]

New Labour campaigners might lack the bluntness of *Socialist Worker* but it is still evident that hunt supporters were also the real object of their hatred. For instance in the various parliamentary debates around the Bill, anti-hunt campaigners repeatedly argued that what most angered them about hunting was the admission by hunt supporters that they took pleasure in the sport.

New Britons cannot abide the pleasures of others

This was a major theme during the second reading of Foster's anti-hunting Bill in November 1997. Labour MP Kevin McNamara admonished Michael Heseltine for suggesting that fox hunting was fun. He complained that 'the Right Hon Member for Henley says that hunting is fun. Hares are pulled to pieces by greyhounds at sporting events. People go to hear the hare squeal for fun. What sort of society has fun in that way?'[2] In case anyone missed the point, the condemnation of the hunter's pleasure was repeated time and time again throughout the debate. In his widely praised maiden speech, Labour Member Dan Norris summed up the sentiment of many when he said that 'ultimately, however it comes down to morality. Before voting, Hon Members should ask "In a civilised society how can anyone be allowed to kill an animal for pleasure?" It is as simple as that.'[3]

If hunt supporters could only adopt the mantle of the 'victim', they would be supported by 'modern Britons'

Clearly it is the behaviour of the hunt rather than the fate of the fox that motivates the anti-hunt campaigners to outlaw the sport. In fact it sometimes seems that if only the hunt were to conduct themselves differently they would arouse less animosity. Hunt supporters are condemned as unethical because their 'tally-ho' outlook and brash values fail to conform to New Labour's politically correct vision of the world. They are 'beyond the pale' because they do not act like worthy citizens. In New Labour's Britain the centre stage of politics is constantly offered to every shade of victim and sufferer. Be they bullied children, traumatised adults or even abused animals, we are repeatedly told to respect the victim. In such a political climate there is simply no place for those who enjoy hunting down their prey and showing absolutely no remorse for their apparently 'abusive' behaviour.

Modern Britons are intolerant of all values other than their own

The new morality that drives the debate can be seen in other ways. We are told by anti-hunt campaigners that the outlawing of fox hunting is about the creation of a modern Britain for the new millennium. But while this mantra is repeated in all the debates, few have bothered to ask what is meant by this? Surely the energies of those who seek to modernise Britain would be better spent updating our Victorian transport system or upgrading our crumbling housing stock. It is not immediately clear why the banning of fox hunting is likely to propel a modern Britain into the twenty-first century.

But the matter becomes clearer when one looks at what is really being said about the modernisation of Britain. When Michael Foster proposed his Bill, he argued that the modernisation of Britain was actually about the moralisation of Britain around New Labour's ethical codes. He claimed that the British Government's capacity to stand in moral judgement over others is precisely what a modern Britain must be about. He spelt out this point in closing remarks when proposing the Bill to the House. With a less than modest sense of self importance, he said:

> How can we pass judgement on Pakistan, where they set dogs on bears, or on Spanish bull fighting, when we allow dogs to be set on deer? When we were elected to the House we all wanted to change the world, or at least a small part of it. Today we have an opportunity to create a modern Britain. The House will be judged by future generations by what we do today.[4]

Foster and his supporters were clear. By turning hunt supporters into moral outcasts, New Labour's own position as the guardians and

70

arbitrators of society's morals would be enhanced. The modernisation of Britain is all about creating this kind of moral authority both at home and abroad. By outlawing and criminalising politically incorrect hunters, New Labour's credentials as politically correct, ethical policemen can only be enhanced.

Being opposed to hunting has become a sign of virtue in 'modern Britain'

It is only when the debate about fox hunting is understood as a moral witch hunt that the postures and positioning of the new anti-hunt brigade can be understood. Throughout the debate, anti-hunt campaigners were not only smug and sanctimonious towards their opponents, they were also totally impervious to any of the old arguments that hunt supporters threw at them about tolerance and freedom. Once hunting became a matter of the new morality such arguments held little sway. In the past a 'live and let live' attitude might have been seen as a virtue but from the perspective of the new morality such an approach is condemned as passive and dangerous. Today's heroes are those who do most to regulate and ban those whom they find morally reprehensible. In fact, once any kind of behaviour is deemed to be outside the new morality, be it smoking, eating red meat or hunting, it is only a matter of time before the practice will be regulated and banned by those who seek to lord it over us.

Given the kind of morality that was attached to the issue, it was inevitable that the left and New Labour joined the anti-hunting campaign with such venom. Despite the fact that Foster's Bill was meant to be a free vote for all MPs, it was a foregone conclusion that New Labour's moralists would be unable to resist this particular crusade. Yesterday's left has spent much of the recent past redefining itself as the guardians of the new morality. Free vote or not, the banning of fox hunting encapsulates what the old left and new Labour have become. Not only did the measure capture the killjoy spirit that we have come to expect from the new Government. It also provided an opportunity for New Labour to flaunt its intolerant authoritarianism with the prospect of using the criminal law to assert its moral righteousness.

Attack on hunting is an attack on freedom of all, not just hunt supporters

The truth is there is nothing modern or progressive about the banning of fox hunting. For all the sanctimony that surrounds the issue, those of us who would like to see a better world should have nothing but contempt for the new anti-hunt lobby. This is not because there is anything especially good or progressive about hunting itself. Hunting is not the issue here. It is rather that the campaign that seeks to ban hunting and outlaw the hunters poses a serious threat to all of us. Once we accept that the state has the right to outlaw private activities that it deems to be morally unacceptable, then we are abandoning one of the few remaining freedoms that we have. Our right to make any decisions for ourselves is severely threatened.

The tragedy of this campaign is that a word like freedom has become a dirty word. It is clear that the old left and New Labour have abandoned any pretence of being in the business of social progress, when the most forthright champions of freedom and liberty are the likes of Michael Heseltine and John Gummer. As someone who has long fought for freedom and civil liberties, I think we should have nothing but contempt for those who wish to tell us how to live our lives and dictate to us all what values are and are not acceptable. You don't have to give a jot about hunting to feel passionately about that.

12

'The right to roam': a new name for an old class hatred

Robin Hanbury-Tenison

Activists are demanding that statutory access is granted to ramblers over private land. They portray this as a conflict between the dispossessed urban multitudes and rural aristocrats wanting to keep the beauty of the countryside all to themselves. The landowners are subject to the kind of infantile caricatures entrepreneurs once were. Yet Robin Hanbury-Tenison shows that voluntary agreements already provide ramblers with access to around 2.5 million acres of private land. Quality access can only be provided with the co-operation of farmers and landowners, who want to give the urban populace an insight into how the countryside really works. Legislation and compulsion will merely antagonise landowners and turn all discussions of access into unnecessary conflicts.

Activists portray 'right to roam' as class issue

In the rich mythology of the British countryside, access and the 'right to roam' have a special place because there is a college of myth-makers and storytellers to propagate the fantasies. A hard core inside the Ramblers' Association and a quaint new pressure-group called The Land is Ours have been busy wreathing the countryside in a simplistic, outdated fable of 'them and us', 'big guy versus little guy', and variations on the class-conflict theme. The modern countryside is diverse and more accessible now than it was 20 years ago. It is about communities, business and conservation; new service industries and high technology cheek-by-jowl with traditional ways of life. Yet the militant rambling rhetoric places rural landowners in the same frame as the archetypal capitalists pictured in the hate-sessions of George Orwell's *Nineteen Eighty-Four*, where children were taught that the Capitalists were 'fat, evil men with wicked faces, wearing black top hats'. Nobody harbours such a crude stereotype of urban businessmen these days, but swap the top hat for tweeds, and there you have the level of debate used by some proponents of a 'right to roam'.

David Beskine of the Ramblers' Association says that new access legislation 'strikes at the very heart of landed aristocracy'. Sounds like this rambler wants to walk softly, and carry a big stick, as the saying goes. The sedentary firebrand George Monbiot, who runs The Land is Ours strikes the same chord: 'Our exclusion from rural Britain is the most manifest of class barriers', he declaims. Well, the fact is that the Duke of Westminster is no more allowed to trespass in George Monbiot's garden than George Monbiot is allowed to trespass on the Duke's estate. Property rights are the same for suburban gardeners and local authorities, for landed aristos, lottery winners and pop-squires such as Sir Paul McCartney. Class has nothing to do with it. Changing key to smart alec socio-babble, Mr Monbiot says: 'What we're getting in the countryside is not just a biological monoculture, but a social monoculture as well'. Hasn't he heard that there's a net migration of 1,700 people per week into the countryside from the towns?

'Right to roam' based upon misconceptions – voluntary access already provides what the public wants

Fully unpacked from their wrappings, the militant roamer myths are these: The public wants and expects coercive new laws to let them go wombling free. Landowners are all toffs who want to keep the commoners in their place. Landowners will never open up unless they are made to. Farmers are useless as conservationists and therefore don't deserve consideration. The public has already paid for access in the form of farming subsidies. There is a huge bank of private land that is ready to be opened up by new rights-based law. All of this is bunk.

Monbiot and Co suffer the usual tragedy of PhD revolutionaries; that they have plenty of leaders but no followers. Yes, there is a clear appetite for more access. 80 per cent of people want to see more access according to a poll for the Country Landowners' Association but there is no sense of militancy in this expectation. The class-conscious mass trespasses of the 1930s are as obsolete as a 60-year-old tractor. All people want is well-managed access for leisure, where they can have some recreation and some unobtrusive facilities, such as maps, guides, signposts, and sometimes parking, toilets and ranger services, where appropriate. There is no stomach in Britain for the 'blood and soil' rhetoric of the rambling fanatics. That is why the Countryside Alliance favours voluntary access – landowners providing access in partnership with walkers and local authorities. Landowners who are happy with a fair new deal on access will provide quality access, and do their bit to make walkers comfortable and secure. Landowners who feel coerced and exploited will obviously do less. They will be less keen to maintain pathways and signs, and less keen to keep the routes that walkers use beautiful and tranquil. Experience shows that voluntary access will deliver what the public wants: around 2.5 million acres are already open due to landowners' permission, and since 1990 220,000 new acres have been opened up by agreement.

Roamers tried to hijack Countryside March

There is no mandate from the public for a legally imposed, top-down 'right to roam'. But the Ramblers' Association evidently wishes it had people-power behind it. On the eve of the Countryside March, organised by the Countryside Alliance, the Ramblers' President Janet Street-Porter shrilled: 'The hunting lobby has hijacked the ramblers' march!' The whole march was organised in the office below mine, and I can say with certainty that the Ramblers' Association wasn't invited. More than 284,000 people turned up to declare for the countryside, and one of the published aims of the March was to oppose a blanket right to roam. I do not think that the militant ramblers could muster a tenth of that number, and I believe that most of the Ramblers' Association members would be well satisfied with practical increased access rather than an explicit new legal right.

Legislation simply unnecessary to provide extensive access

The Government has matured considerably since the 1997 Election. It has faced down some of the pushiest, most strident pressure groups, including the anti-hunting groups whose militancy and huge money-power can seriously interfere with the business of professional government. The Government has rightly taken the role of honest broker in the access debate, and published a consultation paper that offers up for criticism the two approaches to increasing access: legislative and voluntary. It is disappointing that the paper favours the legislative approach, and explicitly asks the parties who favour voluntary access to work harder to make their case. I think this shows that some of the myths pushed by the rambler elite have made their mark. It is they who should prove that a legal right of access to country areas will work. Voluntary access already has a portfolio of successes. The Duke of Buccleuch's is a model of voluntary access. The estate has worked with Dumfries and Galloway Council, and focused on local needs. There are 25 forest walks and nature trails, seven cycle trails and three horse trails on the estate, and well-maintained maps and information boards. Wheelchair routes and routes suitable for the elderly have been laid out. A right to roam edict would not magically create any of these benefits. Only partnership and goodwill can do so much.

At least the Government's paper serves to detonate some rambling mythology. It reveals that any proposed new right to roam legislation would take in a total of 3,062,800 acres. Impressive, except that access already exists to 2,230,000 acres. The 'open land' that stands to be taken in by new legislation comes to only eight per cent of England and Wales. The rest is city, suburb and cultivated farmland anyway. The picture of city people confined to a few little ruts, just waiting for the state to give them the key to the huge new horizons is a false one, a professionally marketed myth.

Right to roamers portray farmers as cartoon villains

It is a shame that rambling zealots have adopted farmer-bashing as a means to assert their views. Farmers have been wrecking the countryside, they say. If they can't manage it properly, where is their right to exclude others? Despite the pressures of CAP, British farmers have been doing remarkably well for conservation. Farming subsidy is a postwar monster that has distorted business and family life for three generations of farmers. It sets arbitrary rules, and if you don't play by the rules, you don't play at all. Unless you are very lucky, you cannot opt out and run your farm according to the reality of the world food market or your ecological ideals. Your farm goes bust and your family has to find somewhere else to live. Much still remains of Britain's traditional landscape. Elsewhere in Europe, the picture is not so pretty. Take a look at rural France from the Eurostar. Take a look round any city, and see how urban centres have been trashed in the same period without any pressure comparable to CAP. Farmers deserve their claim to be guardians of the countryside, and that means having a strong say in who walks their land.

The right to roam that the Government is considering would not affect the most obviously cultivated land, swaying with ripe corn. And that's an improvement on the doctrinaire proposals from the Ramblers' Association. Their 1995 draft Bill for a right to roam does not automatically exclude 'open' land which is being used for agriculture from its catchment. It makes the presumption of a right to roam, and merely only permits farmers to 'make application for a declaration of non-conformity' to except their land from the right to roam.

Not always obvious which land is used for agriculture

Yet the 77 per cent of English land area used for agriculture is not always so easily identifiable. Like the Ramblers' Association, the Government proposals talk of 'open land' in terms of 'mountains, moors, heath, downs and commons'. Most of those areas are used for agriculture some or all of the time, and it's hard for the layman to tell. If there is to be a 'presumption of access' conferred by a right to roam, walkers will inevitably damage farming and conservation efforts and cause ill-feeling. Right to roam proposals may allow temporary suspension of roaming rights to meet certain needs, but it is a very heavy burden for an active land-user to have to specify all the times and places where explorers will do no harm. Alternatively, if farmers and landowners are encouraged to allow access on their own initiative, time sharing and space sharing with the public can be achieved.

Quality access requires co-operation of farmers and land owners

The Government acknowledges that imposing a crude right to roam will not in itself give the public the quality access that it deserves. There will need to be voluntary arrangements anyway to give people the managed recreation that they want, according to polls. Landowners want the public to see how the countryside works, so as to dispel the many rural myths that distort public opinion and public policy on farming, hunting and rural social conditions. Landowners are walking the walk, while militant ramblers only talk the talk.

13

'The right to roam':
the expropriation of land

Jan Lester

What does it mean to own land? If it means anything, it means deciding who may and who may not have access to it; who may and who may not enjoy it. This is axiomatic of private property; it does not depend upon whether one is talking of a back garden or of 10,000 acres. Dr Jan Lester argues that the imposition of a statutory 'right to roam' amounts to the expropriation of land without compensation. In essence it is no different from the demands of socialists of previous generations to nationalise industry; it is merely less honest. Ramblers should not expect their leisure activity to be free any more than the man going down to the pub does. Charging for access would compensate the landowner and would probably lead to improved walking for the rambler.

The 'right to roam' open and uncultivated countryside is a campaign that is gaining pace and which seems set to become legislation sooner or later. This would be immoral folly. I have no objection to roaming, or rambling, as such – as long as it is not compulsory either to roam or to suffer roamers. As the healthists are slightly less powerful than the egalitarians, the arguments in favour of making it compulsory to suffer roamers are making greater headway.

A brief outline of the case for a 'right to roam'
Arguments for the 'right to roam' the countryside certainly have a great deal of common sense on their side. They are not thereby mistaken, of course, though that fact should alert the sceptical intellect. Let me first outline the general case for the 'right to roam', as put across by advocates in the mass media, the Ramblers' Association,

politicians, and one government department.

The great landowners of England did not create the land that they own. These landowners are often personally rich and merely being selfish killjoys by denying others access to such natural beauty ('Access to this part of our common heritage is something which should be enjoyed by the many, not the few'[1]). They have often inherited their land from ancestors who themselves had a dubious claim to it. If they bought it with this as a background, then that does not make much difference. In any case, 'individuals may hold the legal title, but really the land is owned by us all'.[2] So we should be able to roam all over any uncultivated parts, even away from any traditional public footpaths. Ramblers should not have to pay the landowners and neither should the landowners normally be compensated for this in any way (such as by tax relief). There should also be facilities for the disabled as far as this is practical. The overall result will be that 'access to the open countryside will make a significant contribution to improving public health and reducing social divisions...'[3]

Why these arguments are wrong

In all this there is little substantial argument; mainly mere presumption and whimsy. It is a combination of egalitarian bigotry and irrelevant pro-health waffle. But, if only for the enlightenment of the elected oligarchs who might impose this 'right' on us, let us now consider this 'roamish' propaganda in a little more detail.

There are oft repeated arguments putting forward the health virtues of rambling. But all these are irrelevant unless there is no other way for people to be healthy and no way that land access could be voluntary. These two possibilities are patently not the case. So these health arguments can simply be put aside immediately.

The great landowners of England often did and do, to varying extents, create what is worth enjoying about the land that they own. The land is not always in a natural state, but is often well developed and maintained. Without the owners there would often be no easy movement across the land or views to see. That the landowners are often personally rich cannot itself be a reason for imposing on them. Or if it is, then there needs to be some independent argument concerning this rather than just an appeal to envious Procrusteanism.

Ramblers should not expect their leisure activity to be free

Neither is there any reason to think that the landowners exclude people from their land for no good reason. There is no way that having indefinite numbers of people walking across their land cannot impose costs on the owners in terms of physical damage and loss of privacy (owners regularly attest to both). Perhaps it is not usually as bad from a privacy viewpoint as having people walk around your back garden without your permission, but the general principle is the same and the financial losses through damage can certainly be far higher.

Once this elementary point is grasped, one can see that if people are not prepared to pay the landowners the price that those owners would set for access to their land, then that is good evidence that the would-be roamers are simply imposing a cost in excess of any value that they will receive from their roaming. The only way to be fairly sure we are avoiding this is for the roamers to freely negotiate to buy or rent any right of way or general access that they choose. Instead, the roamers want to enjoy their pursuits at other people's imposed expense. This is likely to have a negative sum result, in broadly utilitarian terms. Hence it is anti-social. Roamers think they can get away with this because the owners are generally an unpopular minority – the 'rich' – whose interests it is politically safe to discount. Like anti-fox hunting, the 'right to roam' has no serious case. The anti-fox hunters do not offer a more humane alternative to hunting the pest (shooting and poisoning it would clearly be worse), and they usually turn a blind eye to the suffering the fox itself inflicts on other small mammals. They also often perceive members of the hunt as being from despised 'privileged' (really, advantaged) backgrounds. The 'right to roam' similarly includes some combination of superficial sentiment about 'nature' and malicious political classism (which seems no more defensible than political racism or sexism – as opposed to private discrimination or freedom of association).

If an existing owner's claims to the land are in any way dubious, then that is a good reason to present a detailed case on an individual basis and to challenge the property claims in the courts. If successful, the property should then be returned to the legitimate owners. Dubious property claims are not a good reason to introduce an indiscriminate licence to trespass.

What the 'roamers' are demanding is a licence to trespass, not a 'right to roam'

Why do I call this 'licence'? Because there is a crucial distinction between liberty and licence. 'Liberty' means, roughly, not being interfered with by others in your person and property. 'Licence' means, roughly, interfering with the person or property of others – such as walking across someone's land against his wishes. But how, it might be asked, can it be 'trespass' if the state allows it? For two reasons. First, assuming that the land is legitimately owned, the interference is objective, whether it is allowed by the state or not. Secondly, state legislation allowing such roaming would only be lawful if the command (or 'big stick') theory of law is correct. And if that theory is correct then everything that the Nazis did, for instance, must be held to be perfectly lawful. But I don't see that the 'law' is simply whatever rules people with power can impose on others. Laws are primarily spontaneous social rules which have evolved for the common good; state legislation is conceptually dependent on, and corrupting of, these laws. But these philosophical waters are too deep to enter into seriously here.

Reasonable rights of movement must require that there be some pathways through some properties where the owner would otherwise be being a mere obstacle to the free movement of other people. A very clear case of this would be if someone were to buy a thin strip of land with no other intention than to start charging a toll without adding any service. But such necessary rights of movement are few and far between in the cases under consideration. They are not what the roamers are normally claiming.

If landowners charged for access, 'roamers' would also benefit

Once we understand the great general social value of exclusive property rights, we should be very reluctant to ride roughshod over such rights in any particular case without very strong reason (David Hume's *An Enquiry Concerning the Principles of Morals*, 1751, is a good exposition of the social utility of private property). We should be especially reluctant when there is a clearly efficient voluntary alternative, as there is here: simply allowing the landowners to charge for and regulate access to their property. The landowners are unlikely to be able to charge very much, given that the service is hardly essential. They are unlikely to refuse altogether provided that people are prepared to pay a price that covers their costs. The landowners might even improve the facilities (maps, guides, toilets, cafes,...) and advertise. Thus no one will be imposed on and both sides to the trade will gain (as is normal with all trade).

Contrary to activists' claims, disabled not a special case

As they are often mentioned – such as in the DETR consultation paper *Access to the Open Countryside in England and Wales* – what about the disabled? Those who are truly disabled are rightly objects of our compassion and, sometimes, charity. But to allow them to impose claims against innocent people is to turn them into social parasites who will eventually risk becoming despised – if they are not already becoming so. There is usually no amount of money that can compensate people for severe disabilities. Does this mean that they must be given rights to ever more of what others possess? Taken to its extreme, there is no stopping point short of the enslavement of the able by the disabled (even this might not be enough compensation to achieve equality of welfare). And every step on the way towards this is both immoral and inefficient. With the 'right to roam', as elsewhere, the seriously disabled should only be helped charitably – where the market will not suffice – if we are to avoid this additional egalitarian disaster. That charity is often resented by the recipients is a social boon and a spur to maintain independence; the 'welfare rights' the state gives foster both arrogance and dependence.

Problem is not lack of access, but excess of publicly-owned land

In fact, we can go much further in our rejection of this bogus 'right to roam'. Far from allowing a 'right to roam' on private properties, we should do the exact opposite of what these 'rambler communists' are advocating. We should positively add to private property wherever this is possible. All those state-owned properties that currently allow unrestricted access should be sold off so that these resources can also be properly husbanded: maintained and developed, instead of being stuck in a 'tragedy of the commons' (where all have only an incentive to overuse). What of all the existing heaths and parks that are neglectfully owned by the state, or local authorities, for the reckless use of all? These should be sold or given away forthwith to private individuals, charitable trusts, or businesses, so that they can be added to the social efficiency that only private property and the market can generate. But much so-called private property is, in any case, so hedged about with state regulations that the putative owners' property claims are severely compromised. So these regulations must also be abolished.

It might be suggested that at least some public right to access, such as public footpaths, would seem to come traditionally and legitimately with the ownership of some land. However, that also seems to be an argument for some form of common ownership (though imposing worst on the landowner) which, similarly, cannot really improve liberty or welfare. It would be better if some people were allowed to own these rights privately, though that could always be through a charitable trust.

Activists fail to grasp basic economic concepts

Like most political problems, the main source of error here is a lack of understanding of basic economics and property concepts. This lack, though, is often shared by professors of economics, who reject the implications of free-market economics just because they are 'too extreme' – ie, counter to common sense. The solution will only be found in educating people about the economics and about the philosophical inadequacy of some common sense. Any discussion of 'rights' that does not have economic and philosophical clarification as a background, is likely to generate more heat than light.

Under no circumstances should the mythical 'right to roam' be incorporated into the legislation of this country. In reality, it is clearly a mere licence to trespass. Armed with the appropriate economic and philosophical arguments, we should eventually be able to offer an effective counter-attack with a movement for the 'right to own' privately every last one of the state-controlled commons, heaths, hills, mountains, downs, woodlands, rivers, beaches, and footpaths. As a result, there will be no imposition on legitimate landowners and more access to better resources for ramblers.

14

Urban perception and the 'contaminated countryside'

Richard North

Risk of cancer from eating meat or 'mutant vegetables' makes for good copy. 'Our food is safer than ever before' is not a good story. This has brought about an urban perception that much of our food is poisoned and that the countryside is 'contaminated' by farmers using 'unnatural' methods. Richard North argues that, contrary to this perception, food is very safe in the UK. Food poisoning directly results in only 50 deaths per year in the UK out of a total death toll of 500,000. Yet ever greater sums are spent on 'food safety' and the burgeoning 'food safety' regulators. They do not make already safe food any safer and in instances – such as meat inspection – cause contamination. If the money spent on food safety were spent on other measures far more lives could be saved.

Reading the media, one would think all our food is poisoned

Whether it be salmonella in eggs, listeria in cheese, E.coli O157, BSE in cows, or even cancer risks from eating meat, for the last decade our newspapers and airwaves have rarely been without dire warnings relating to our consumption of food. Faced with the barrage of media 'concern', it would be hard not to take the view that our food is an ever-present source of danger, and that each mouthful brings us closer to an unpleasant and lingering death.

Barely concealed behind the unending stream of reports is the implication that the source of our food – our countryside – is poisoned by filthy, feather-bedded, profit-driven farmers and producers, and their fellow conspirators in the slaughterhouses and processing industries, all of which provides fertile ground for the regulators who revel in new and more stringent controls, each time the media indulges in another of its orgasmic bouts of indignation over imaginary perils on our plate.

Hardly surprisingly, a largely urban myth has emerged, driven forward by clichés like 'from plough to plate', which epitomise a desire to extend 'wider and deeper' controls over what is termed 'the food chain', in the interests of food safety. And so ingrained has become the myth of our dangerous food that the Government is establishing what may well become the biggest quango ever launched, the Food Standards Agency, as an answer to the 'problem'.

Regulators have self-interest in hyping dangers

Behind all this, however, is an even more pernicious myth, which effectively styles the regulators as being on the side of the angels, a disinterested body of men and women who only have the interests of the public at heart.

That myth is effectively exploded by the formation of what is in reality an entirely new – even modern – kind of government body, which has been dubbed the 'Self-financing regulatory agency', or Sefra for short. The archetypal model is the Meat Hygiene Service, set up in 1995 to take over the inspection of meat and the control of hygiene standards in abattoirs.

Regulation a vast industry which uses every scare as an excuse to expand

Courtesy of the (then) government and EU Directive 91/497, there has been created a brand new business opportunity, an organisation of over 1,000 officials dedicated solely to law enforcement, with a £60 million turnover. It gains its income from the imposition of fees on its 'customers' for compulsory inspection. Thereby, every slaughterhouse in the land has full-time inspection by meat inspectors (grandly titled 'meat hygiene inspectors'), supervised daily by veterinary surgeons charging £60 plus per hour, many of whom have little grasp of the mechanics of meat production. Regulation has become big – and profitable – business.

The activities of this agency came to a head after the now infamous E.coli outbreak in Lanarkshire in 1997, which killed 21 people and poisoned over 400. On the back of the wave of public concern, the Meat Hygiene Service launched a new reign of terror on livestock farmers and slaughterhouses alike, demanding clean animals be presented at slaughterhouses – and doubling up its inspections to enforce its new code.

But, when the inquiry on the outbreak convened in June 1998, it transpired that the cause of the outbreak was massive cross-contamination in the butcher's shop from which the outbreak emanated, the premises being inspected only annually (without charge), in this case by a recently-qualified officer. Meat hygiene standards and conditions on the farms were ruled out as a cause, at a very early stage in the inquiry. Predictably, the response has been to charge butchers for their inspections.

Meat inspectors a source of contamination

Thus, behind the hype of the contaminated countryside, which has so often spawned major and damaging food scares, the reality is savagely different from what is portrayed. For example, a clinical analysis of the controls over primary produce suggests that current meat inspection techniques in the UK are the single most important – and unavoidable – source of contamination in the meat industry, occasioned by meat inspectors pawing freshly killed carcasses – with hands clad in unsterilised chain main gloves – and slashing at the meat with their similarly unsterilised knives, all in the search of bacteria which are invisible to the naked eye. The officials are the problem, not the solution.

Out of 500,000 deaths per year in UK, only 50 due to food poisoning

And, in any case, the whole food safety issue is vastly overblown. Taking the most extreme consequence of failures in food safety – ie, death – it is difficult to make out a case for there being the crisis which is so often portrayed. The estimated death rate from all types of food-poisoning is about 50 a year, although it might be higher, at about 200 if you include all those persons who were at death's door through other causes – usually extreme old age, but also including those suffering from AIDS – and the very small number of people who have died from the so-called new variant CJD, attributed to the consumption of BSE-infected cattle.

By contrast, the total deaths in the nation each year amount to approximately 500,000 – from all causes. Of the relatively small proportion of premature deaths, one of the most serious contributors is the common ailment, influenza. Putting the food poisoning figures sharply into context, during a major flu epidemic of the last ten years – in the one week ending 22 December, 1989 – 782 people died from the illness. More significantly, a later study argued that half the deaths were preventable, had vaccines been properly targeted on vulnerable people.

The costs of regulation ignored – costs to the food industry exceed one billion pounds

Nevertheless, advocates of more controls to increase food safety will argue that, on top of its health implications, the burden of food-borne illness imposes significant economic costs, with figures for the annual costs of salmonella food poisoning estimated at £331 million, of which £220 million is attributed to lost production, as workers take time off sick. This is taken to justify the increasing regulatory burden.

But what is rarely taken into account is the cost of so-called prevention. Something in excess of £200 million a year is spent by public authorities on surveillance and implementing regulatory measures, in addition to which the meat industry is forced to pay over £60 million annually on compulsory inspection fees. Compliance costs for the food industry probably exceed one billion pounds a year, without taking into account loss of production from workers involved in non-revenue earning, hygiene-related occupations.

And vast costs to agriculture

Costs to agriculture are more difficult to estimate, but it is known that the salmonella scare cost the egg industry alone an estimated £70 million in the first eight months of 1989. Controls on animal feed and veterinary monitoring probably cost several hundred million, and the feed industry is similarly burdened. And the newly introduced salmonella vaccination programme for laying hens will cost the industry over six million pounds a year.

All of this expenditure, it should be remembered, is devoted to reducing the food poisoning threat, in the context of an annual death toll of a maximum of 200, a figure which has remained steady for many years.

Food risks insignificant when compared to other risks

The extent of the dangerous food myth, however, can only best be appreciated when contrasted with other threats. For instance, in 1997 it was revealed that poor hygiene in hospitals kills something like 5,000 people a year. Consider the implications: in a day and age when something like 3,500 people are killed on the roads each year, hospitals

– which are supposed to make us better – kill 1,500 more – each and every year.

Contrast also the hue and cry over a recent fatal train crash in the UK, the Southall incident, where pundits were quick to argue that expenditure by the rail network of one billion pounds plus on automated safety systems could have prevented six deaths, those deaths making 11 killed in the three previous years – against over 10,000 killed on the roads and 15,000 in hospitals during the same period.

If money spent on food safety were spent on other risks many deaths could be prevented

Against that, how does the three billion pounds plus spent on BSE measures compare, when all the scientists can offer us is 26 deaths over four years for so-called 'new-strain' CJD, with no proof whatsoever that there is any link between the two diseases? A tiny fraction of that money spent would have protected many thousands from a much more deadly killer – ie, the flu – leaving billions to sort out many other pressing health problems – not least hospital infection.

Pork pies better protected than hospital patients

It is interesting, therefore, if not instructive, that we had to learn from a former food safety specialist how dangerous hospitals really are, at the 1998 British Medical Association conference. How appropriate that it was Dr Joe Kearns, former head of food safety for Joe Lyons, who noted that pork pies are better protected from infection than hospital patients.

That is the essence of the myth, and its measure. While untold millions are spent on countering the threat of dangerous food, the truth of the matter is that pork pies – and a whole range of other foods – are and have been far better protected from infection than hospital patients. Yet, while the sick and vulnerable in hospitals are dying in their thousands, unlamented and unmourned, the concerned media continues to peddle the myth of the contaminated countryside, while the officials rake in the fees.

15

Organic Farming: no option for mainstream agriculture?

Leanda de Lisle

Urban perception divides farmers into saintly organic producers and Frankensteins unleashing ever new horrors upon the unsuspecting consumer. If only all farmers were to adopt organic methods, the thinking goes, the countryside would be safe for future generations to enjoy. But Leanda de Lisle shows that organic farming simply does not offer a future for mainstream agriculture. Urban consumers will protest in surveys that they are willing to pay extra for organic produce, but when it comes to the supermarket the vast majority are unwilling to spend the extra money. Who then is responsible for organic farming not being more widespread – the urban consumer demanding ever cheaper food or the farmer merely meeting this demand?

Organic farming receiving ever more public and media attention

Farmers aren't very popular. Those who are rich are assumed to have succeeded at the expense of the rest of us. They have cheated us, poisoned us, destroyed the very earth we live on, so they can lord it over us from their horses and Range Rovers. Those who are poor are considered too backward and stupid to succeed at anything. The best place for the lot of them is in the stocks of television comedy. Except, that is, for organic farmers. Fashionable opinion is that farming should be as it was depicted by the German romantic movement of the 1930s: full of big, pink people cutting wheat by hand. We are told the past is the future and it's organic. But the truth is, this is neither feasible or desirable. The way forward lies in a new way of farming that's good for the earth and good for people. One that's already been practised

89

all over the country.

A mere 0.3 per cent of land in Britain, and 0.06 per cent of agricultural output, is farmed organically. This is due, in part, to the innate conservatism of farmers. Farming is a highly geared industry that offers a low return on capital. Few can afford to take big risks. It could cost them their jobs, their home and their way of life, their heritage and their children's future. Knowing this, farmers think long and hard before they go into something like organic farming from which there is no short route back. Until now those who farmed organically have tended to be early, fervent followers of the Green movement or the Trust Fund Babes of the farming community – people like Prince Charles. But the BSE tragedy, public disquiet about industrial farming methods and the high, positive profile of organic farming have led farmers to look again at the organic option. The number of those farming organically or applying to the Soil Association to do so has increased by 40 per cent in one year.

But organic farming will always remain a minority interest, not because of government policy, but because of lack of consumer demand

There is no doubt that we could and should have more organic farms. Despite the commonly held belief that the EU discriminates against organic farmers, EU subsidies have been paid per acre rather than per ton produced since 1993. This means organic farms are on a level playing field with conventional farms. In addition an organic aid scheme subsidises the costs of converting to the organic system, and the much derided set aside scheme pays organic (but not ordinary) farmers to grow clover to improve productivity. Being few and scattered, organic farms have crippling distribution costs and offer unreliable supply of goods.

Demand for organic produce is not, therefore, being satisfied. But once they have reached a critical mass, organic farmers will find it easier to meet the demand. This will, in turn, increase demand. But by how much? The truth is, telling farmers that the organic system is the way forward is like telling grocers that Fauchon's is the Sainsbury's of the future.

CWS agriculture (the farming wing of the Co-op) set up an organic farm in Leicestershire in order to look critically at the issues surrounding organic farming. The first concern of most farmers is whether they can grow organic crops successfully. At CWS they were pleased to discover that they could and without great difficulty. Yields were down, as expected. In the case of wheat they were down 56 per cent. Inevitably that meant organic food would be premium priced. But people pay premium prices for glossy packaging at Marks and Spencer, so perhaps that wouldn't matter. It did. The real problem with organic produce, proved to be not growing it, but marketing it. According to project manager, Alastair Leake, 'all the surveys we've done show that people think organic farming is wonderful and if they were faced with the choice of buying organic food, then they would buy it. But when you face them with the reality, which is that the product is sometimes inferior to look at and always more expensive, then people start to shift.'

Most customers simply not interested in whether food is grown organically

The middle-class people who order boxed organic produce may get depressed after weeks of finding nothing but potatoes and cabbages in their food parcels. But at least they are happy for food to look as if it once grew in the ground or walked upon it. Most people aren't. The supermarkets go to great lengths to place meat in absorbent packaging, so that no free blood is visible under the cling film. Fruit and vegetables are washed and waxed so they look bright and clean. The aim is to make food look as if it arrived on earth as a ready meal. The public is more than happy to pay extra for a hamburger that's already in its bun, ready for the micro-wave. They are not so keen to pay extra for a perfectly dull, organic turnip. 'But what about people's concerns about their health? What about their concerns about animal welfare?' you might ask. These are factors certainly, but they are not necessarily complementary and the cost benefit analysis differs widely between economic groups.

People are more worried about dying from a heart attack than getting BSE, salmonella or some yet undiscovered disease spread by cheap sprouts. White meat like chicken has grown in popularity over the years at the expense of red meat like lamb. Yet it's lamb that's invariably free range. The public demands lean pork. Yet the leaner the meat the more likely it has come from a crated pig. Organic pigs in addition to being fatty, often have hair and the follicles can start right down in the meat. Consequently if you can't find an organic market for an organic pig, you won't be able to sell the meat at all. People should be persuaded to eat greener, kinder food but the evidence suggests that only a minority will pay more for a clean conscience and a dirty spud. Alastair Leake's view is that, with luck, organic farms could account for five per cent of the land area. The Soil Association hopes to reach this target in about 2002. What then is the future for the remaining 95 per cent of British land?

Organic farming has its own environmental problems

In the long term the Soil Association would like to see the world 100 per cent organically farmed. But would this really be the triumph some suppose? It's far more difficult to control pests in tropical climates than temperate ones. The green pioneer Dr Norman Borlaug has complained that environmentalists have paralysed attempts to prevent starvation in the third world by denying farmers access to disease resistant seeds and crop protection chemicals. It is imperialism of the worst kind. The only 'natural' way to compensate for lower yields is to plough up more land, much of which may be unsuitable for cultivation. We are already seeing the environmental consequences of this in countries like Brazil and Indonesia where the rain forest is being slashed and burned to make way for new farm land. It would be both greener and more humane to give third world farmers access to technical knowledge that would enable them to feed their countrymen with the farm land they already have.

In Britain, we'd be unlikely to starve if all our farmland was managed organically. However, we'd be more dependent on imports and people would have to get used to spending far more on food. It's common for journalists to say that farm subsidies mean British families have to carry a terrible financial burden to support British farms. Actually British families spend a lower percentage of their income on basic food than they ever have. And it would surely be better if people were persuaded to eat well by foodies and animal lovers, rather than being forced to by politicians? Not least because organic food is not the only animal and environmentally-friendly produce out there and people deserve a choice. Organic farming is more a religion than a science. Farmers will use copper sulphate and sulphur on their crops because they are natural, yet their toxicological profiles show that they are considerably more harmful than some of the man-made chemicals used on conventional crops.

'Integrated crop management' may offer farming 'third way'

But there is a new method of farming which is both based on science and rooted in a respect for the environment. 'Integrated crop management' takes the completely natural system of crop rotation and many other of our ancestor's farming practices and integrates them with the latest technology. Hedges are encouraged rather than ripped out, because they are the natural habitat of creatures which feed on destructive pests. The pesticides that are used, are to DDT what electricity is to the wood fire. They have excellent environmental profiles and are targeted rather than used prophetically. At CWS they have found that where ICM has been practised, yields have been slightly down (eight per cent on wheat), but as so little pesticide is used, costs have also declined. As a result performance is equivalent to or better than the conventional system. ICM removes many concerns about modern farming methods. It allows the farmer to make a profit and the customer gets affordable, quality produce. For Bob Hilborn, head of Primary Agriculture at Sainsbury's, 'it's a clear win-win for farmers and customers alike'.

Customers have yet to be told about ICM, but farmers are already enthusiastic about this 'third way'. It's promoted nationally by a charitable organisation called LEAF (Linking the Environment and Farming). LEAF has about 1,200 farming members, whose subscriptions help to support the organisation. Most of them hail from eastern counties like Cambridgeshire and Lincolnshire, the supposed home of demonic grain barons, who like nothing better than to rip up a hedge before settling down to a breakfast of Jack snipe (a protected species). LEAF sees itself as setting the standard for mainstream farmers and are keen supporters of independent verification schemes that offer customer guarantees. The majority of them thus far have been set up by the NFU and are known as Farm Assured schemes. They began six years ago with a scheme for fruit and vegetables which included strict environmental as well as quality guarantees. Six thousand farmers have signed up to it. It was followed with a scheme for beef and lamb and then, more recently, pigs. These resemble the RSPCA's Freedom Foods (which is popular with mainstream farmers). Emphasis is based on animal welfare issues and traceability. The recently launched Combined Crop Assured Scheme has attracted 5,000 out of 30,000 grain farmers in its first six months.

It's time to stop bashing farmers

The rapidity and apparent ease with which these schemes are being taken up indicates that the average farmer is not the animal and vegetable torturer he is portrayed to be by those all too happy to bite the hand that feeds them. If there is to be a debate about the future of farming let it centre on the role ICM can play in it.

There is a saying that 'the man who has food has many worries, but the man who is hungry has only one'. To a large extent British farmers have been victims of their own success. During the Second World War and it's aftermath they were asked to increase food production and they did so. By the 1970s they discovered that they could completely control pest diseases in wheat and grow it year in, year out, without rotation. We now know the consequences of that were environmental degradation. But we cannot go forward by throwing away everything that has been achieved in the last 50 years. Insisting that 'organic farming' is the only right way to farm damns the people who will produce the bulk of our food for the foreseeable future, or damns us to a time when food will again be expensive and scarce. It is a flat earth entreaty, as helpful as Marie Antoinette's suggestion that the poor eat cake. Like the rest of us, farmers need to learn from the past and build upon it. A system which integrates natural and scientific methods of food production does just that. It will help everyone do the right thing.

16

Agrochemicals and biotechnology: true friends of the earth

Robin Malim

The activist and the sentimentalist both object to innovation in agriculture. They object to anything they deem 'unnatural'– be it the use of pesticides or, more recently, biotechnology – and seem to think that if farmers could only return to the practices of their great-grandfathers all would be well. Yet Robin Malim shows that innovation in agriculture means that a fraction of those once employed on the land can now produce more varied, better quality, cheaper food to cater for the ever-fussier demands of the urban consumer. With a growing world population, abandoning scientific advances in agricultural methods is simply not a viable option. Why should scientific advances be appropriate in telecommunications, for example, but not in agriculture?

New agricultural technologies offer the only hope of feeding a growing global population

Although it is widely believed that global agriculture will always be able to supply the food that is demanded by a rising population, this must be open to question. The world population, which now stands at around 5.7 billion, is forecast to increase to between nine and ten billion by the year 2035. Concurrent with this increase the standard of living in the developing world is also expected to rise and this will create greater expectations, both in terms of food quantity and quality.

In spite of the recent economic downturn in Asia, countries in the Pacific Rim are experiencing an unprecedented change in economic activity. China, which is a good barometer of this change, is experiencing new freedoms in political activity which will lead to greatly increased expectations amongst its people. Demand for better quality food with a higher protein content has already led to a rapid increase in pig and poultry production in that country and, even if one ignores the effect of rising population, this alone will inevitably lead to a rapid increase in grain consumption.

During the period from 1950 to 1995 world protein use rose from around 30 million tons a year to a staggering 195 million tons a year. The land area available to global agriculture is comparatively static. In 1975 the area under grain production throughout the world was around 705 million hectares, by 1995 the area had in fact fallen marginally to 679 million hectares.

Greater production from roughly the same area of land has been the consequence of increasing demand but these increases in yield have inevitably led to increases in water consumption. Water is now becoming one of the scarce resources and could well become the major limiting factor. Agriculture is being forced by urban and industrial users to compete for available supply. The demand for water appears to be insatiable.

In the developed world consumer demands are also changing. Fears about the environment and fears surrounding food quality have led to resistance to the new technologies. Biotechnology and genetic engineering, both the subject of great public scrutiny, must be the real hope for the increases in production which will be needed by future generations.

Opposition to new technologies grows when people know they will have enough to eat

As the world becomes less hungry the resistance to modern technology appears to grow. The old Byzantine proverb, which states that a man with a full belly has many problems but that he with an empty belly has only one, appears to have a great deal of truth in it.

It is amazing how quickly media attention can focus public opinion, which quickly demands the curtailment of the new agricultural practices. Perhaps if the public had been sensitised to these concerns 30 years earlier, the techniques that brought about the yield increases which have been so vital in feeding the growing world population would never have been developed and food would be in much shorter supply.

Without use of pesticides food production would be insufficient to meet today's needs

The development of the use of pesticides, combined with better knowledge and better practice in the field of plant nutrition has led to a doubling of yield in many of the more advanced agricultural areas over the past 30 years.

Without these increases in yield the world would not have been able to feed a population which has risen from under three billion in 1950 to its present 5.7 billion. Grain use has risen from 631 million tons in 1950 to 1,841 million tons in 1996. The world population has doubled, but grain use has nearly tripled during this period.

Unfortunately the incentive to develop new technologies against this tide of ill-informed public opinion has been reduced. The multinational chemical companies, who have played a major part in developing these new techniques, have undoubtedly lost some of their enthusiasm in this endeavour as the cost of the development has risen to satisfy the demands of those ranged against them.

If GM food production is curtailed, future food supplies will be insufficient

The time-scale built into the pattern of demographic growth is such that time lost could be critical in the fight against hunger. The hope must lie in the development of biotechnology and genetic engineering. If the growth of these sciences is delayed, those who create this delay, however well-meaning, may well have their actions described as criminal by future generations.

It is only through continued development and constant refining of both the objectives and the processes that real security can be achieved. Comparison between current practice and the early use of pesticides in agriculture demonstrates conclusively the strides which have been made both in terms of safety and yield increases.

New technologies make food safer

Over the years the development of high technology farming has seen the application of plant protection products containing less active ingredients as better and safer chemistry has been developed. At the same time, the farmer has learned how best to use these powerful tools which are under his control.

Few people pause to think that, in its natural state, the plant puts out its own defence mechanism against insect or disease attack. The chemistry of this 'natural' defence mechanism is often akin to those that have been developed by the chemist for the farmer's use. In the natural state these chemicals are often produced in such quantity that their residues remain as toxins in the plant. Very little work has been done to investigate the effects of these naturally-occurring toxins.

The risk of consuming residues from pesticides applied by the farmer is certainly no more dangerous than consuming naturally-occurring toxins. The latter are very likely to be present in great quantity in a plant with no farmer applied protection.

Modern methods of measurement are so accurate that it is possible to measure infinitesimal amounts of any chemical to be found in a plant. A great deal of effort is made to measure the residues of applied chemicals. The chemistry of naturally-occurring toxins appears to have attracted very little attention.

Notion that presticides can cause cancer not supported by evidence

There is strong medical evidence that proves that a diet containing quantities of fresh fruit and vegetables is the best way to remain healthy and to protect against bowel cancer and heart disease.

One of the world's leading cancer specialists, Dr Bruce Ames, states that 'Pollution seems to me to be mostly a red herring as a cause of cancer...Environmentalists are forever issuing scare reports based on very shallow science...99.9 per cent of the toxic chemicals we're exposed to are completely natural...We are shooting ourselves in the foot with environmental regulations that cost [in the US] over two per cent of the GNP, much of it to regulate trivia.'

Modern agricultural pesticides have reduced food prices and thus enabled more people to have a better diet

It is undoubtedly essential that fresh fruit and vegetables should be available at the lowest possible cost to the greatest possible number of people. The quantity and the price will be determined by the utilisation of the best modern technology.

However strong the emotional appeal of 'untreated' food, the reality is that the development of modern farming technologies have greatly reduced the cost of food and allowed many more people to benefit from a better and cheaper diet.

Organic farming will never be anything other than a small niche market

In reality it would appear that most organic systems require an extended rotation. This, together with the inevitable yield penalties inherent in organic farming systems, demands a price premium of nearly 50 per cent in order to equate the profit margins obtained by the more technically-minded farmer.

Although many shoppers may pay lip service to the idea of buying organic food, when it comes to the crunch it would appear that price and appearance control their buying habits.

I believe that it is most unlikely that organic food will ever appeal to more than a small minority of shoppers although the organic niche market will hold onto its dedicated band of supporters. This makes it doubly surprising that the zealots, who at present benefit from the premiums which they themselves have created by developing this market, now appear hell-bent on destroying their own opportunity by encouraging the rest of the farming fraternity to join them in their endeavours.

Farming and the agrochemical industry must educate the public in the achievements of modern agriculture

Because of the high level of misinformation it is difficult to see how misconceptions can be dispelled, but it is essential that the farming industry and governments realise the gravity of the situation and institute measures aimed at putting things right.

Undoubtedly the new Food Standards Agency has a major part to play, both in investigation and regulation. When it is satisfied that a new technology is safe, then it must do everything it can to reassure the consuming public. The farming industry must double and re-double its efforts to inform and educate the public about its practices. It should cease to be reactive and defensive and plan to capture public confidence in both its words and deeds. The agrochemical industry must take the same route and should link with agriculture and the Food Standards Agency to promote safe new technologies. It will take time and money to repair the damage of the past and to create the new way forward. There is no time to be lost.

17

Drink-driving, gesture politics and the attack upon rural livelihoods

John Maloney

Drink-driving leads to death on the roads. The activist is rightly concerned by these fatalities and demands that further 'action' be taken. But what action? The sensible thing would be to crack down on the small number of hardened habitual drink-drivers who are the real threat. But this would be difficult. Why not instead show one's 'concern' over fatalities by reducing the legal drink-drive limit from 80mg per 100ml (about two pints of beer) to 50mg per 100ml (about 1¼ pints). Dr John Maloney shows that there is no evidence for believing that such a reduction would save any lives. But it would have a massive impact upon country pubs. Many have too few customers within walking distance to be viable. Lowering drink-drive levels could destroy the livelihoods of thousands of publicans and remove one of the focal points of village community life without bringing any benefits, without saving any lives.

The Government is thinking of cutting the maximum legal level of blood alcohol for drivers from 80mg per 100ml (the state you're in after two pints of beer) to 50mg (about 1¼ pints). Actually, at the moment, if you stay in the pub long enough, you might be able to drink a bit more than two pints. As soon as you start drinking, you start losing the equivalent of half a pint of beer per hour from your bloodstream, so that the formula for those of average metabolism is P = 2+H/2, where P is the number of pints that puts you at the limit and H is the number of hours the session has lasted. But, because everyone's metabolism is so different, you would be highly unwise to go up to this limit. Under the new laws, unless you plan an extremely long stint, you would be silly to drink more than a pint if you are going to drive.

Whatever happens to drink-drive figures, police use them to call for more resources and tougher drink-driving laws
This is exactly what the police want. And, little as one wants gratuitously to insult the police, the question has to be asked: has 'new' Labour been advising Scotland Yard? Because every police force in the country, it seems, now has a standardised 'rapid response' to its Christmas drink-drive figures – or rather a set of four responses, one for each possible case.

- More breath tests, increased proportion positive – motorists are getting complacent about the laws and must be jolted by making the laws more severe.

- More breath tests, reduced proportion positive – the police are catching the wrong people and need to extend their activities in the hope of catching the right ones.

- Fewer breath tests, increased proportion positive – more resources must be put into breath testing and motorists must be jolted by making the law more severe.

- Fewer breath tests, reduced proportion positive – drunken drivers are obviously getting away with it – more resources and tougher laws are needed.

Sir Karl Popper might well have asked a chief constable or two, 'under what circumstances would you reject the hypothesis that the laws need to get tighter?' No doubt if ten million motorists were breathalysed one Christmas, and none were positive, that would merely prove the Satanic cunning of offenders in avoiding detection.

Government drink-driving statistics frequently misleading
At least Whitehall, by comparison, has improved. Not so long ago, its main contribution was to cite the number of drink-related road accidents to show the need for more repressive laws. The fact that these figures included, for example, drunken pedestrians run down

by teetotal drivers, was no deterrent. Indeed one senior policeman, a few years ago, even branded drunken pedestrians as drunk-drivers *manqué*, unscrupulously outwitting the laws by walking home, and called for further measures to combat this menace.

. One recent Whitehall document[1] is notably more determined to get at the truth. It makes a heroic effort, albeit interspersed by assumptions of breathtaking arbitrariness, to estimate exactly how many road deaths (a) involve drivers with 50-80mg of alcohol per 100ml of blood and (b) would not have happened had the limit been lower. Its starting point is evidence from those coroners (practice varies between courts) who routinely perform a blood test on drivers killed on the roads. By assuming that coroners who do not do this would have got the same kind of results, the Ministry estimates that 100 drivers die every year with between 50 and 80mg of alcohol in their blood. It then makes two bold guesses: first that if the limit had been lowered, half of these drivers would have complied, and second that half of those complying would have saved their own lives. Number of lives saved so far: 25.

And backed up with untested hypotheses
But, the Ministry goes on, some of the motorists testing at over 80mg (and thus breaking the law even as it stands) might have drunk less had the limit been lower. Presumably some of those only just over the 80mg limit had miscalculated, and imagined they were underneath it. Lower the limit and these people will be trying, and failing, to stay below 50mg instead of 80mg. This somewhat notional category gets roughly the same treatment as the 50 to 80s. Coroners' reports (plus the same dose of induction to cope with non-respondents) indicate that another 100 dead drivers had alcohol limits of 80-110mg. These, the ministry assumes, include all the drivers who might conceivably imagine they were under 80 mg. Again, imagine that half of them change their behaviour with a lower limit, and of these half save their lives. Here are the other 25 recruits who make up the official estimate of 50 lives saved if the limit goes down. However, as the DETR website itself points out, international evidence is divided on whether cutting the limit has any detectable effect on those who were already above the old one.

Case for lowering drink-drive limits relies on just two US surveys – one of which finds no safety grounds for reduction
It may sound unfair to talk about the Ministry 'guessing' how many

lives would be saved if drivers drank less, when its consultative document cites two extensive surveys on the subject as a basis for its estimates. But these surveys need careful scrutiny. One is the Grand Rapids study of 1962.[2] Here researchers flagged down about 8,000 motorists and breathalysed them after assuring them that no prosecution could result, whatever the score. They then compared this profile of randomly-selected drivers with that of drivers involved in an accident.

The Grand Rapids report is 240 pages long and full of fascinating facts. The more often you go to church, the less likely that you will be drunk at the wheel. Motorists who have a drink most days are, as you would expect, more likely to test positive but, for any given level of alcohol in the bloodstream, are less likely to be involved in an accident than those who only drink occasionally. Women, minors and the uneducated are all more of a menace with three drinks inside them than the rest of the population. White drunks drive as badly as black ones, though whites have fewer accidents when sober.

But the report's basic conclusion is summed up in a sentence: 'The effects of alcohol on accident experience in this study, using the test described, became statistically detectable at the 0.08 per cent alcohol level class'. In other words at 80mg per 100ml: the existing limit. Indeed this was how the Grand Rapids report persuaded the then government back in the 1960s that an 80mg limit was the right one.

Second report based on limited numbers, some in excess of existing limits

The other survey cited by the DETR was carried out across the USA in 1986, and its results published by A K Lund and A C Wolfe.[3] This one is organised around the concept of 'relative crash rates'. Suppose your control panel of randomly-stopped motorists includes 40 people with a blood alcohol level over 80mg, and your accident-involved 'panel' contains 100. Then the crash rate for this category is $100/40 = 2.5$. Suppose now that the control group and the accident group respectively contain 2,000 people and 1,000 people who have drunk nothing at all. The crash rate for the abstainers is thus 0.5. The relative crash rate for the over-80s is $2.5/0.5 = 5$. So being over the 80mg limit will make you five times as likely to crash.

Lund and Wolfe's survey, in fact, is of limited value in estimating how many accidents would be prevented if Britain lowered the limit to 50mg. For one thing, it specialises almost entirely in single-vehicle accidents, many if not most of which will involve no-one but the driver. If our focus, as it should be, is on drunk-drivers killing and maiming innocent victims, we want a more general picture which includes all accidents. Lund and Wolfe do provide this, but, for some reason, only for male drivers aged 25 or over, and only for the 50-100mg bracket, not 50-80mg. Doing this, they get a relative crash ratio of 4.1. This figure, however, must be treated with caution. Only 91 drivers in the control group fell into the 'male 25+' and the '50-100mg' categories. (The number between 50 and 80, which is what interests us, is unrecorded but will of course be smaller). This is a meagre sample to work with.

And the results are distorted by those drivers who refused to co-operate with the study
And all this is before the distorting effects of the eight per cent who refused are considered. As the authors themselves say, people who did not co-operate were much more likely to be drunk than people who did. Clearly, if drunk-drivers disappear in this way from the control panel but not from the accident panel, crash rates will be an overestimate. And the eight per cent of respondents who refused the test outnumbers the 6.4 per cent who tested at over 50mg. Had they all been over 50mg and all been tested, the crash rate (and therefore also the relative crash rate) for this category would have fallen by more than half.

To be fair, Lund and Wolfe do try to allow for this factor. Their researchers employed 'an electrochemical fuel-cell sensor' which was 'held for five seconds about six inches from the mouth of a talking subject' – presumably while he was refusing to be tested. 'However', Lund and Wolfe admit, 'such things as turned heads, discontinuous speech, strong wind, rain and only partially lowered windows often made reliable readings difficult to accomplish'. In other words, if you don't want to give a breath test, make sure it's a fine night, wind the windows all the way down, look straight at the interviewer, don't stop to draw breath, and don't worry about the contraption held level with your eyes. Then your refusal won't hold up their research.

UK surveys suggest that lowering drink-drive limits will not reduce accidents
With one American survey which raises as many questions as it answers and one which yields no grounds for changing the law, you might

have expected the DETR to examine recent British evidence more closely. The consultative document in fact does present the raw results from two surveys. Curiously, it then abstains from deriving crash rates and risk factors. Let us do the job for them. Roadside surveys carried out by the DETR between 1988 and 1990 found that 2.3 per cent of motorists had breath alcohol levels equivalent to blood alcohol between 40 and 80mg/100ml. (Since, in marked contrast to the last survey mentioned, only 0.8 per cent of motorists refused the test, this should be a reliable figure.[4]) When drivers involved in accidents were tested at the Radcliffe Infirmary over the same period, a slightly lower proportion (2.1 per cent) were between 40 and 80.[5] Does this mean we pass a law requiring a minimum blood-alcohol level before anyone is allowed to drive? No, because the difference between 2.3 per cent and 2.1 per cent is unlikely to be statistically significant, so the safest inference from this pair of surveys would be that having between 40 and 80mg in your blood has no effect on the chance of an accident.

To sum up, the DETR has ignored a pair of recent British surveys which, taken together, suggest that lowering the limit will have no effect on casualties. Of the two surveys it does use, one also concludes that alcohol is not a statistically significant cause of accidents below the 80mg level – and indeed has been officially cited up to now as the main evidence for not changing the law. The remaining survey does claim a significant effect in the 50 to 100 category, but has only 91 motorists in this category and has more motorists refusing the test than testing at over 50mg, quite apart from the substantial number of motorists, also disproportionately likely to be drunk, who, the researchers admit, wheeled round or went off down a side street when they saw the sign 'Traffic Survey Ahead'. A country publican might well see all this as precarious grounds for taking his job away.

Village pub a focus for community life
And now that the bus, the shop and the school have most probably gone, the pub is the last remaining focus for social life in the country. Until recently I lived in a small village of about 100 people, with its own pub. Take away everyone in the village who was too young, too old, too sick of the sight of their neighbours or too Methodist, and there were still a lot of us who used it regularly and would have seen little or nothing of one another without it. We were all, of course, in walking distance. But without the motorists we would not have had a pub – I doubt if more than 10 per cent of the turnover came from

people who lived within walking distance. The pub needed the motorist from the town and from the countryside around; the motorists from the countryside around needed the pub. Now some might say to these people that, after all, they would still be able to have a pint in the pub and drive home even if the law does change, and, if a rural pub is such an amenity, they should not need a second pint to help them enjoy it. The trouble with this argument is that it misses the point. Perhaps drivers ought to feel like that, no doubt many of them do feel like that but if others stay away because of the change in the law, no one will even be able to have a half in the pub because it won't be there any longer.

Livelihoods and pleasures of country people threatened on the flimsiest of evidence

Trying to estimate the number of pubs which will close is even trickier than trying to estimate the number of lives saved. What can be said is that everyone but fanatics will have some kind of a tradeoff between the two. If changing the law saved 1,000 lives a year at the expense of one pub in 100 closing, we would all support the change. If it saved one life a year and closed 1,000 pubs, most of us would want to leave the law as it was, though anyone who said so would doubtless be invited to a confrontation on television with the relatives of victims of drunk drivers (and why not?). It is notable that the brewing trade and their PR men have not at any point suggested that a handful of lives is an acceptable price to pay for keeping thousands of pubs open. They cannot afford to say this and hence, when pinned down, argue that changing the law would save no lives at all. In fact they defend their position reasonably adeptly, pointing out for example that, given the Government's reluctance to give the police any more money (sorry, 'resources'), lowering the limit may just mean that breath tests on relatively sober drivers will displace breath tests on some of the genuine drunks, in which case more lives are likely to be lost.

At a time when isolation and depression in the countryside, and the high suicide rate among farmers, have been much in the news, thousands of country-dwellers are to be criminalised for enjoying the pleasure – and in sadder cases, consolation – of a couple of pints in the nearest pub followed by a careful drive back along quiet roads. Some pub goers might welcome this. As Betjeman remarked, the trouble with village pubs is village bores, and everyone who has patronised their own country 'local' can think of fellow customers they would be delighted to confine to base (though the landlord the late Jeffrey Bernard expelled from his own pub for being tedious was in central London). But the pleasures of the country pub far outweigh any faint risk of boredom. If a government really wants to persuade rural areas that reducing the legal blood alcohol level is justified, something more than vivid official imagination applied to a sample of 91 American motorists is going to be needed. When Britain has the lowest road casualty rate in Europe[6], when drink-related accidents have fallen by two-thirds in the past 20 years[7], when British (as opposed to American) surveys seem to indicate that changing the law would prevent no accidents, and when 100 country pubs a year are already closing[8], is it not time to leave well alone? Reputedly Mr Blair has gazed aghast at the prospect of leading, or – far worse – being written up as leading, the most bossy and sanctimonious government in history. Now is the time to start struggling against this imminent fate.

Road builders: the real defenders of the countryside

Keith Madelin

The road protester has become the symbol of activism in the 1990s. The protesters claim they are defending the countryside. But defending the countryside for whom? Certainly not the people living in the countryside. Keith Madelin shows that an improved road system is essential if rural life is to be sustained. Rural roads are facing the fastest growth in traffic volumes. If rural roads are not improved the road system will simply be unable to cope. This will damage the environment and reduce the standard of living in rural areas. Improved public transport is a policy option for densely populated cities; it is not an option for rural communities. Road protesters, far from protecting the countryside, are doing their best to destroy it.

The countryside needs a better road system

The media suggest that popular opinion is now opposed to road construction. Road protesters have enjoyed considerable publicity and government has taken the opportunity to save money by stopping road schemes. But it is a myth to assume that those who live and work in the countryside are opposed to road construction. Rural communities are more likely to press for better roads than oppose them. My own conclusion, having been responsible for developing sustainable transport policies in Shropshire for many years, is that the countryside needs a better road system to protect it and enable rural life to be sustained.

Rural areas face fastest growth in traffic and greatest pressure on road system

The concept of rural and urban life is understood though difficult to define. It is estimated that about 11 per cent of people live in settlements of less than 3,000 population, but those living in free-standing market towns are also part of the rural community. What is clear is that those living in urban areas now far exceed those who in live in rural areas.

Transport is linked to land use and few people travel simply for the benefit of the journey. Travel provides access and increases choice of jobs, shops, schools and recreation. Since we are all limited to the amount of time we have at our disposal, we choose to travel when the benefits outweigh the time and cost involved. The majority of journeys are from one urban area to another but these journeys have to pass through the countryside. The problem of transport in rural areas has been the subject of study by Oxford University and a number of interesting issues emerged. For example they found that traffic was growing much faster in rural areas than in urban areas. There was a 79 per cent growth in traffic on minor rural roads over a ten year period prior to 1987 which, the report suggested, pointed to these roads being used as rat runs. Whilst the motorway network carried 27 per cent of all extra traffic, and another 27 per cent was carried on urban roads, 46 per cent was carried on non-motorway rural roads. The study concluded that if these trends were to continue then by the year 2019, urban roads would be carrying 1½ times their 1989 traffic load but rural main roads would be carrying over three times as much traffic. This would lead to a nightmare scenario since rural main roads could not cope and traffic would then spread onto B roads and country lanes. If you think the possibility to be exaggerated then consider the growing popularity of travel books which show short cuts along rural roads to avoid motorway congestion. The next generation of cars and lorries will be fitted with congestion warning systems such as *TrafficMaster* and most alternative routes will use rural roads. The trend of exceptional traffic growth is confirmed in Shropshire where traffic on rural main roads nearly doubled between 1980 and 1995.

Government road policies cater to urban, not rural, concerns

Government policy is now to discourage traffic growth by land-use policies and by increasing the cost of travel, either directly through fuel tax or indirectly through parking charges and restrictions. These measures are welcome but are more likely to reduce car use in urban areas than rural areas.

The growth in traffic in rural areas is already having a major affect on rural communities and the most consistent complaint is about speed of traffic and road safety. Very few villages and market towns have a by-pass as the Civic Trust discovered a few years ago. Now that the government intends less road construction, long planned by-passes are being abandoned much to the anger of local people. A march in 1998 in Alderley Edge, Cheshire, led by Martin Bell MP was a protest against the abandonment of their village by-pass. This was a very significant act and one likely to be repeated more frequently as traffic growth on rural roads affects villages across the country.

A poor road system increases accident fatalities

Road safety is another serious issue and a recent study in Cambridgeshire has shown that 90 per cent of fatal accidents occur on rural roads. Road safety is often viewed as an urban problem but accidents on rural roads are more severe due both to the extra speed and the poor quality of the road. Many rural roads are single carriageways with poor visibility, two-way traffic flow, frequent junctions and a mixture of slow farm traffic and faster longer distant traffic. 3,500 people are killed and 40,000 seriously injured each year on our roads. These figures are a national disgrace because lives could be saved by developing a modern road system. The safest and most environmentally efficient roads are motorways and dual carriageways. You are three times more likely to have an injury accident on a rural single carriageway road than on a motorway. The Cambridge study estimated that the cost of accidents on rural main roads to be about £175,000 per kilometre per year but, the real cost is human misery and suffering.

Improved public transport not an option for the countryside

Improved public transport will provide very little protection for the countryside. Maximum use should be made of the rail network but even a doubling in rail passengers and freight will have little impact on road traffic in rural areas. This is because rail traffic carries only five per cent of total passenger travel and about nine per cent of inland freight. The expansion of the railway network will also raise the same protests as road construction. The new rail link to the channel tunnel and the abortive plan for a freight link to Leicester produced the same level of objection as any new motorway.

There has been a rapid growth in longer distance coach travel and the market is likely to expand but the popularity of the modern air-conditioned coach has followed on from the provision of the national motorway network. There is an argument for developing bus only lanes on the motorway network but there is also an argument for expanding the network. Villagers can see very little difference between the large modern coaches and heavy lorries. Both pose the same problems when squeezing down a narrow village street.

Patterns of rural life make reliance on the car inevitable
Employment in traditional rural industries has declined over many years and resulted in a general move towards urban settlements. It is very rare for rural employment opportunities to match the local population and so commuting to nearby towns and cities has become an accepted reality today. This imbalance is made worse by those with urban employment choosing to live in rural communities. Commuting may have stabilised or even reversed the drift away from rural areas but it has added to the demand for travel which has been met largely by car-based journeys.

Rural communities have also been affected by the economic pressures for larger units of production, distribution and service. Shopping centres, schools and hospitals have become remote and the result is longer journeys. This is confirmed by statistics from the Department of Transport which show that people living in rural areas tend to travel further than those in urban areas. Car ownership in rural areas is one third higher than urban areas and the average rural based car travels nearly 10,000 miles a year compared with 8,000 miles for an urban based car. In 1991 only 19 per cent of rural families did not have access to a car and this figure will fall further as more women acquire a driving licence and the proportion of elderly drivers increases. The future growth in road traffic will largely be driven by these two trends. The number of male drivers and the mileage driven by them has almost reached saturation point and any government policy towards reducing future traffic growth must not discriminate against women or the elderly. Traffic reduction measures could therefore become more of a social and political issue than currently envisaged.

Bus services always have been – and will inevitably continue to be – poor in rural areas
Rural residents have little alternative to the use of the car and even those with no direct car access will organise travel to benefit from car sharing with a friend. Public transport has never been a major factor

in rural areas. Even in the golden days of the 1930s to the 1950s, many rural bus services were subsidised from profitable urban services. Bus operators have wrestled with the rural problem for many years but the density and location of settlement is not conducive to frequent and profitable services. Bus de-regulation has made matters worse and virtually eliminated cross subsidy between urban and rural areas. Those services which are not commercially viable but are deemed socially necessary are subsidised by the local authority. Subsidies are now falling as local authority budgets are put under pressure. The recent announcement of additional government support is welcomed but is unlikely to have much impact.

There is now more transport available in rural areas than at any other time and exists in the form of cars, local delivery vans, social service buses and school buses. The challenge is to use modern communication systems to link those in need with those who can provide transport. The resolution of this problem will enhance rural life but will not necessarily diminish existing or future levels of car travel. Better public transport tends to generate extra journeys rather than encourage a transfer from car to bus.

Modern agricultural machinery and changing land use will increase pressure on rural roads

Rural life depends on local industry even though commuting to urban areas will continue. The changing needs of agriculture mean that large heavy goods vehicles require access to individual fields to deliver seed and harvest crops. Farming also depends on large and heavy machinery accessing rural areas and so it is no surprise that narrow rural roads are being damaged. Sixty per cent of the road network in Shropshire is made up of narrow country lanes about ten feet wide and the poor state of these roads is a major local issue.

The increasing need for heavy lorries to access rural areas also arises from changing land-use patterns. Redundant farm buildings are being turned into freight depots, small factories or recreation facilities. It is difficult to resist any change of use which provides new employment in the rural area even when the adjacent road system is unsuitable.

A popular policy in Shropshire is to widen and strengthen a network of rural lanes whilst seeking to retain their character and alignment. The aim is to provide safe access at lower speed and connect these lanes to a network of main roads which in turn access the national trunk and motorway network. Millions of pounds are required for even this modest improvement.

By-passes popular with local residents

Every rural area requires a basic network of efficient and congestion free trunk roads to attract new employment and to keep through traffic off rural main roads. The rejuvenation of South Wales would not have been possible without the M4 and the Severn bridges and every agency seeking to attract new jobs stresses the benefit of good road access. Rural main roads must be developed for the local traffic movement and simple by-passes provided around villages and market towns. This will enable the villages and towns to be turned back to the people by using traffic calming and pedestrian streets. In my experience, every village and town by-pass has been welcomed by the local community. The Bridgnorth by-pass was celebrated by erecting a marquee on the new river bridge and holding a charity dance. Newport by-pass was the occasion for an ox roast in the old high street. Shrewsbury by-pass has enabled park and ride schemes and the pedestrianisation of town centre streets. Whitchurch by-pass has enabled a complete remodelling of town centre streets, reducing space for cars and increasing space for pedestrians, cyclists and buses.

Twyford Down M3 development both locally popular and environmentally friendly

There is no doubt that public opinion has been influenced by protesters and road schemes such as Twyford Down and Newbury. But have these road schemes really damaged the local environment or is it a case of yet another myth?

The original A33 was a by-pass of Winchester built in the 1930s but it was very unpopular because it formed a barrier between the town and the local countryside of St Catherine's Hill and the historic Plague Pits Valley. The barrier effect was reinforced by traffic volumes of 60,000 vehicles a day and congestion became commonplace. Local roads became rat runs and pedestrian access to the downs was via a muddy underpass.

The construction of the new M3 has enabled the A33 to be reclaimed and incorporated into the local countryside. The old road is now buried under thousands of tonnes of chalk which came from the new cutting on Twyford Down. One and a half hectares of transplanted turf and a quarter of a tonne of wild-flower seeds has completed the transformation and reunited Winchester with its countryside. The new M3 has also enabled existing roads to be downgraded. There are no longer any class A roads within the conservation areas of Winchester, St Cross and Twyford, and the former A31 has become a local road.

Two Sites of Special Scientific Interest (SSSI) required careful attention. The use of environmental consultants resulted in proposals to create new downland habitats on former agricultural land and translocate turf from the areas to be lost. Three years after completion the new habitats are thriving and are expected to become SSSI in their own right. The people of Winchester are very pleased with the end result.

As is the Newbury by-pass – the road protestors caused more environmental damage than the road

The residents of Newbury have long looked forward to the completion of their local by-pass. Newbury was the only town without a by-pass on the route from Southampton to the Midlands and the North. The town itself not only became congested and polluted but traffic found alternative routes on many local roads around Newbury and even further afield. The by-pass will reduce accidents, enable roads in the town to revert back to local traffic, facilitate pedestrian areas and improve public transport. The cost was the use of agricultural land and the effect on a number of SSSI. The environmental protection measures at Newbury are impressive yet rarely reported. Not only are new sites for wildlife being created but the process is being managed by ornithologists and environmental experts to fit in with breeding seasons. River bridges have been widened to allow wildlife to flourish and animals to pass along both river banks. A colony of rare snails has been moved and is now flourishing in new wet land areas on what was originally waste ground. Nine new drainage ponds have been built to protect the local rivers from any risk of pollution and the ponds themselves will become new habitats.

Protestors at Newbury were particularly vicious, burning equipment and setting booby traps designed to maim construction workers. The occupation of woodland and SSSI by protestors caused more environmental damage than the actual building of the by-pass.

Imagination and new technologies make road building yet more environmentally friendly

Prior to the protest movement, construction in the countryside could be unsympathetic to environmental issues with projects justified mainly by financial cost benefit evaluation. Environmental issues are now high on the agenda, and blind opposition to construction, whether in town or country, is environmentally counter productive. Road vehicles are now being designed to use sustainable energy sources and are becoming pollutant free. Even Greenpeace has recognised that the car is here to stay and therefore every effort should be made to design an environmentally acceptable car. This they did successfully and their pioneering work has been endorsed by other motor manufacturers. Technology is showing how transport can be environmentally sustainable and modern roads can be designed to complement the countryside. During a recent visit to Austria I stood on a hillside and found it difficult to identify the motorway which I knew was routed along the valley. A mixture of mature planting, landscaping, tunnels and viaducts plus a noise-reducing road surface called whisper concrete showed just what could be achieved.

Austria and Switzerland, together with most mainland continental countries, have continued to develop a high class rural road network in spite of severe natural difficulties. The key to success has been a system of adequate funding which could sustain a high quality of design and construction. The Swiss even had a national referendum to approve the need for a modern road system paid for by an extra petrol tax. The environmental debate is now about how much should be spent to reduce or eliminate environmental effects rather than opposing road construction in principle.

Responsible environmentalists must work with responsible road builders, not against them
There is still much to be done but to pretend that the human demand for accessibility will go away or can be suppressed is environmentally irresponsible. A modern road network, particularly in rural areas, will always form the backbone of any future sustainable transport system.

An official of an environmental lobby group was once invited to see how modern design and construction could actually protect the environment, but replied 'I am not interested in the facts. My job is to oppose any construction'.

Road protesters must move on from blinkered opposition, and join in a serious environmental debate. They must now understand the environmental damage that will be caused if a modern road system is not developed in this country.

19

Britain's old roads:
neglected by conservationists

Charles Clover

Are roads necessarily eyesores? There are all sorts of societies to protect this part of our heritage or that kind of hedge, but no-one stands up for England's historic roads. Some modern roads, although necessary, are undoubtedly aesthetically displeasing. But Charles Clover points out that many roads are masterpieces of engineering, spectacularly cutting through magnificent countryside. They can be objects of real beauty. Others are at least as historically significant as many of Britain's great houses. Perhaps it is time not just to defend roads on utilitarian grounds but actively to embrace them as an integral part of our heritage.

If collared by a pollster and asked for our views about roads, most of us would say that roads are a shameful necessity. An increasing number of us would also say that we don't see the need to build any more. In Europe the car – though almost universal – has become such an object of fashionable disapproval, because of its ability to pollute and cause Macadam sprawl, that the enjoyment of roads has become a guilty thing, not to be admitted in public. Yet who does not admit to enjoying a view of the countryside from the train?

Roads far more popular than might at first be thought
Guilt about roads is historically new. It is partly the result of the post-Rio age of environmental awareness, partly a reaction against a previous political generation in Britain which seemed to measure progress in concrete and tyres. This guilt, however, is only skin-deep. Ask us in a different way what we think about roads and we answer differently. Look, for instance, at the advertising which sells cars. A winding – and

empty – road stretches through the vineyards. It is down this road that Nicole joyously revs her hot little hatchback to meet Papa.

In truth, we are all of us a little in love with roads – at least characterful roads, which for me rules out multi-lane highways like the M25. We long to travel along roads, to see what is over the crest of the hill or around the next bend. As a society we are in denial of the fact – for the rational, politically-correct reason that we know that we cannot all have what we want without destroying the thing we love – without that winding, empty road through countryside, shaded by a canopy of trees, becoming a concrete highway.

There is good and bad road design, just as there is good and bad architecture

As someone with environmental sympathies who happens to be fascinated by roads, my plea is a simple one. For heaven's sake let us dispel this myth that all roads are unattractive blanks in the landscape which we would rather weren't there. Let us embrace the fact that many roads are a pleasant way of enjoying the landscape, whether countryside, desert, mountain or metropolis, whether it is by car, on a bicycle or on foot. But let us accept that it is only certain kinds of road which have this quality – which is why 'upgrading' kerbs, sodium lighting and roundabouts are to be abhorred. So too are crass and unnecessary roads which devour and dominate unspoilt, wonderful landscapes.

I fear that unless we celebrate our relationship with roads – and define precisely what makes some roads attractive and others not – we will encourage bureaucrats to turn all roads into the kind of soulless necessities we pretend them to be, to the further impoverishment of the landscape. In a civilised country – which must these days include the notion of ecological sustainability – people should express their own opinions about road design, just as they now do about architecture, rather than leave this to the homogenising vision of professional highway engineers. There is even a 'green' message her. Paradoxically, we need to celebrate old roads more, to want new ones less.

England was shaped by its road system

It is astonishing, when you consider it, how little we do celebrate old and beautiful roads, given that they are usually the oldest man-made things in the landscape. We know from the great landscape historian, W G Hoskins, that everything in the landscape is older than we think it is. Oliver Rackham, the countryside historian, tells us that Roman roads, which we think of as built in the heat of war, surveyed from hilltops, and constructed straight to convey the legions to the front line, were not always new. Others, built later in settled times, meandered almost as much as the prehistoric roads, and before them the sheep-walks whose line they took.

We know from Hoskins, too, that the pattern of settlement of England was pretty much fixed by the end of the Saxon era. This means that the road system was too. In England, most country lanes have a longer and more distinguished history than the mediaeval towns, the ancient cathedrals, that they serve.

Every twist and turn of a pre-twentieth-century road is the result of a confrontation with natural obstacles – and the local landowner's view on whether the road should cross his land. Geology and land-ownership formed the road network, though its anthem will always be G K Chesterton's poem, 'The rolling English drunkard made the rolling English road'. The materials which make the walls by a road, the canopy of trees which meets so satisfyingly over it, the width of the drovers' verge and the composition of species in the hedgerow, all give the landscape its local character. Roadside verges contain what remains unsprayed of the *flora Britannica*.

But roads ignored by the heritage industry

The difference between roads and buildings is that roads do not bear the imprint of those who have passed along them, even lived on them. Ancient roads may have no obvious engineering or architectural merit, by contrast with road bridges which are often fine works by known architects and engineers. It has therefore been possible for the heritage industry to ignore the importance of roads as fine man-made structures.

There are few roads registered as ancient monuments. There are no learned societies dedicated to cataloguing old roads, or seeking to record the vestiges of old roads in new roads, such as the A1. There are no signs saying this road was the way taken by King John or King Edward I, two restless kings, no sign saying this was the road to London taken by the Young Pretender. Old roads are, by and large, victims of the next whim of the Highways Agency or the local authority's highway engineers. And in heritage-crazy Britain, where tourism is the number one industry, and you can't get windows altered on a Grade II listed cottage without permission in writing, that is more than a little odd.

Clearly utility and, more recently, a bureaucratic obsession with safety, conquered all until now. Currently air pollution, congestion, noise, and a sense that new roads have already damaged many of the landscapes of our crowded island, have forced us to reflect on what we want from roads. The question we should be asking is whether we should not be counting history and beauty as things we want from roads, as well as minimising noise and pollution. Is not that line of ancient oaks beside the A5 on the way to Shrewsbury at least as valid a reason for not 'improving' the road as the greenhouse effect? These questions are still going to be as relevant, perhaps more so, in 100 years time when we have virtually stopped using fossil fuels and cars are powered by low-emission fuel cells.

Roads can enable us to enjoy spectacular landscapes

It is true, few twentieth-century roads have the quality I am seeking to celebrate. But it is possible to think of a small number which have the ability to involve the traveller in experiencing the contour-line, the geology, the sense of discovering a new landscape – because they cannot dominate that landscape. Most of these are roads into the mountains or across the contour-line. There are the awesome bridges on the M62 through the Pennines, the corniches of the south of France, the awesome roads up into the French Alps Maritimes, even some cuttings on the M20 through the North Downs. There are awesomely-engineered sections of the A9 through narrow glens on the way to Inverness.

All these modern roads creatively attack the contour-line, overcoming yawning chasms with bridges and have sweeping, necessary bends. The character that one celebrates about these roads is not so much the engineering skill of making them, but the sense that engineering has enabled us to experience the landscape, in a not totally dissimilar way to that in which slower, more bucolic or more miserable travellers encountered the same contours on foot or horseback.

Motorways usually less interesting because they've lost the road's geographical and historical connections

What is it about modern arterial roads which makes them so ugly? Arguably that they obliterate everything else. Or is that just a subjective judgement which will be reappraised in future? Do our new roads have to be so cultureless, featureless, historically bankrupt? Perhaps they do, because of the volumes of traffic they have to carry, but it is a question which must be asked nonetheless.

A case in point is the A1, currently being upgraded to a motorway. The present alignment of the Great North Road from London to Edinburgh is, as far as it is possible to work it out, a mixture of the Roman road – the Ermine Street as it was known in the Middle Ages – drovers' roads and eighteenth-century turnpike. The present route is a relatively straight one, barring an incongruous bend at Sandy, Bedfordshire, over the Grand Union Canal.

There is a sense, on the unimproved parts of the A1, of a road with different manners to a modern motorway. There is, in the gently winding route and the rising and falling contour, a sense of real connection to the land which is passing on either side. Limestone and brick farmsteads, dating from the eighteenth century or before, face onto the road, reminding one of a time when travellers and new faces were welcome as company or a source of custom. Now most of the inns and farmsteads along the sections which are becoming motorway are boarded-up and await demolition. No-one wants to live in them because of the noise of the road. Before the earth-movers rolled in, the volume of traffic had already brought an end to 1,000 years of history.

The earth-moving machines are now defying what contours are left, the chalk hills and limestone downs have been rolled out as with a rolling pin. The new road will be seductively easy and quick to drive on in heavy traffic, and, no doubt, safer than before. But there is no sense of history. You might as well be anywhere. You could nod off, as a passenger, wake up, and not know where you were, except for the road signs. It will be necessary to turn off and take old roads to experience the history, the geology, the flora of the counties you are passing through.

Road protestors should defend old roads

No-one has yet chained themselves to the earth-movers on the A1. Perhaps they should. There are, in fact, precedents for the defence of old roads, indeed the history of road protest can often be seen as the defence of old roads in the face of the new. The protesters who defended Twyford Down outside Winchester – unsuccessfully – against the earth-movers, who provoked the present heart-searching about road-building, called themselves the Dongas Tribe. This was after the deep iron-age trackways on the Down which they were seeking to protect.

There are few who do not now wish, now the Down has been disfigured with a great chalk gash, that the protesters did not achieve their modest aim of placing the M3 in a tunnel.

The Department of Transport (as it was then called) did – to do it justice – produce an admirable book, the *Good Roads Guide* in 1992, which showed the best ways of setting a road into the landscape, planting beside it and replacing signs of local distinctiveness such as stone walls. Little of what it preached seems to have been taken to heart on the M3 – or indeed on the A1. There is a case, at least, for a few heritage signs in motorway service stations celebrating the antiquity of the route.

Road 'improvement' and the obsession with safety

A word about safety. Safety has been the reason for the mutilation of many old roads by highway engineers. There are still instances, even though the roads programme is supposedly on hold, of proposals to destroy beautiful, historic roads for spurious safety reasons. One of the best examples is the straightening of the A5 as it enters the Snowdonia National Park. Telford built the A5, then the main road to Holyhead, at the height of the picturesque era in art, when a man of culture, as he was, could not but be affected by the cult of landscape. Telford built the bends along the banks of the Conwy in wide loops which are still safe at over 45mph today. Proposals still exist for a bypass behind the Padog bends, though the accident record would not seem conclusive, and the improvement of the road more a matter of local politics than safety. As so often, safety could be achieved much more cheaply – and a historic route better understood – with better signs and driving manners more schooled in the hazards of older routes.

Interest in old roads gradually increasing

A heartening sign of a long-overdue interest in the recording of old roads is Valerie Belsey's *The Green Lanes of England*. This book, admirable in intent and partly in execution, celebrates the unmetalled roads which have shrunk back into the landscape. The drovers' roads, salt ways and trackways gouged by centuries of carts, sledges, horses and cattle are now being rediscovered as routes for a new generation of ramblers. Belsey's proposition is that there should be a register of information about these old roads, many of which merit protection. But it seems perverse to confine such a register to 'green lanes' and ignore metalled roads, some of which are at least equally ancient. If roads deserve greater respect, then the national register should record information about all roads, even if this information should one day prove inconvenient to the plans of highway engineers.

Time for an Old Road Society?

A national register of roads would be a first base. It might persuade English Heritage, the Countryside Commission and their sister bodies to think creatively about preserving the character of old roads and, who knows, in time, to perhaps inform the development of new ones. But no government agency achieves much without a pressure group snapping at its heels. Old roads need a champion. The Council for the Protection of Rural England ought to be up to the task. It has complained about the lost tranquillity of country lanes, but it has not really taken up the challenge. I suspect what is needed is a new learned body, an Old Roads Society. Anyone want to join?

20

Greenbelts and the blighting of rural England

Mark Pennington

When politicians claim to be defending the countryside, they often speak of their commitment to greenbelts. But Dr Mark Pennington shows that far from protecting the countryside, greenbelts have led to the kind of monotonous, poorly designed, tightly-packed development conservationists most abhor. 'As opportunities for new building on greenfield sites have been restricted by greenbelts, developers have responded to the shortage by cramming as many houses as possible onto the remaining sites in the countryside and the market towns which are actually granted planning permission.'

Greenbelts have become one of the sacred cows of British land-use planning and environmental policy more generally. The recent furore stirred up by the attempt to accommodate the requirement of 4.4 million new homes by the year 2016, illustrates the depth of public commitment to this core of the British planning system. It would appear that few other environmental issues can generate the degree of public response as the threatened loss of greenbelt land for housing and the allegedly inexorable spread of urban sprawl. It is the contention of this essay, however, that public and political support for greenbelts is based on a serious misunderstanding of the facts. In short, it is a myth that greenbelts have been an effective instrument of environmental protection. On the contrary, they have actually contributed to many of the environmental problems affecting both the countryside and the cities alike.

The origin of the greenbelts
Greenbelt policy in Britain is a throwback to Atlee's post war socialist

experiment and the nationalisation of development rights under the 1947 Town & Country Planning Act, one of the few elements of that programme yet to be unwound. First proposed in the Barlow (1940) and Scott (1942) reports, a key priority of planning controls in the post-war era has been an attempt to restrict the outward growth of urban areas through the designation of sites where urban developments are unlikely to be permitted. The greenbelt is probably the most famous of these and was originally recommended to local planning authorities by Duncan Sandys in the Ministry of Housing & Local Government Circular 42/1955.

The greenbelts grow

In the intervening years the area of designated greenbelt has increased substantially and currently accounts for about 14 per cent of the land area of England and Wales. It is a testament to the power of the greenbelt concept, that the Thatcher Government, supposedly committed to a strategy of de-regulation, actually presided over the biggest expansion of the greenbelt system at any time since 1947. Between 1979 and 1991, the area of designated land increased from 1.7 to 4.2 million acres (+147 per cent) and contrary to popular opinion the rate of rural to urban conversion was lower than at any time since the war.[1] Partly as a result of this strategy the vast majority of the land area (89 per cent) remains in rural and in particular agricultural uses.[2] It is far from clear, however, that the benefits of this policy actually outweigh the environmental costs. In particular, it appears that greenbelts have generated various unintended consequences which have been detrimental to environmental quality in both the countryside and in the towns.

Greenbelts favour agricultural land-use without rationale

Any analysis of the effectiveness of greenbelts as an environmental protection tool must first ask what it is that they are supposed to be protecting. Although it is often thought that greenbelts are an instrument of environmental policy, in practice they have been confined purely to a preoccupation with preventing any kind of urban development in the countryside surrounding the cities, to the neglect of what actually happens in the countryside itself. In most cases greenbelt land is held in agricultural uses, which due to the subsidies available under the Common Agricultural Policy have been nothing short of an environmental disaster

The grubbing up of hedgerows and other side effects of intensive farming have been well documented elsewhere,[3] but the role of greenbelts and other restrictive land-use designations in contributing to these problems is rarely, if ever recognised. In particular, by forbidding the development of non-agricultural land uses greenbelts have reinforced the privileged position of subsidised agriculture and have prevented the transfer of land to more highly valued and in many cases less environmentally damaging uses. As Reynolds suggested more than 30 years ago,[4] greenbelts may have been instituted with the goal of preserving the landscape around towns, but one could be forgiven for thinking that their principal contribution has been the perpetuation of the cabbage patch.

Assumption that underlies greenbelts is that housing development is a bad thing

Advocates of greenbelts will doubtless reply that the solution to the excesses of the farming sector is to subject agricultural land uses to the same planning requirements as currently govern urban uses. But the weakness of this argument lies in the implicit assumption that urban developments such as housing, however badly needed, are always bad for the environment. Low density housing or leisure development, for example, interspersed with woodland are perfectly compatible with maintaining habitat and species diversity and would often represent a considerable environmental improvement on the agricultural monoculture which they might replace. As Professor Evans has suggested,[5] it is not at all clear that in countries such as France and Italy, where planning controls are more relaxed, that the more numerous houses spoil the rural landscape. 'Those who travel outside Britain do not seem to think that the landscapes of Tuscany, Umbria, Brittany or the Loire Valley have been irretrievably ruined by piecemeal development. On the contrary, they seem to be pleased that villas and *gites* exist which are relatively cheap and which allow them to live in rural surroundings.' Greenbelts by contrast have discriminated against this type of environmentally sensitive development and are thus responsible for a second undesirable feature of the British system of land-use planning.

Greenbelts lead to poor quality, densely packed housing

Following the seminal analysis by Hall et al,[6] it has become widely accepted that greenbelts and other land-use designations have so restricted the supply of land for housing that land prices and as a result house prices have been artificially inflated. The principal beneficiaries have been those individuals fortunate enough to own property and especially houses in designated areas. The principal losers have been the marginal consumers no longer able to afford to buy a house and the mass of the urban population who pay higher prices and are subject to the increasing congestion and air pollution brought about by the cramming of development into the towns. It is less well recognised, however, that one of the major effects of the shortage of development land brought about by greenbelts has been the encouragement of the very type of poorly designed and monotonous suburban housing developments which are the *bête noire* of groups such as the Council for the Protection of Rural England.

As opportunities for new building on greenfield sites have been restricted by greenbelts, developers have responded to the shortage by cramming as many houses as possible onto the remaining sites in the countryside and the market towns which are actually granted planning permission. This 'rabbit hutches on postage stamps' syndrome[7] is the proximate cause of the high density suburban estates, characterised by poor architectural quality and a lack of garden space which periodically spring up on the outskirts of towns. Nor need developers worry about their ability to make a profit from the sale of these dismal creations, for the planning system has created such a scarcity of development that more or less any kind of property can be put up and sold. In a more liberal system, by contrast, developers would have to compete on quality, including the environmental/ aesthetic quality of their developments. Such a situation would be more likely to encourage environmentally sensitive, lower density development, with larger gardens and attractive landscaping rather than the high density monotony so often produced today.

Greenbelts have contributed to traffic problems

In addition to the above problems it is now increasingly apparent that greenbelt policy has contributed significantly to the environmental problems associated with transport congestion and the growth of long distance commuting. Although much of the growth in the demand for commuting may be attributed to the effects of a subsidised road system and in particular the absence of mechanisms for road pricing, analysis has confirmed that greenbelts and equivalent controls have exacerbated these trends.[8]

The major effect of greenbelts in the UK has been the physical containment of urban areas, but this has not prevented the functional decentralisation of cities and of the population itself. On the contrary, throughout the entire post-war period there has been an important shift away from the major conurbations towards the commuter towns outside the older metropolitan areas. In turn as people have left the older cities they have been accommodated in suburban estates in the commuter towns. This outward flow of resident populations has not, however, been matched by a concurrent shift in the pattern of employment, with most people continuing to work in the major metropolitan areas. The result has been an increase in the proportion of employment opportunities taken by commuters, often living a substantial distance away from their place of work. Greenbelts and other designations which restrict the development on the rural/urban fringe have acted to push this development pressure still further out into the areas beyond the greenbelt, increasing the distance between work and home and thus raising the demand for longer distance commuting and hence more roads. Add to this the effects of urban congestion in the commuter towns themselves, brought about by 'town cramming' and it can be seen that greenbelts have contributed significantly to the transport chaos so characteristic of urban Britain today.

Time to abolish greenbelts
The type of housing greenbelts have encouraged, and the traffic chaos they have contributed to, should act as a salutary lesson to those environmentalists who, in defending greenbelts, claim superior foresight with regard to conservation than those who would put the countryside to alternative uses. Far from being an unambiguous protector of the environment it would appear that greenbelts have acted to protect the position of the subsidised farming industry, have contributed to the production of monotonous housing developments and have added to the transport chaos which is a prime feature of our towns and cities.

Given these manifest shortcomings, policy-makers should begin to look at longer term solutions to these problems and in particular should examine the ways of dismantling the cumbersome planning apparatus and of replacing it with an alternative based on privatised development rights.[9] In the meantime, a more realistic 'short-term' solution would see the abandonment of greenbelt policy and would encourage local authorities to judge individual planning applications on their environmental merits rather than according to blanket land-use designations which half a century of experience suggests are 'green' in name only.

21

Land-use planning: a penalty on the poor

Linda Whetstone

Think of ten buildings in the countryside which you love and ten buildings in the countryside which you hate. For most people most of the buildings in the first category will have been built before 1948, most in the second after 1948. 1948 was the year in which wholesale land-use planning was introduced. 'The countryside as we know and love it owes almost everything to the actions of private individuals pre-1948 and almost nothing to government regulation post-1948'. So if planning controls have not conserved the countryside, what have they achieved? They have driven land prices up, and thus housing prices up. This has meant that young country people have found it more and more difficult to buy, or even rent, property in rural areas. Organic communities of those working and living in the countryside have thus been undermined in favour of weekend cottage owners. Land-use planning is a penalty on the poor, but it does not conserve the countryside.

What is most loved in the countryside owes nothing to government regulation

Consider what the Town and Country Planning laws were invented to preserve. All of it was created without the benefit of government intervention. Private actions created that which government intervention has been invoked to preserve. Had that government intervention existed a thousand years before most aspects of our countryside that the preservation lobby seek to keep would never have been created in the first place.

It is only the resources developed in both towns and the countryside which have generated the wealth to enable each generation to live better

129

lives for more years than the preceding one. Had the current restrictive development policies been implemented in the year 1000 AD or the year 1500 AD, the Industrial Revolution would never have taken place and that wealth would not exist. Had the housing stock at those times been conserved in the way that today's planning laws would have us conserve so much, would earlier houses have been replaced, for instance, by the lovely Georgian houses that are much admired today. Almost certainly not.

The diversity that we enjoy and seek to preserve was created by individuals acting in their own interests and, through market pricing mechanisms, serving the needs of others. It was not created by government control. This control can preserve but at a cost and as the years pass and the controlled resources become increasingly like a museum rather than a living developing entity so the cost increases.

Almost everyone can name post 1948 – the year in which wholesale land-use planning was introduced – developments in the countryside that they hate, but try and get them to name ten such developments which they would feel moved to create the planning controls (had they not yet existed) to protect. So the countryside as we know and love it owes almost everything to the action of private individuals pre-1948 and almost nothing to government control of development.

When government planning has so clearly failed elsewhere, why is it still seen as appropriate for housing development?
We must consider what might have happened in the absence of such controls and, yes, development would have been different but would it have been better or worse and who is to judge? Who would it have been better or worse for? Who wants to do it differently and why? The stock answer is 'greedy developers of course', who make the money when planning consents are granted. But the only reason they can make apparently windfall gains is the way the planning system works.

Our system is very restrictive and forces up the price of existing stocks. Admittedly the quantity of land in any country is limited but so are the stocks of every other resource relative to the potentially unlimited demands upon them. In other areas it is the market pricing system that allocates the use of these scarce resources and very importantly directs users to be more or less sparing with their use according to their price, which is the measure of scarcity.

For example oil is a scarce resource and we hear horror stories that it will run out at some future date but that date is continually moving forward and away. This is because the market price tells us to use it sparingly and encourages manufacturers of oil-using products to use it more efficiently and the oil industry to extract more from a given reserve. Imagine if the stock of oil had been treated as finite and government decided to allocate the available stocks by means of rationing. What would have happened to our standard of living? And the higher the oil price rises, so the reward for intensive or unlikely exploration increase and hence more oil is found. The market discovers!

The UK's land planning system is one of the final and finer examples of government rationing. If you look at the UK land planning system it is virtually guaranteed to have a restricting effect which in turn forces up land and house prices.

Demand for new housing created by people wanting somewhere to live, not greedy developers

The demand for development land is created, not by greedy developers, but by men and women who want somewhere to live or to work. The high prices and windfall profits enjoyed by landowners who are given planning consents are entirely due to the system. For example house prices in the South East indicate that there is a demand for more housing. So businessmen are looking for opportunities to satisfy that demand and trying to find land which might be developed.

They submit plans to the District Council to ask for permission to develop and then a lengthy procedure takes place which has a high chance of producing a negative response. Those living anywhere near the proposed site perceive that the value of their own property maybe devalued by it. More houses in the village, a restricted view, more traffic, more children in an already full school are all reasons why existing residents object and they do this most vociferously.

Planning controls only give a voice to existing home-owners...

It costs them virtually nothing to object. They are already inside the drawbridge and enjoy the benefits of living in a charming 'protected' village etc. They only see the potential reduction in the quality of their lives or the value of their properties as there is nothing in the system that allows those who are disenfranchised by it to be represented. Other than by someone in business, via the pricing mechanism, who is trying to satisfy his own needs/self interest.

Most people believe the planning process protects them but it offers little real protection and absolutely no opportunity of any gain, or compensation, even when that perceived protection fails as it often must. What does planning really offer? There are some winners and many more losers.

The developer is the only person usually perceived to benefit from a positive response and local politicians are leant on by their electors to vote against. It is an unequal contest and is the reason for the very high costs of development land and of new development. And also the high value of existing development whether it is seen in housing rents or purchase prices or the rents and/or purchase costs of offices, factories, warehouses etc.

And are a government perk only enjoyed by middle classes
The high cost of property in many parts of the UK is directly attributable to the tight grip on planning afforded to those who have every interest in restricting development and the complete lack of representation of those who would prefer more personal space as against a countryside set in aspic. The planning controls can rightly be accused of being an invention of the middle classes for the maintenance of their status quo. Those that already 'have' use them to keep what they have got and to keep those who are not in such a fortunate position in circumstances from which they would like to escape.

But the less advantaged are hurt by planning controls
We should ask ourselves who 'they' are and how it affects them. The worst affected are those at the bottom of the heap in terms of jobs, housing, schooling, recreational facilities etc. They would not be the ones who were going to come and live in the villages or the countryside because their incomes would not afford them such pleasant surroundings under any system, but they might dearly love more space where they are and the limited amount of development allowed further out has a knock on affect on the cost of all development and property.

For instance planning, and the associated cost of land, has led to the social deprivation inflicted upon families by high rise flats. Whatever the cost of the actual building may be, as you add the cost of an acre of development land – approximately £200,000 – and divide it between the units, it pushes their prices beyond the range of many.

Furthermore the high cost of development opportunities and developed property is a drag on employment and affects the competitiveness of everything we do in the UK. Admittedly we are not alone in this situation but the higher the total cost of a product the less of it will be sold and the cost of rent is an important part of this equation.

What would happen to the countryside without planning controls?

So if government planning is so costly in opportunities foregone, how else can the countryside be protected? Perhaps we should consider whether government should be involved at all and what might happen in its absence.

A typical response might be that the whole of the South East would be covered in bungalows with quarter-acre plots and the countryside as we know it would vanish, which in turn raises two issues. Firstly would it happen and secondly if that is what most people want who should be given a position to stop it?

Consumer demand dictates what is produced in virtually the whole economy – why not housing?

To take the second point first, planning controls give power to vested interests to enhance their position. Perhaps we are so used to government acting in this way that we no longer question it, but should we meekly accept that government largely exists to appease the interests of whoever pushes hardest? Should we accept the replacement of the Rule of Law by the rule of those in government through a very subjective decision-making process that is neither predictable nor transparent? This is definitely the case in planning decisions.

Why not replace planning by government with resource allocation via the market, which is the system that has increasingly been used in so many other spheres and with such obvious benefit. If this produced the predicted number of bungalows then how could you argue that it is not as optimal an allocation of land as is possible?

Without planning controls, England would not be covered in concrete

But would an end to planning controls mean that every green space was covered in concrete? I think not. Currently in England, (ie, excluding Scotland and Wales) less than 12 per cent of our land is covered in bricks and mortar, concrete, etc, so we are a lot further from saturation point than many preservationists would have us believe.

There is no law prohibiting farmers from selling off their land in any size plots that they choose and in the South East, at least, the smaller the plots the higher the per acre price tends to be. But most farmers do not do this because they value the larger size of their holding.

If there is a chance of getting planning on some of their land the price goes up in quantum leaps. £2,000 an acre for agricultural land and upwards of £200,000 for land with development permission would almost certainly tempt them to sell. But if builders could build anywhere the price of land for building would drop to approximately the agricultural figures, with premiums for particularly special locations. So if most landowners do not sell the odd acre for the smaller plot premium currently available, why would they start doing so simply because planning restrictions had gone?

The answer is they would not, but there is a problem of conception here. We are so used to building land being worth huge figures and most people do not associate that with the involvement of government in land-use planning. We find it hard to conceive of a world where, because you can build anywhere, the land on which you build has no premium over other land.

But cost of housing would fall

As the cost of the building plot is a high percentage of the eventual value/cost of the property the reduction in this cost would greatly reduce the cost of the new building. Following on it would also reduce the value of all existing properties and once again we come up against the problem that the ending of government rationing of development land would threaten the 'haves' on two fronts.

First, there would be more building, which could threaten the amenity value of those living near it and of those who we are told come out of the towns at the week-ends to enjoy it. Secondly, not only the value of new but also the value of existing property would be reduced.

Covenants could be adopted to restrict future development in specific areas

Ways exist whereby people can protect what they value in an area and these would develop if the Town and Country Planning Acts were abolished or drastically reformed. When an area is developed a covenant can be placed on all properties sold in it to ensure that future owners do not alter the character of the area so anyone buying a property in it can be assured that the value of their investment will be maintained. The system of covenants has been shown to work very well indeed in preserving streets in London, amongst other cities, which are currently just as they were built so many years ago and even all painted the same colour and yet in different ownership. Government is not even needed to preserve the original colour schemes as it has all been done through voluntary agreements.

Groups or individuals can, and already do, buy property to protect whatever aspect of it they cherish. The Royal Society for the Protection of Birds buys up sites as bird sanctuaries, those against stag hunting buy up areas which they keep as refuges for deer and thousands of individuals in the UK support the National Trust which protects and maintains huge areas of land and many special buildings.

Land-use planning protects vested interests to the detriment of UK as a whole

In summary the Town & Country Planning Acts impose a great cost on many members of society who are not those in a position to do much about it, while they are seen by those who already enjoy living in protected areas as essential to the very existence of the countryside. But these people have no idea, or may not care, that their desire to preserve and protect adversely effects the living conditions of others by keeping property prices high and making UK Plc less competitive.

22

Developing the countryside: for townies to play in or country people to live in?

Jane Wright

The countryside is viewed by many urbanites as a pleasant tranquil place where they can relax from the rigours of city life. But Jane Wright shows that this view of the countryside clashes with the desires of those who live and work there. The countryside cannot be 'preserved' in some romanticised image of a non-existent past golden age. Housing, commercial development and modern agriculture are all essential requirements if real communities are to survive in the countryside. Already many of the poorest in Britain reside in the countryside. Development must be allowed to continue if the situation is not to get worse.

On 14th July 1997, and again on 1st March 1998, the countryside took to the streets, staging marches to express dissatisfaction with the current political agenda. The aim of these demonstrations was to draw to the attention of the urban community and Westminster that the countryside is not solely their playing field but actually provides raw materials, an industrial base and employment.

Urban sentimentalism about the countryside no help to country dwellers

The romantic sentimentalism of city dwellers for the British countryside has, over the recent past, conditioned life in rural communities through its influence on policy formulation. Its counterpart is a misguided, paternalistic, belief that the urban dweller must assume responsibility for maintenance and conservation of the countryside. Policy makers have paid attention to those who philosophise on rural activity while turning a deaf ear to those affected by it. This is due to a perception of the rural community as 'second-rate citizens', unworthy of consultation. The rural community has every right, and indeed a responsibility, to ensure that it is treated with the same degree of consideration and understanding as any other business community.

While it comforts the urban dweller to think of the countryside with picture-postcard imagery – the landed gentry residing in stately homes and riding across the rolling hills, obeying only the call of the hunting horn – this far from mirrors reality. However, while such perceptions are held, how can the rural community expect their cries for urban sympathy and government assistance to be taken seriously? After all, more political capital can be gained by injecting public funds into derelict inner city areas rather than assisting those believed to be enjoying a self-reliant life of luxury. The time is long overdue for another William Cobbett to dispel this idealistic myth and open people's eyes to the harsh realities of rural life.

Poverty in the countryside
Eleven million people in England – over one fifth of the population – live and work in rural areas and, in 20 per cent of cases they are living in or on the margins of poverty.[1] These figures are only set to get worse as the impact of the BSE crisis and strong pound drive more and more farming families out of business. In 1997 farming incomes were slashed, down 47 per cent, and the situation became even worse throughout 1998.[2] This fall in incomes is set against the background of rural work commanding low wage rates compared with urban employment. The decline in farming incomes has a widespread impact on the rural community as the survival of local shops, pubs etc are all dependent on the incomes of local people. Therefore, a fall in farming incomes can start a negative multiplier which then eats away at the livelihood of the whole community.

Newcomers often do not want to live in the 'real' countryside
Some could therefore argue that the recent trend of wealthy townsfolk moving to the villages and commuting to work should be welcomed by the locals as it brings in a fresh injection of money and ideas. However, it is often the case that commuter families do not wish to

live in the real countryside, just a mythical, idealised dreamland. Consequently they complain about the cockerel crowing at the break of dawn, the smell of the muckspreader and the potential danger farming machinery and chemicals may have on their children or pets. All of this, however, is as much a part of rural life as the flora and fauna, hedgerows and streams are. It is also a sad situation that although commuters may have attributes that could be put to good use in the administrative tasks of the village or small town, the majority choose to remain peripheral to local activities. This may occur for a range of reasons. First, it may be true that although the commuters wish to become involved they are too busy and tired by the time they return home to dedicate time to community activity. Secondly, it may be that the commuter families feel little association with their village as they send their children away to school and use the cities for entertainment. Thirdly, it may simply be that the commuters do not wish to be part of the community as they have moved to the country to escape. All of these reasons draw the same conclusion, that the benefits of the rural community and essential work in maintaining the life of the village is lost when urban commuters displace the original rural residents.

Popular urban image of farmers is unjust

It is not only the view of committed eco-warriors, but also popular belief, that the farming community has no interest in the preservation of the countryside. Farmers' intentions are perceived to be to squeeze maximum short-term profit from the land while taking no responsibility for the long-term consequences – raping the fields for subsidies and polluting the rivers as a side-effect of increasing crop yields. This stirs up the paternalistic belief in urban dwellers and Westminster that they must intervene, adopting the responsibility shirked by the farmers, in the maintenance of rural Britain. This belief, however, is not only misguided but also illogical.

Farmers do respect the countryside. After all, it is the farming families and other members of the rural community who are affected most by any decline in the beauty and productivity of the countryside. Consequently, they have put resources into planting more trees and adapting farming methods to encourage more biodiversity.[3] Eighty per cent of the UK's landscape is cared for everyday by British farmers.[4] These farmers have voluntarily entered 1.2 million hectares of their land into conservation agreements that will manage the countryside in ways that benefit landscapes, wildlife, public access and archaeology.[5]

Alongside this the rural community has put effort and money into planting and restoring hedgerows. Between 1990 and 1993, government surveys showed that every year 4,400km of new planting took place and 5,700km of derelict hedgerows were restored.[6]

Country people realise that countryside cannot be preserved in aspic

However, the difference between the 'traditional' rural dweller and the passive admirer of the countryside is this; while both appreciate the beauty of nature, true country people also accept the need for development. They realise their dependency on sustaining a livelihood from the countryside and look for ways to improve competitiveness. Progress has come in many forms over the past few decades: farming practices have been mechanised; intensive methods of production have been introduced for livestock and poultry, while arable farmers have biologically engineered crops to increase yields and used chemicals to decrease the risk from pests and disease. While those working the land accept these as necessary competitive advances, the onlookers have viewed such developments with contempt.

Problems are intensified when those who have no involvement with the countryside, other than the occasional weekend away, believe their views should influence rural policy. So, what is it that makes people with no knowledge or understanding of country methods and practices believe they have a right to drive rural policy and restrict country activity? The urban dweller may allege that his intentions lie in maintaining habitat and vital resources for future generations, however, many would be reluctant to accept this argument. The real urban objection stems from much less honourable desire: purely the current interest of that individual. The city dwellers wish to keep the English countryside as a place to escape from the industry and commerce of the city: they do not wish to drive through an intensively-farmed region which reminds them of the environment they are trying to escape. Therefore they wish to ring-fence the countryside from development and technological advances so as to ensure that tranquillity and picturesque landscapes are maintained. If successful, this imposes restrictions on those already operating in tight economic conditions. However, it also enables urbanites on their weekends away to revel in their private wealth as well as the richness of the countryside; assuming they can ignore the poverty they have inflicted on its inhabitants.

The rural community do not object to people taking a break from the city to enjoy the countryside. After all, the numerous guest houses, holiday cottages and craft shops are dependent on the tourist trade. There is also a comprehensive network of public footpaths and rights of way to enable country and townsfolk alike to absorb the country ambience. However, conflict does arise when visitors expect their one-off requirement for tranquillity to rank as a higher priority than the livelihood of the people who live and work in the country every day.

The subsidies of the Common Agricultural Policy have allowed politicians to ignore wider concerns of country people

While it is human nature to attempt to influence decisions in one's own favour, even if this means others lose out, why and how did the rural community lose its voice in Parliament? This can, almost entirely, be seen as a side-effect to the UK's membership of the Common Agricultural Policy (CAP). The subsidies and the protectionist policies extended to agricultural producers by the CAP have destroyed any sympathy the urban population had with the farming community. Complaints came from other declining industrial sectors questioning why agricultural incomes were guaranteed while their sector was failing in the face of competition. Consumers complained about the additional cost the subsidies add to food prices. Tolerance of agricultural complaints decreased even further when the set-aside policy presented farmers with financial incentives not to farm the land. The CAP has therefore lead the urban dweller to consider the rural community as an expense. Therefore any further cries for assistance are, at best, ignored.

However, the CAP has been a 'wolf in sheep's clothing' for many farmers. The imposition of quotas has penalised farmers for increased productivity and rendered them unable to gain profit from improved efficiency. Set-aside has resulted in land degenerating into beds of weeds which then grow their way into surrounding fields of crops. Therefore, while consumers have objected to the additional costs of the CAP, the benefits have not necessarily been reaped by the producers.

Membership of the CAP has given successive administrations the opportunity to hand over responsibility for agricultural production to Brussels. This has not only increased the distance between the policy makers and farmers themselves, but has also given Westminster an excuse for its knowledge vacuum on rural issues. This void should never have occurred. After all, the rural economy is much more than just farming.

Political centralisation has led to the further ignoring of rural communities

How then has the Government been able not only to pass over responsibility for agriculture to Brussels, but to ignore the existence and needs of the rest of the rural community? Trends in government over the last ten years, have shown a continuing shift of power away from local government towards centralised administration. Although this may be argued by some as more efficient, it has had a negative effect on the representation of the countryside. It is inevitable that a legislative body made up predominantly of urban constituencies places more weight on the urban voice. The very nature of constituency boundaries heightens this bias with the dense few square miles of the Cities of London and Westminster and the vast tracts of Ross, Cromarty and Skye both being represented by a single member.

Fashionable 'green' policies are response to urban, not rural, demands

How has Westminster hidden its ignorance of country issues for so long? Governments have avoided addressing the real country issues by implementing fashionably acceptable 'green' policies instead. Green policies have been mis-sold as being beneficial to the countryside. It is simple to understand the burden many green policies place on the rural community. First, take the supposed environmental policy of increasing tax on fuel. This, obviously, drives up the cost of private transport. The additional costs of this policy fall disproportionately on country dwellers as they often have no alternative to using private transport because of limited public services. It is this community that has to travel the furthest to reach essential amenities such as shops and schools.

Greenbelts are another example where environmental policy has been imposed without assessing the potential impact this has on rural communities. Greenbelts create an artificial shortage in supply of land for housing. Therefore any increases in demand immediately filter through as price rises. As demand pressures on country dwellings have heightened over the last ten years, with an ever increasing number of city workers choosing to take advantage of country living and commuting to work, house prices have escalated beyond the reserves of many rural workers. As a consequence of the higher prices, rural workers have been displaced from their local communities and forced to reverse commute to their village job from the local town.

Few MPs have a real understanding of the countryside
The problems of the countryside continue to fall on hostile minds. Since Labour's overwhelming General Election victory of May 1st 1997, the cries from the countryside have been met with more adverse proposed legislation. This has occurred as very few Labour members of Parliament have a real understanding or first hand experience of the countryside. This Government appears to be more susceptible than previous administrations to the views of the pressure groups. Although this may, in the short term, result in achieving popular headlines, it does little to address the underlying problems. A typical example of an attempt to appease the rural community without fully considering policy effects can be seen in the proposed implementation of regional development agencies. Although this regionalisation may be a step in the right direction as far as recognising diversity, it is still clear that funding will be focused on the areas of urban concentration within the region.

Until educational and cultural attitudes are changed to embrace the realities of the countryside rather than fostering an outmoded sentimental image, rural communities will continue to be downtrodden. It is essential that the rural argument is given the weight it deserves in policy formulation. This will require the rural agenda to be considered in its widest form. If this does not occur both the 'traditional' rural community and the 'city's playing field' will be lost.

23

Hill farming: not so much the 'good life' as the hard life

Jeremy Hunt

Many sentimentalists dream of leaving their arduous urban jobs, moving to the countryside and living a carefree and contemplative existence in harmony with nature. They call this 'downshifting'. But while it is much dreamt and talked about, few take it any further. If they were to 'downshift' they would soon realise that rural life can be much harsher than they thought. Jeremy Hunt shows that many rural dwellers must work much longer hours, much more arduously, for much less money than most city dwellers. The hill farmer, for example, may earn as little as £8,000 per year. And for this he must contend with the vagaries of the weather and the changing – these days inevitably falling – price of sheep. The image and reality of the hill farmer's life may be wider apart than that of most country occupations, but it is symptomatic of the wider picture.

The sentimentalised image of the hill farmer

Staring out over the wild, open spaces of the hills, leaning on the carefully-crafted, curved horn of his crook, loyal sheepdog by his side – the picture of the contemplative hill shepherd, entrusted with our upland heritage, a life of springtime lambs, summer haymaking and a cosy farmhouse with a welcoming Aga to warm away the worst of the winter. And if that isn't enough, the hill shepherd has almost become venerated by a populace who perceive something religious about his selfless lifestyle and undying devotion to the care of his flock.

Hill shepherds are undoubtedly wise men. They have to be. While some may serve as lay preachers and take to the pulpit in the local chapel each Sunday morning – and in summer they will probably be spreading the Gospel to more ramblers than fellow farmers – their inherent wisdom is now a lifeline to their survival. Today's hill shepherd needs to be wise to the ways of the modern world that now invades and infringes his unique workplace.

Hill farmers may earn as little as £8,000

Average hill-farm incomes are at a dangerously low level – some farmers are ekeing out a living from incomes of little more than £8,000. Were it not for the subsidies paid to hill shepherds through EC livestock and environmental schemes, many thousands would simply sell-up and leave. To those who live and work in towns and cities that may not seem such a drastic step to take; in fact it may seem like a sensible move to some.

Yet they maintain some of the most spectacular countryside in Britain

But the impact of such a mass exodus from the hills would have a devastating effect on the upland landscape; a wilderness of stunning beauty, one that has been created and maintained over centuries of hill shepherding, would be deprived of those who have fashioned its austere beauty.

Without the constant grazing of sheep the rounded, close-cropped mowing of the highest hills and fells that make up some of the UK's most dramatic and internationally-famous scenery, would be lost. The rate at which scrub and birch woodland would invade and colonise these areas would be dramatic. The only thing that stops it happening is the year-round shepherding of sheep, often many thousands of sheep, by a breed of men who are irreplacable as trustees of that most majestic of landscapes – our highest hills.

Borderway Mart and the Shepherd's Inn

One of the largest livestock auction marts in the UK is at Carlisle. Just of the M6 is Borderway Mart, an internationally-known centre for livestock selling, a place where millions of sheep have been sold, and a great meeting place for farmers from both the hills and the lowlands.

Adjoining the market is the Shepherd's Inn, equally famous as the source of food and succour for those who may have travelled hundreds of miles and been up well before the sun to ensure their stock was loaded and delivered to the market on time. Outside the Shepherd's Inn there is a large and colourful sign depicting a well-known northern shepherd and his dogs. That image, pleasing though it is to all who visit, typifies the public's image of the hill shepherd. While this glimpse of rural tranquillity may enhance the facade of the Shepherd's Inn, it is a far cry from reality.

Hill farmers must contend with factors beyond their control: the weather, isolation, environmentalists and currency fluctuations

Life in the hills is hard. Those nights by the Aga with a wind whistling around a remote stone steading are far from restful. Outside your sole source of income could be battling against a biting blizzard, hunched up against a wall, helpless against a tide of drifting snow, fighting for life against all the odds. But sheep, like those who tend them, are hardy creatures, showing a defiance for the elements that seem to wage a constant war with all living things, out in the remote expanses of the hills.

Some hill sheep farmers may own their own land; a large number rent their farms from major land-owning institutions such as the National Trust or are tenants of large landowners whose primary interest for owning such farms lies in their potential to provide shooting. So the option of selling-up and cashing-in on the value of their land is not an option open to a large percentage of hill farmers.

Doggedly pursuing a way of life, more than a way of earning a living, they battle not only against the weather and the harshness of their isolation, but against less tangible threats like the fluctuations of European currency and the effect that has on the value of the stock, and the pressures from environmental groups whose vision of a perfect countryside all-too-often fails to acknowledge the influence wielded by traditional agricultural practices.

Hill farming involves very different calculations to lowland farming

Owning or renting a large hill farm does not signify affluence. Large areas of these desolate grazings offer only meagre food supplies to sheep; that means the stocking rate – the number of sheep that can be kept per acre of land – is very low. Compared with a lowland farm which may carry six ewes to each acre of grassland, the hard hill farm may only be able to support one.

So a hill farmer has to run many hundreds, or often several thousand sheep to generate sufficient income from a vast acreage of poor land. Just like those who shepherd them, the breeds of sheep that have evolved over thousands of years to exist in these conditions are independent and single-minded.

While lowland farmers expect a ewe to rear twin lambs to provide a fair return on capital invested, the hill shepherd would not thank you for two lambs from his pure-bred horned ewes. One is quite sufficient. It takes the ewe all her time to keep herself and her embryonic lamb alive in winter; and in spring and summer she needs to build herself up again in readiness for the winter, as well as feed her growing offspring.

Even though many lowland flocks could thrive outside all winter, many are brought in for at least the run-up to lambing in early spring. Very few hill shepherds can afford, or are even allowed, to erect buildings large enough to handle ewe flocks numbering four figures. Their sheep have to remain outside all winter. That demands a tough shepherding regime. The quad-bike is looked upon by some as the 'new toy' of the hill shepherd. In reality it is an absolutely essential aid to modern shepherding and enables man and dogs to cover huge distances of inaccessible fells and hills, keeping tabs on ewes and delivering feed supplies in the hardest weather.

Tourism a mixed blessing

Gathering a flock of over 1,000 ewes for clipping, dipping or to sort out lambs at weaning time in late summer, when they are grazing over several thousand acres of remote fell, is an arduous task. Although neighbouring farmers usually give each other a helping hand for these important seasonal stock tasks, for much of the year the routine husbandry has to be undertaken by the lone shepherd. Tourism, while considered by many to have been a source of income for hill farmers who offer bed and breakfast, has its downside. Ask any hill shepherd with 500 lambs to move down narrow lanes in a National Park in midsummer and you realise that not all visitors are totally sympathetic to the fact that, while they enjoy a holiday, this place is the farmer's workshop.

Problems faced by the hill farmer

While some hill shepherds may have help from an agricultural student looking for practical experience at lambing time, such assistance is a luxury at most other times of the year. Farmers' sons, now through choice and often necessity, often seek employment away from the farm. This deprivation of family help – help which used to be on hand for the 365-days a year that good shepherding demands – can no longer be relied upon. A hill shepherd's wife is now more likely to be found with a heavy bale of hay on her back feeding ewes in a biting winter gale, rather than sitting in a rocking chair by the Aga baking scones.

At lambing time hill ewes are brought down off the higher land to lamb in the relative comfort of sheltered 'in-bye' or lowland fields. While this makes shepherding more accessible, it does not reduce the long days and nights spent monitoring pregnant ewes, assisting difficult deliveries and administering to sickly sheep and weak lambs.

And even when the lambs are born the risk to life is not over. Marauding foxes, often vixens with cubs, see lambs on remote hill farms as a readily available food source. And danger can strike from the skies as attacks from crows and magpies can leave a sickly lamb with eyes mercilessly pecked out. Distances of 20 miles and more a day may be covered by the shepherd at this time of year. Vigilance is his watchword, sleep a luxury.

The unpredictability of the weather is the hill farmer's greatest concern. Early winter blizzards can disrupt tupping time which, in turn, can delay lambing time. While lambing in the hills is traditionally in late spring to avoid the worst of the weather, an unseasonal April snowstorm can bury ewes and lambs and, within a few short hours, account for a big slice of the annual income if lamb losses are heavy.

While lowland farmers make hay and silage from mid-May onwards and can still be cutting grass in autumn to conserve for winter fodder, hill shepherds may have only one 'bite' at a crop of hay. Their limited acres of lowland pastures will have been grazed bare by ewes and lambs which will not have been turned back on to the higher land until May. By July those acres will have to provide sufficient grass to be cut and baled to supply the entire flock with winter fodder. A wet summer or even a wet spell that coincides with grass newly cut for hay, can be disastrous for hill farmers. At best it means poor quality winter feed; at worst it means empty barns. The pressure on the hill farmer is constant. With a large flock covering a vast track of remote hills and fells, every shepherding task involves detailed planning and hours of back-breaking work on steep slopes and unyielding terrain.

Hill farmers cannot easily diversify
The lifestyle of the hill farmer has an in-built inflexibility. While those pundits who recommend and advise our farming community talk glibly of diversification into new farming systems to boost income, hill farmers

are restricted by their landscape, their location and all-too-often by the environmental restrictions or rules imposed by their situation or a National Park authority.

They cannot grow crops because the land is unsuitable; they cannot milk cows because there is insufficient grass and daily milk collection is unprofitable for dairy companies. They are in a straight-jacket that allows them only to graze sheep and perhaps keep a few suckler cows.

The hill farmer only paid once a year

Income for the true hill shepherd comes but once a year when lambs and draft ewes – those that are usually in the mid-life stage and will fare better on lowland farms – are sold. Most of the lambs will be sold as 'stores' and not as 'prime' lamb. Prime lambs have a higher value but store lamb income depends on other farmers with more advantageous holdings to make an investment in these lambs for further fattening. Hill farmers have no option but to sell their store lambs in the autumn. They cannot take them home if the price is low, they have no grass or 'keep' for them to eat. They have to take what the buyers are prepared to pay on the day. It's a big risk to place almost your entire annual income on a couple of days trading at an auction mart.

So spare a thought for the hill shepherd – food producer, countryside manager, environmentalist, tourism officer, but first and foremost a resolute farmer and dedicated stockman.

24

Children in the countryside: is it the best place to bring them up

Diana Winsor

Children joyfully and innocently playing on summer days in meadows and woods; this is a widespread urban image of what life is like in the countryside for children. Diana Winsor points out that this idyllic image has more in common with the countryside as it is portrayed by such authors as H E Bates and Laurie Lee than with the countryside as it is today. Bringing up children in the countryside undoubtedly has its advantages. But so does bringing up children in cities. Parents in the countryside have as many concerns and worries as urban parents. Yet many urban parents want to bring their children up in the countryside in the hope of rediscovering an innocence they themselves have lost.

'I want them to grow up close to Nature, with the freedom to play in the fields and woods. I want them to be safe, to be part of a small community where everyone knows everyone else'. I remember saying that; before I had children.

Image of idyllic countryside drawn from novels
Most of us create our childhood idylls of the countryside from books. Old books. I imagined my children making a cowslip-ball as they did in Miss Mitford's *Our Village* – 'Everyone knows the process: to nip the tuft of flowerets just below the top of the stalk and hang each cluster nicely balanced across a riband, till you have a long string like a garland. What a concentration of fragrance and beauty it was!' And when Miss Mitford's little companions made a mess of their cowslip-ball they simply threw away the first lot and started again, there were so many, and mothers carried bucketfuls home for cowslip wine. That

was almost 200 years ago, of course. Few children now can know the pleasurable sensation of cool stems bunched in a small fist. These days the best place to find cowslips growing wild is along motorways, where they have been planted, and where no-one can pick them.

Not all the books were so old. Laurie Lee filled us all with longing, lying on his back in June-high grass, 'a massed entanglement of species, crested with flowers and spears of wild wheat, and coiled with clambering vetches, the whole of it humming with blundering bees and flickering with scarlet butterflies.' In Miss Read's books about her village school in Fairacre the children dawdle along country lanes to school, eating young hawthorn leaves they called 'bread and cheese'. If you went through H E Bates's Uncle Silas's garden you came to a wood 'where primroses grew so richly in spring that they blotted out the floor of oak and hazel leaves. In summer wild strawberries followed the primroses and by July the meadows beyond the wood were frothy with meadowsweet, red clover and the seed of tall soft grasses.'

This countryside has gone, if it ever existed outside the imagination

I knew a wood like that. As a child I spent my summers on the edge of Romney Marsh in Kent, where my uncle still farms. Unaware of country codes or designated footpaths, careless of farm boundaries, I explored on foot and bicycle, sometimes a pony, that airy flatness of sheep and larks and yellow-flagged dykes. When I was 18 I painted it. The picture bears little resemblance to what it is become. Wheat grows there now, between the summer cracks in the Kentish clay, and the pumping stations hum louder than the insects. This abundant Nature I thought would embrace my children in the countryside has become elusive, secretive.

Yet when I took the children to London we walked through Hyde Park and found the squirrels so tame they came to us to be fed. Municipal parks are the secret jewels of urban living. A recent study of bird species in town and country recorded both much greater diversity and abundance in urban areas. Not only in parks and gardens but along city canals and industrial sites thrive moorhens, kingfishers, goldfinches on thistleheads. Trees have room to grow. I can remember the elms that suckered along every hedge, ghostly boles in headlights' beam at night along every lane: now they are gone, and hedges that might become field maple, hazel, ash and spindle are cut to fraying ribbons.

Countryside not a place of innocence

But if Nature has retreated, what of freedom? My children went to the village primary school, but out of the 120 that attended, only a handful arrived on foot. The rest came by school bus or car. A hundred years ago the roll of pupils was almost the same, 120, but then all walked to school, because they all lived within the parish boundary. Now many neighbouring schools have closed, and the catchment area increased. For two weeks we did try to walk to school, but were defeated by the stretch along the A443 and the buffeting slipstream of lorries and cars. Further afield now, at the local comprehensive school, transport is essential. There are no public bus services, so the children must use the school bus. In that unsupervised limbo, Golding's *Lord of the Flies* is curtailed only by the time it takes to get to your stop.

City children are socialised in the dangers of the adult world

Living in a city, as I did as a child, meant that I could use regular bus services. I could walk to the library, swimming pool, shops; a group of us often went to a cafe. We were part of a wider society, absorbing knowledge of the adult world. We became aware that people were not all the same in their actions and reactions as those we know: we learned almost by osmosis the etiquette of queues, handling cash, dealing with unexpected situations. We recognised the signals of unwelcome attention. Home was a base, not a prison. All these things can be taught by parents who themselves have the experience and time to do so, but theory still requires practical experiment.

The simple statistics of population may mean a greater risk to any child from some disordered human being in a city, but that risk is minute in any case, and perhaps the *nous* to deal with dangerous situations is the vital element.

Country roads more dangerous

The child who has grown up with busy roads in a city is probably at lower risk from a traffic accident than its country cousin. Besides, there are other dangers in the countryside. Once, being brought up on a farm was everyone's ideal: now there are 200hp tractors, slurry pits and chemicals in the barn. Rather, the children are whisked away to playgroups and the pictures, not the reality, of the farmyard.

Farming families, or those with enough money, can afford ponies, and there is no doubt that many children enjoy riding. But for their parents the current rate of road accidents involving horses makes it a nerve-wracking business. As for cycling – few of us can forget that childhood freedom, recaptured whenever one gets back on a bike and sails down a hill again. Now my children look at suburban cul-de-sacs and envy those who can still ride their bikes unsupervised. Like a million others, we have a cycle carrier on the back of the car so that we can take the children to some safe designated place like the Camel Trail in Cornwall.

Even walking in the countryside is not the blithely spontaneous activity it once was. I gave up many attempts to explore local footpaths with two small children, so often finding them blocked by wire or vegetation, gates or stiles difficult to negotiate. It only takes a couple of hostile farmers to unnerve a wary walker, however justifiable their territorial instinct may be, and where is the pleasure of walking across a field if you are afraid to let your children stray a little from the path to look at a flower? I remember meeting three women pushing their infants in buggies along a road in the flat fields of Lincolnshire. Was there nowhere else to walk? No, they said, They were afraid to use the footpaths in the fields because they did not know with what they had been sprayed. So they walked their children along the windy, treeless road.

Poor country dwellers often resent the arrival of wealthy townies

What then of that sense of safety and security found in a small rural community, where everyone knows everyone else? Like other incomers to our village I became an enthusiastic member of the hall committee, a parish councillor, a school governor. One afternoon, planting daffodils at the village hall, I became aware of someone standing over me. 'Too many of these new people' a voice said grimly, 'Never see 'em taking part in the village. *Commuters*', it added: the final condemnation. With the guilt of the townie I made some sound of assent and continued shoving the bulbs into the earth.

In the city, poverty may mean deprivation. In the countryside, inevitably, it also means isolation. Public transport competes in cities: in the country it scarcely exists and, indeed, only fantacists can visualise when it could ever provide the mobility and freedom of the private car. A recent study for the Joseph Rowntree Foundation observed that richer people are moving into and poorer people out of rural areas, and in our own village the only new houses built in recent years have been way beyond the means of local inhabitants. All have been bought by commuting families. And families are smaller than they used to be. Children, if not entirely cut off from others, or from clubs, sports and discos, must be chauffeured everywhere – thus creating the increasing traffic in what were once quiet country lanes. So few now walk or cycle along country lanes, especially children. The road that bisects our village is so busy that its narrow pavements remain empty. No-one chats across a garden gate. It is a vicious circle of loneliness for those old people, for the poor, and for children, and it accentuates the gulf between them and the affluent two-car (one of them a 4x4) middle class. It was their voice, the voice of the dispossessed that accused me.

The country village exhibits all the best and worst traits of small communities

Nevertheless our village is, on the whole, a friendly place. People do talk to each other in the post office and at the school gate. In cities, there is greater wariness: what burdens of confidence, of intimacy, might one invite by a casual 'good morning' at the bus stop? Yet bitter feuds burn here that could not survive in the city. There, they are diluted simply by the number of people and the escape routes from confrontation thus provided.

Parents often want the countryside for their children to rediscover an innocence they themselves have lost

And at the end of it all there is a paradox. We who want the countryside for our children find that they often reject it. They would rather be driven to town to see a film or go shopping than go for a walk – just as we, so often town children, longed for the excitement of fields and woods. 'The toads have laid toadspawn in the pond!' I cry to my offspring. 'Great mum,' they say indulgently. And I wonder if they might appreciate the beauty around them more if they did not actually live in it, but simply visited it in the holidays, as I used to in my childhood. Perhaps that is why I remember so many golden summers, and, through my children, try to find them again.

I don't think the countryside is the best place to bring up children, although it may have been once. But then, nor is the inner city. In the end, the best place to bring up children is in a happy home. If it makes their parents happier to live in the countryside, then that is probably all that the children themselves, if asked, would want.

25

The incomer and rural life: a question of values, not of birth

David Edelsten

The incomer has long been a focus of rural hate. Many of the problems of the countryside have been blamed on incomers. But this is unfair. David Edelsten shows that most country people are incomers to some degree or other. And many of these incomers take a full part in the local community and enjoy country pursuits. The conflict between townies and country people is not one of origin, but one of values. Those that took part in the 1998 Countryside March were united by their values, not by where they were born.

The incomer as hate figure

Do you remember the odious and officious Mrs Elton, in Jane Austen's *Emma*, the daughter of a Bristol merchant, who came to Highbury, in then rural Surrey, 'with superior knowledge of the world, to enliven and improve a country neighbourhood'? Did you ever hear the term 'incomer' used other than pejoratively? Much more probably you heard it in relation to some grotesquery such as a report of rooster-rage, seized on by the media because it made good copy.

The incomer has become a hate figure in rural mythology, a scapegoat, in stereotype an evangelist of urban ways and urban values. But is such demonizing of these immigrants fair: not if my own experience in north Dorset is any guide? And are we country dwellers not ourselves anyway all incomers?

But the great majority of country people are incomers

If like me you live in a rural parish, try this test. When next in church look around you, count the adult members of the congregation who were born within the parochial boundaries. I would be very surprised if, in a congregation of, say, 20, they numbered more than one or two. Ask yourself next where the parents of those few were born; almost certainly you will soon find yourself all but clean out of natives.

Then study the memorials in view, many will be of, or will mention, recent immigrants. Our church boasts a Ham-stone effigy of a Norman cleric whose family gave its name to the village: he most certainly was not born here. Nor was our most famous 'son', brought here in infancy, the great Duke of Marlborough.

Have you rumbled that it is not a fair test that I have set you; at least, it would not be fair where I live, in what Thomas Hardy called the Vale of Little Dairies? Our farmers, nearly all parish-born, are traditionally excused church attendance on grounds of milking, or its vestigial indulgence. Take your poll at Easter, Christmas, or at the Harvest Festival, and you will get a truer figure; but still, I suggest, you will find that the great majority of adult country folk are this generation's migrants. Look closer, and you will also see that it is they who run the village.

Our Church Wardens, in succession to my father and myself, are a retired teacher, married to a farmer, but herself from 12 miles away in Puddletown, and a one-time stockbroker, a Scot born somewhere about the Empire. The Lord of the Manor, a noted cattle judge, came here 15 years ago from the home counties: the Rector, thanks be to God a hunting man, came originally from Chard, in the neighbouring county, and his PCC lay vice-chairman, his second-in-command, is the village's obligatory brigadier: the organist is also an import from Somerset, and so on, and on. The Chairman of our Parish Meeting, not a churchman, is a retired Schools Inspector, recently settled here: its Secretary however, and her husband, the Captain of the Bells, prove the rule, they are another farmer and his wife, natives both.

Incomers active in defending and assisting the village community

Three times in recent years our tiny parish, adult population 150, has had to clear the decks for war, or gird up its loins to mount a great endeavour. With neighbouring communities we had to fend off a potentially disastrous 'development', by a local farmer-turned-businessman, seeing the thing through the whole ruinous gamut of dissent to a public enquiry. And, again in an alliance, we had to prevent our own County Council from siting a massive mound of the county's ordure in our midst, and buy the land in question from them, to prevent their trying the same wretched brainless, bureaucrat-dreamed-up trick again. Then on our own, at vast cost, we re-hung, and augmented from four to six, our peal of bells.

On each occasion, the leadership, the knowhow, the hands-on-strings, and to a generous extent the hands-in-hip-pockets, were those of the recently arrived, the newest incomers. Without them, these turncoats from another world, we would have been defenceless, and we would still have just four bells, and they not safe to ring. This village would have died without its new blood. But fortunately we country folk are in the most part not a settled people, in the longer term we are on the move, and on the make, arrivistes one and all.

The incomer as scapegoat
If the incomer as a bugbear proves to have the elusive qualities of a snark, how does he rate as scapegoat? Go back to the miracle of St David's Day, I mean of course the 1998 Countryside March: I do not intend irony, the march was a phenomenon without blemish and without par. Remember those placards and banners, those epigrammatic messages from embattled hearts, 'Hands off...', 'Say no...', Send home...'? We felt ourselves to be fighting against outsiders.

It was sobering I found, amongst the aftermath, to observe how others saw us. A letter from London SW in the following week's *Spectator* asked 'Who is it exactly who grubs up our hedgerows and replaces old stone walls with wire? Who demolishes old farm buildings, replaces them with tin and corrugated iron? Who slashes the country lanes with flails? Who poisons the wild flowers? Who fills the carparks of the out-of-town supermarkets?'

Allowing for the writer's Mary Poppins view of rural economics and technology (who is to rebuild the walls, who pay for them, has not wire fencing been a fact of farming life for a century and more?), and discounting the inbuilt assumption of a duty on farmers to keep the countryside looking as London residents might, on their occasional visits, wish to find it, she had a point. '*Touché*', I conceded, who but we ourselves do all these things that most of us regret?

Blackmore Vale from Thomas Hardy to the present
When my father, a country doctor released from World War II, bought the local practice and moved us down here, on the way to our new home he stopped the family car where the old coaching road from

Dorchester to Sherborne joins the prehistoric Ridgeway, to show us the country we were come to live in. I can see the place from my window as I write. It is a magic spot, where the Dorset downs cease their march northward from the sea, and give way to the Blackmore Vale. On a fair day the view is tremendous, west to Exmoor almost, north to Alfred's Tower at Stourhead, and east, if you must look east, to Bulbarrow.

Tess passed that way on her fated tramp to visit her in-laws, one frosty Sunday a hundred years ago. Hardy describes the scene,

> In time she reached the edge of the vast escarpment below which stretched the loamy Vale of Blackmoor [sic], now lying misty and still in the dawn. Instead of the colourless air of the uplands the atmosphere down there was a deep blue. Instead of the great enclosures of a hundred acres...there were little fields below her...so numerous that they looked from this height like the meshes of a net. Here the landscape was whitey-brown; down there...it was always green.

The view, a typical sudden modulation in the classical symphony of the English countryside, remains much the same today, at least in its impact, if not in detail: but of the foreground a different story must be told. Tess, we must suppose, followed an old, unfenced track, little used then and now, that lies like a strap along the ridge. I have known it, ridden it, walked it, picnic'd, played and had pleasure there since first my father showed it to us.

Ravens nest there, the old trees are a delight, and there are flinty earthworks to explore – but no longer. The once free-sided track, where you might pick your way if you chose among the trees, has recently been corsetted with hideous barbed-wire, to keep out 'travellers': the latest embellishment of this once lovely place is a radio mast. (I was riding there this morning, contractors are busy still, erecting chain upon chain of wire fencing, grubbing up stumps and long-fallen timber, tidying the place up, Surrificating Dorset so that any visitors from modern Highbury will feel at home.)

Developers as likely to be locals as outsiders

And who is responsible for all this? Not, I assure you, any recent incomer. Here, as in the case of the 'development' our local parishes successfully saw off, and of the great pat of garbage, until we stopped it, the Council planned to dump at the foot of that escarpment, it is a home-grown agency at work, a much-respected, long-established, land-owning family.

A question of values, not birth

One recent winter's Monday morning, driving our clapped-out horse-box to a local riding school, where a guru advises on delinquent horses, I found myself stopped at traffic lights, behind the expensive limo of a recently-arrived new neighbour. His road lay straight ahead, eastward to Blandford, Salisbury and London, mine left, over Sturminster Newton's storied and ancient bridge into the borders of North Dorset. His preoccupation is television drama, including the most recent *Tess*; mine our young-stock, home-bred, home-broken, stabled through the winter, a treasured leg-iron, like having a baby in the house. Just for a moment, until the lights changed, I had a dyptich before me, of our two so different but overlapping lives – we are becoming friends.

Remembering the Christmas party at his house, where I encountered people of great interest whom I would never otherwise have met, I thought of the varied riches such a family brings to a retired rural quarter. Just as my father, London bred, came west, a young man, in abdication year, to enjoy the country and to be a countryman, and, although 30 years dead, is till spoken of round here as a loved and skilled physician, artist, and mad-keen hunting man, so, I believe, will these newly-arrived neighbours enliven and improve our country neighbourhood.

26

Modern Britain
and the subsidy culture:
no salvation
for the countryside

Leo McInstry

One of the hallmarks of Modern Britain is the subsidy culture. Everyone with a grievance seems to believe that they deserve – that they have a 'right' to – a handout from the state. Whatever the problem is, it can be solved by extravagant public subsidy. Leo McInstry warns the countryside not to fall into this trap. The subsidy culture offers no salvation to the countryside. It only offers a road to dependency upon the whims of urban politicians, as farmers are learning to their cost. The countryside must revel in its traditions, customs and way of life. It will not have won if all it gains is subsidies for post offices and village shops.

A fundamental contradiction lies at the heart of the present debate about the countryside. On the one hand, rural dwellers demand – rightly, in my view – that the Government should stop interfering in their lives. End the destruction of our landscape by sprawling urban estates, they cry; drop the proposal to ban fox hunting; ditch plans for a right to roam across our lands. On the other hand, in direct contrast to this call to be left alone, the protesters moan about lack of support from the Government. Their litany of complaints includes inadequate support for farmers, poor public services, closure of local hospitals, schools, and bus routes, and lack of local jobs. Parading this rag-bag of grievances, the countryside activists want the Government to 'stop ignoring us' and 'listen to our needs'.

Countryside at risk of adopting modern welfare mentality

I believe this contradiction has arisen largely because the rural movement has been gripped by the same querulous mentality which characterises modern welfare Britain. Like so many other elements of our society, the protestors appear to believe that the Government has a duty to provide for them in every circumstance, to guarantee their living standards and to alleviate every misfortune they might suffer. These demands are entirely in line with the development of the infantilised state, whose citizens seek ever greater independence while, paradoxically, becoming ever more dependent upon government. This drift towards infantilisation was predicted by Alexis de Tocqueville, writing in 1835, in *Democracy in America*: 'Over this kind of men stands an immense protective power which is alone responsible for securing their enjoyment and watching over their fate. That power is absolute, thoughtful of detail, orderly, provident and gentle. It would resemble parental authority if, father-like, it tried to prepare its charges for a man's life but, on the contrary, it only tries to keep them in perpetual childhood.'

There is a direct parallel between the demands from the countryside for more state action and the demands from welfare recipients for more state help. In both cases, the Government is already providing lavish funding: in the countryside through, for example, subsidies to farms and roads; and in the social security system through bloated allowances for, say, single parent families. But this largesse appears only to breed resentment. Far from expressing any gratitude, the beneficiaries wallow in their anger against the Government, moaning about their lot and seeking more from the state.

Welfare mentality already found in farming, forestry and housing

Farming has been the foremost victim of the welfare mentality in the countryside – and the most widely commented upon. But there are other instances. Forestry has suffered the negative consequences of large-scale intervention, with the Forestry Commission proving an inadequate tool for the protection of our woodlands. As Alan Duncan and Dominic Hobson argue in their book *Saturn's Children*: 'State ownership and management of the forests is a disaster for the landscape and the natural environment. The Commission itself has covered much of the countryside with unsightly conifers rather than the broad-leafed trees now in favour among environmentalists. Many private forests of conifers were also planted with state help in the shape of tax subsidy.'

The same can be said of the grisly housing developments which now scar the rural landscape. Now it might be argued that private housing is an example of the free-market in operation, with developers putting up new homes to meet the demands of the public. In practice, this is far from the truth. In fact, rural housing has been driven by government edict. Four years ago, civil servants in the Department of the Environment decided that an extra 4.4 million homes would be built in Britain by 2016 to 'meet the needs' of a changing population – and two million would have to go up in the countryside. The bureaucratic practice of 'researching and addressing needs' is well-known to social work departments and other welfare agencies. It is the complete reversal of a true market approach. Instead of gearing the supply to meet demand, the demand is built around the supply. And central government diktat plays a key role in achieving the level of supply. In West Sussex, for example, the county council decided it would need to build 38,000 new homes by 2011. But like some Soviet-style central planners, the Department of the Environment said that the West Sussex structure plan was 'unsatisfactory' and ordered the county to incorporate another 12,000 homes into their proposals. As so often happens with central planning, the sums do not always add up. In Gloucestershire, chartered town planner and academic John Allinson estimates that the county is providing 6,000 more homes than it requires. The drive for a vast expansion in housing has achieved pernicious results. One has been the decline in the quality and variation of rural architecture, with the same dismal semi-detached homes springing up in cul-de-sacs throughout the country, from Cumbria to Cornwall. Another has been the creation of more traffic and rail congestion, as millions are encouraged to buy properties far from their workplace. Not only does this create networks of dormitory villages in even quite remote areas, but it also leads to demands for yet more state spending on public transport and roads. A third, even more serious problem, is the incentive given for the break-up of the family, since it is seen as the duty of government – both local and national – to provide 'affordable housing for all', whether it be married couples splitting up or young people leaving the parental home. If housing were less widely available, ('move in now for just £10' is the slogan emblazoned across several new estates near my home in rural Essex) many people might not be so relaxed about reneging on their responsibilities to their families.

If country people want to save local shops and services they must use them and not call for government support
What is so depressing is that many in the countryside have already fallen into the welfare mentality by their refusal to acknowledge the level of financial support already provided by the urban taxpayer. The protestors are outraged at the closure of rural post offices, yet they never mention the subsidies required to maintain postal services in rural areas. The same can be said of rural roads, schools, hospitals and libraries. And this ingratitude is all-too-often allied with hypocrisy. Some of the very people who bemoan the decline of economic life in their own villages can be found eagerly pushing their trolleys around a vast out-of-town supermarket, stocking up on their low-price Chardonnay without a thought for their local off-licence.

The countryside can thrive without government handouts and interference
But it would be wrong to tar all country dwellers with this brush. For the contradictory nature of the protests should not be taken as representative of rural Britain as a whole. Like all modernist pressure groups, the countryside movement trades in pessimism. In order to justify its existence, it has to present a picture of precipitous rustic decline. But just as the claims of the welfare lobby about the growth of poverty in modern Britain – usually voiced to accompany demands for yet more benefits expenditure – have proved to be baseless, so doom-laden warnings about the disappearance of the countryside have been grossly exaggerated. That is certainly my experience. I moved to a village in East Anglia about three years ago. Contrary to all the stories about rural depression, I found a flourishing rural community. With a population of around 4,000, the village has no less than six restaurants, four pubs, two teashops, a garden centre, an off-licence, two grocery stores, a garage, two butcher's shops, a greengrocer, two newsagents, a glass factory, a road haulage warehouse, a post office, two clothes shops, a bookshop, an electrical store, a pharmacy, two estate agents, a travel agency, and a string of antique shops. On Thursday mornings, the centre of the village is taken over by a traditional – and highly successful – market. On top of all this retailing, there is also a well-attended Anglican church, a newly built health centre, a fire station, a municipal library, a primary and a secondary school, and a community centre which is in almost constant use for events like adult education classes, craft fairs, and scout evenings. For me, what seems to

characterise the village above all is the spirit of enterprise. Local people do not sit back and demand that the council or the Government sort out their problems. Instead, they use their own initiative. The best example of this is the village community bus which is operated by local residents and provides an excellent, reliable service. There are other instances of this approach, such as the Summer Carnival and the Christmas Festival. No doubt other towns and villages throughout the land can boast the same spirit. And they can show the way ahead for the countryside. The road leading to yet more state intervention is a dead end. Country people should resist the temptation of government subsidies. It is merely the other side of the coin from government interference in the rural way of life. But beyond the clenched fist of grievance and the outstretched palm of subsidy, the future could yet be a rich one.

Agricultural subsidies and falling farm incomes: how one has led to the other

Richard Howarth

The Common Agricultural Policy has been attacked for its manifold failings. Cutting farmers' incomes is not usually one of these. One would have thought that this vast, highly expensive regime of agricultural subsidies would at the very least boost farmers' incomes. But Dr Richard Howarth demonstrates that the CAP has not even achieved this. In fact farming must be the only industry in which real incomes fell between 1970 and 1990; and fell by over 50 per cent.

Aggregate income falling

In the spring of 1998, British farming was in crisis. The leader of the National Farmers' Union (NFU) was calling on the Government to fund an early retirement scheme to enable his beleaguered members to make a 'dignified' exit from the industry. Dairy farming, normally one of the most profitable sectors of agriculture, was facing a predicted slump in income to as little as £2,500 for an average 120-cow herd in 1998, compared with £47,500 in 1996.[1]

The rollercoaster of national farm income had plunged by 45 per cent to the point at which aggregate *farming income*[2] was, in real terms, back to its 1989 level, which itself was less than half that of 1970. Having reached a post-war peak in 1973, the year of Britain's entry to the EEC, real farming income fluctuated downwards throughout the remainder of the 1970s, the whole of the 1980s and into the early 1990s, picked up briefly and sharply in 1993-95 – when it doubled from the 1991-92 level – only to halve again during 1997.

Relative income falling

Moreover, the relative income of British agriculture (GDP per worker in agriculture as a percentage of GDP per worker in the economy as a whole) had also fallen. In the 1950s, 1960s, and through to the mid-1970s, Britain was highly unusual in having a relative agricultural income of around 100 per cent, ie, agricultural income was equal to average income in the economy as a whole, signifying a relatively healthy agricultural sector compared to that of most other countries where the percentage had long and persistently tended to be 50 to 55 per cent.[3]

But, since 1976, British relative agricultural income has steadily fallen to around 80 per cent in the early 1980s, 70 per cent in the late 1980s, 67 per cent in 1990 and an all-time low of 55 per cent in 1997, when the two per cent of the total workforce which is engaged in agriculture contributed only 1.1 per cent of GDP. Our relative farm income has therefore now fallen to the long-term levels of that of France, Germany, Italy and the EU as a whole, having previously been double theirs.

Instability increasing

To make matters worse for farmers, instability of income has tended to increase as its overall level has fallen. Those working in other industries would find the fluctuations in farming income hard to believe. The average annual variation in UK real farming income per full-time farmer was 8.9 per cent in the 1960s, 13.4 per cent in the 1970s and 29.7 per cent in the 1980s; from 1990-97 it was 21.5 per cent, with the biggest rise being 42.4 per cent in 1993 and the biggest fall 46.1 per cent in 1997. Within individual sectors of farming the variations have been much greater.

Budgetary cost and degree of protection rising

And yet, at the same time, British public spending on agriculture, which is mostly under the CAP, but also on some remaining national grants and subsidies, has continued its inexorable rise from £392 million in 1970 to one billion pounds in 1980, £1.9 billion in 1990 and £4.3 billion in 1996; whilst the total budgetary cost of the CAP, for all EU members, has risen from three billion pounds in 1970, to seven billion in 1980, £20 billion in 1990 and currently stands at some £30 billion.

The increase in budgetary cost has, not surprisingly, been accompanied by increases in the degree of agricultural protection. From figures published by OECD and other bodies[4], it is possible to estimate the *nominal tariff equivalent* (NTE) of all agricultural support measures in the EU and other countries. For the six countries which later formed the EEC, the NTE was 16 per cent in 1956, whilst that for the UK was double that figure – 32 per cent. But by 1966, when the CAP was under way, the EEC figure had jumped to 52 per cent while that of the UK had fallen to 28 per cent. By 1986, the NTE for the EU, with Britain part of it, was 108 per cent.

In 1990 the NTE for the EU was 96 per cent; for the USA 41 per cent; for New Zealand a negligible five per cent following the virtual abolition of agricultural support after 1984; and for Japan, of the major countries the world's worst agricultural protectionist, 194 per cent. As world commodity prices rose from 1993 to 1995, NTEs fell sharply, only to rise steeply again from 1996 to 1998.

Farm subsidies have failed to achieve any of their aims

Aggregate and relative income have been falling, whilst instability, budgetary cost and the degree of protection have been increasing – all these statistics point to a major long-run failure of agricultural policy under the Agriculture Act (1947), the guiding light of British agricultural policy until accession to the EEC in 1973, and particularly under the CAP since then. Both of these policies have had as their major aims the stabilisation and the raising of farm incomes: in the words of the actual legislation – 'promoting and maintaining a stable...agricultural industry' and 'proper remuneration...for farmers' in the 1947 Act, and 'to stabilise markets' and 'to ensure a fair standard of living for the agricultural community' in the 1957 Treaty of Rome.

In both cases, the main policy instrument used to achieve those aims has been protected, guaranteed or 'supported' prices (ie, prices higher than the market would otherwise have determined) for most farm products. Such policies have been practised in France, Germany and Italy since the 1870s, and in the USA and Britain since the 1930s. Since the Second World War virtually every developed country has had an agricultural support policy and the degree of support has been steadily increased. Indeed, one of the most significant economic features of the post-war period has been the marked contrast between the growing liberalisation of world trade in industrial goods – under the auspices of GATT – and growing restrictions on agricultural trade, in the reduction of which no progress was made until the limited progress under the Uruguay Round of GATT which ended in December 1993.

'Bucking' the market

Agricultural policy thus provides one of the best and longest-running examples in economic history of pervasive, extremely costly, yet unsuccessful attempts by government to circumvent the laws of supply and demand (or 'to buck the markets' in Mrs Thatcher's phrase) in relation both to agricultural products and farmers' incomes. The apogee of such attempts is undoubtedly the CAP, which *The Economist* aptly described in 1990 as '...the single most idiotic system of economic mismanagement that the rich western countries have ever devised'.

The many iniquities of the CAP relating to the Third World, international agricultural trade, the burdens of high food prices on poorer households, environmental damage, etc, have frequently been discussed elsewhere.[5] Here we concentrate solely on the reasons for its failure in relation to its main objective of raising farmers' incomes. The arguments which follow are equally applicable to the farm policies of the USA and other developed countries. Indeed, several of the illustrative examples are drawn from outside the EU, but the UK is used as a microcosm to illustrate the general arguments.

Cost of CAP more than twice what farmers gain from it

Since 1978, when Britain became fully integrated into the CAP, the total annual cost to our consumers (in higher food prices) and taxpayers has typically been more than double the gain in *gross* income to our farmers. Why is that so? First, an increasing proportion of the budgetary expenditure of the CAP has been spent on payments to administrators, to private storage agencies, on financing stocks in store, and on export subsidies (much of the cost of which has been incurred in overcoming the depression in world prices caused by the CAP itself) – all of which have been subject to a prodigious degree of fraud.

Secondly, much of the extra expenditure on food by British consumers through higher food prices has not gone to British farmers at all but to continental farmers from whom we have come to import so much. Thirdly, as a major importer of food and of industrial goods, and as a relatively minor recipient from EU funds, Britain pays a large net budgetary contribution (currently some three billion pounds) to the EU, the majority of which is spent on supporting continental farmers, with relatively little going to British farmers.

Taking the EU as a whole, the World Bank's estimate in 1985 was that it cost £1.90 from consumers and taxpayers to transfer one pound to farmers, but an even high ratio of 2.5:1 can be derived from figures given by Harvey.[6] In other words, for every £100 of farm support paid by consumers and taxpayers, only £40 was a gross benefit to farmers. The other £60 was 'wasted' elsewhere: five pounds on administrative costs, £25 in offsetting the depression in world prices as a result of policy, and £30 in storage and processing costs (including £10 in fraudulent claims by middlemen).

Subsidies subsidise success

Some 90 per cent of all farm policy expenditure in the EU is related to production or acreage. Since it is paid per unit of output or per acre, those who produce the largest output and have the largest number of acres obviously receive the most support in absolute terms. Those who produce 2,000 tonnes of wheat or have 2,000 acres of wheat will receive ten times as much as those who produce 200 tonnes or have 200 acres. It is therefore inevitable that the bigger farmers, who tend to be the richer ones, will gain most from the total support system and the smaller ones the least.

As far back as 1957, it was estimated that something like two-thirds of all price subsidies to British farmers went to the one-third of all farms which were the largest. Concentration of production has increased greatly since then and we have now reached the stage where half the total output is produced by less than ten per cent of all holdings and 80 per cent of the output is produced by 20 per cent of all holdings.

The bulk of the £1.3 billion currently spent on arable area payments (including set-aside) to compensate for reduced cereal support prices under the CAP since 1993, is going to a relatively small number of wealthy individuals, many of whom are receiving £250,000 to £500,000 per annum from them. Yet, at the other end of the scale, the Government's Farm Business Survey shows that some Welsh hill farmers still regularly receive net incomes of only £1,000 to £8,000 per year.

Studies have also shown that the wealthiest farms receive the highest support, not only in absolute terms but also proportionately to their income, and the poorest receive the least since the products which the bigger farms produce (cereals and dairy products) are more heavily supported than the products (beef and sheep) generally produced by the smaller farms. A peculiar situation to say the least.

New technologies boost production: a bigger supply means a lower unit price

A more important reason for the general failure of agricultural policy has been that it has attempted to fly in the face of the inexorable long-run trends in agricultural markets. These may be summarised as a virtually static demand for the raw product, coupled with a technology-driven, constantly rising supply. In Adam Smith's words of 1776, 'the desire of food is limited in every man by the narrow capacity of the human stomach', and in all wealthy countries the vast majority of the population have for some time been able to afford to fill their stomachs to capacity with the result that, regardless of increases in income, overall food consumption per head now rises hardly at all. Indeed, with minimal population growth, and, as people become more health and fitness-conscious, consumption can actually fall, and for some products, such as red meat, milk and butter, fall dramatically. The only growth in expenditure on food comes at the retail level from increasingly sophisticated pre-preparation, presentation and packaging, and from the growth in consumption of take-away and restaurant meals; neither of which is of much help to the farmer.

On the supply side, mechanisation, improvements in animal and plant breeding, the huge increase in use of fertilisers, herbicides, pesticides and other agrochemicals and, latterly, biotechnology and genetic engineering, have, over the post-war period, led to a trebling of cereal yields and a quadrupling of sugarbeet yields per acre, a doubling of milk yields per cow and egg yields per bird, with still great technological scope for further increases.[7]

Consequently, the national and international growth of supply of temperate foods has tended to outstrip demand over the past 40 years by around one per cent per year, leading to a gradual depression of agricultural prices on world markets in real terms of around four per cent per year. Thus farmers have had to exchange an increasing amount of farm products, say wheat, to buy a given amount of industrial goods, say a Mini motorcar. In 1960 a Mini cost £500 and the price of a tonne of wheat was £20, so that 25 tonnes of wheat purchased a Mini. But in 1997 a Mini cost £9,000 and a tonne of wheat £80. It now takes 112.5 tonnes of wheat to buy a Mini: four and a half times as much as in 1960. And the same applies to all the industrial inputs – fuel, machinery, chemicals, buildings – which farmers use. This is illustrated in *Table 1)*

To keep pace, farmers must run on a technological treadmill which

Table 1: The farm problem

Some Comparitive Indices Affecting UK Agriculture (all in real terms) 1970–1990

	(1) Farm Product Prices	(2) Farming Income	(3) Land Value (E&W)*	(4) Rents (GB)	(5 Feed- Cos
1964/65–1966/67	109	96	120	86	10
1970	100	100	100	100	10
1971	95	103	97	98	88
1972	96	104	211	101	10
1973	122	139	256	103	14
1974	116	98	182	94	13
1975	115	98	123	86	11
1976	127	108	144	89	13
1977	116	94	170	93	12
1978	108	84	206	100	11
1979	106	69	245	107	11
1980	96	51	204	107	10
1981	95	61	184	113	99
1982	95	72	181	120	97
1983	96	52	196	128	10
1984	92	81	178	135	99
1985	86	37	166	138	91
1986	84	50	139	139	88
1987	81	48	155	137	84
1988	77	33	200	131	84
1989	78	45	184	125	83
1990	74	40	168	119	79

Sources: Annual Review of Agriculture (various)   Agriculture in the United Kingdom (various)
Annual Abstract of Statistics (various)   *The Economist Diary*, 1993

moves ever faster, and the more they produce the more they depress product prices and the more it costs in subsidies to bridge the gap between support prices and market prices. Eventually, as happened under British policy in the 1960s and under the CAP in the 1980s, the cost of support becomes politically unacceptable and support prices have to be reduced or, more likely eroded by inflation, whilst farmers' costs rise in line with general inflation. Farmers are trapped, as it were, between the two blades of a pair of scissors – falling prices and rising

(6) …ilizer …sts	(7) Fuel Costs	(8) Farm Machinery Costs	(9) Farm Labour Costs	(10) Purchasing Power of £	
…9	102	104	83	128	1964/65–1966/67
…0	100	100	100	100	1970
…0	98	99	102	91	1971
…3	99	104	112	87	1972
…5	117	110	131	83	1973
…6	131	113	144	79	1974
…0	127	118	143	56	1975
…9	135	123	146	48	1976
…3	139	132	139	42	1977
…9	127	135	144	38	1978
…0	140	135	150	34	1979
…5	159	133	155	29	1980
…4	174	128	154	26	1981
…7	187	127	155	24	1982
…5	200	128	161	23	1983
…3	197	140	163	22	1984
…5	204	146	166	21	1985
…7	154	147	165	20	1986
…4	143	146	166	19	1987
…1	129	140	164	18	1988
…3	135	147	167	17	1989
…9	141	151	176	16	1990

*England and Wales (vacant possession)

costs – hence the term the 'agrarian scissors'. Price support can act only as a temporary palliative to the wound inflicted by the agrarian scissors and, in the long term, aggravates it.

Farm subsidies merely boost land prices

The final and critical argument against agricultural support relates to its ultimate destination, mainly *not* to farmers' incomes. It has so far been shown that the cost of support is likely to go on increasing indefinitely as technology and artificially high support prices encourage production to outstrip demand and to put farmers in a permanent cost-price squeeze. The only brake on support costs is a political one. It has also been demonstrated that the support system has been extremely inefficient in transferring *gross* income to farmers with perhaps only £40 reaching them out of every £100 of cost to taxpayers and consumers. But what happens to that £40?

If we assume that government artificially increases product prices by, say, ten per cent, empirical studies from America show that, after time for adjustment, over five to ten years, farm output will also increase by around ten per cent (ie, the long-run supply elasticity of farm output is unity). Thus farmers' gross income (receipts) will rise by 21 per cent. But half of that extra revenue will be used on purchasing extra inputs to achieve the increase in output – for example, labour, machinery and, particularly, interest to service the borrowings on additional capital; 42.5 per cent of the extra revenue will be capitalised, mainly into land, and *only 4.8 per cent* will be *net* income to the farmer.[8] An econometric model developed by Professor David Harvey in 1989 suggested that British land prices under the CAP were 46 per cent higher than they would be under a free agricultural market, and that 55 per cent of the producer benefit was capitalised into land values and rents, and therefore captured by landowners. Rents were £13.80 per acre above their free-market level. Of course, many farmers own their own land and, if they have owned it for some time, have the benefit of the capital appreciation if, and only if, they sell it. But only a few can do that at any one time because if the situation ever arose that more than the present one per cent of all farmland were to come on to the market in any year, capital values would fall steeply as they did in the 1930s. In any case, high capital values are a mixed blessing because they represent a barrier to new entrants to farming, and store up the possibility of large future payments of capital gains tax and possibly inheritance tax for present and future owners.

Only one per cent of cost of farm subsidies is of benefit to farmers

The CAP and other countries' farm policies have represented a triumph of political clout over economic logic. This was even recognised by the European Commission in 1987 when it admitted that 'It does therefore seem doubtful whether farmers in fact benefit from support, the effects of which are primarily felt in other socio-economic sectors'. In the late 1980s, other international and national bodies including the IMF, the World Bank, OECD, the USDA, the National Consumer Council and the House of Lords came to similar conclusions. Yet, because of the strength of the German and French farm lobbies, hundreds of billions of pounds have continued to pour into the CAP – to so little avail. If 40 per cent of the total cost reaches farmers and only 2.5 per cent ends up as net income, then only one pound in every £100 paid by consumers and taxpayers is of net benefit to farmers. It is surely a grand irony that never in economic history has so much been given, for so long, by so many, to so few, and to such little effect.

28

The hereditary peerage: a voice for continuity in and for rural England

Ian Crowe

Modern Britain views the countryside as old-fashioned, and the hereditary peerage as one of the most old-fashioned things about it. But the hereditary peerage offers a voice for the countryside. It is a voice of historical continuity standing against rash change. Dr Ian Crowe shows that this was at the core of Edmund Burke's support for property, inheritance, and aristocracy. Burke's writings on this are as relevant today as they have ever been – and politicians of all parties have lost touch with the principles of ordered liberty to a greater extent than ever before. When the hereditary peers are expelled from the House of Lords, the countryside will have lost a powerful voice.

'Some decent regulated pre-eminence, some preference...given to birth, is neither unnatural, nor unjust, nor impolitic'
Edmund Burke, *Reflections on the Revolution in France*

The countryside is no longer a way of life, but an escape from *the* way of life. Ninety per cent of the population, the city-dwellers, view it – or feel they are entitled to view it – as temporary relief from the two chief pressures of the city: the press of numbers, competing for limited space and resources, and of time – that endless succession of irrecoverable and unforgiving deadlines. When they visit the countryside, they take with them the attitudes moulded by these pressures, a sense of the antagonistic roots of social relations: productive and unproductive classes; new politics and the old; the liberated and the blinkered; the Establishment and the people; the people and the peers; the unspeakable and the uneatable. These are antagonisms justly resolved only by a 'majority' seizing the high ground and condemning the minority to the Heritage industry. Under this iron law of the new politics, the ways of the countryside are no longer a way of life, but just a *Heritage*.

It would require then, an extraordinarily brave statesman to seek in the countryside sources of political wisdom. If we look at the constitutional 'debate' on the House of Lords, we recognise that this is not the Age of Statesmanship: here, where the blending of interests through compromise – the *art* of politics – should be the starting point for discussion, we meet only the dreary *science* of psephology and Newspeak, and the key issues are bypassed on the nod for the sake of numbers, or majority rights, and the deadline of the new millennium. How *might* the countryside retain a relevance in political thinking today?

Burke and the organic nature of class

When he purchased his 600-acre Buckinghamshire estate in 1768, Edmund Burke, an aspiring statesman, professed to a friend his intent 'to become a farmer in good earnest'. A sizeable portion of the money used to buy 'Gregories' in Beaconsfield came from farming of a different sort – that is, in the dealings of the East India Company – and Burke was already committed to the professions of the city: first, the law, then Grub Street and, finally, Parliament. By 1768, it could be argued, his political philosophy was broadly set, but his life as a farmer infuses and enriches that philosophy in a way that could be instructive to us today. Ironically, but perhaps not surprisingly, the best example of this, his *Thoughts and Details on Scarcity* (1795), is either dismissed by commentators as un-Burkeian in spirit – and springing from too specific a set of circumstances to offer general lessons – or treated as an early example of the free-market, capitalist mentality that was to subvert the agricultural way of life in the following century.

The central theme of *Thoughts and Details on Scarcity* is that there exists, by a divine plan and a natural, human instinct, a common social orientation, which guides the diverse sections of human society into a process of compromise and harmonisation. In contrast to the divisive 'rights of man' philosophy spreading at the time (and the root of our modern politics of competing classes – clusters of target groups and single-issue interests jostling for their moment), Burke presents a society comprising classes that are distinct from each other in degree, but not in purpose, where the rich 'are trustees for those who labour, and their hoards are the banking houses of the latter'. It is a convergence of interest that he describes emerging through the natural artifices of the agrarian market, where individuals commit themselves to a complex, instinctive web of exchange. He did, indeed, trace here in the countryside, an invisible hand, but not that 'invisible hand' beloved by the amoral city slickers and economic theorists of the 1980s. Burke stresses time and again (as, indeed, did Adam Smith) that this process is never to be divorced from a larger framework of moral sentiment and divine law: '[The] benign and wise Disposer of all things...*obliges* men, whether they will or not, in pursuing their own selfish interests, to connect the general good with their own individual success.'

Compromise between classes at core of Burke's vision of the countryside

Burke believed that an empirical recognition of the underlying harmony of society is the very source of a universal political wisdom: his whole political experience, from Ireland to India and the Paris of the Jacobins, taught him that this wisdom rests on fundamental, unchanging principles of man's social (not some theoretical, Rousseauvian pre-social) nature. These principles are not the inventions of some urban Frankenstein, but they are to be sought and discerned in the diverse landscapes of tradition and customary behaviour; the Jacobin threat brought from Burke their clearest articulation, as liberty, property and trusteeship. Applying these unchanging principles to changing circumstances requires the supreme quality of statesmanship – prudence, which always takes the longer perspective and is not harried into decisions by numbers or deadlines. Burke's countryside was a grand expression of the naturalness of a society without silent majorities waiting for their time to come, and it is inexplicable in the antagonistic terms of the modern politician. (Perhaps this is why the fox hunt is incomprehensible to city people: as a sport, its aesthetic coherence is bound into a longer-term context than the laps of a racing track and its end has no reference in numbers or competing sides.)

By 'liberty', Burke understood the opportunity for private individuals to pursue their own needs through bargaining with each other and thereby discovering their higher mutuality of interest. At first, such freely contracting parties might have conflicting interests in mind, 'but then the contract is of the nature of a compromise; and compromise is founded on circumstances that suppose it the interest of the parties to be reconciled in some medium'. Here is the market as a practical, moral schooling in the relations woven by God: it is liberty to discover our independence on other people. Government has no authority to impede this reconciliation with any visible hand, however benign. Political wisdom and prudence – attending to the longer-term, even in times of dearth – dictate for government the role of enforcer, not creator, of contracts: 'When government appears at market all the laws of market are subverted.'

Property essential for smooth functioning of society and for maintenance of liberty

We are interested in this market, and so drawn to liberty, by private possessions – the property (including our labour) that it is our right to exploit in sale, investment or risk. Burke had emphasised the vital role of private property in social welfare when writing in Ireland in his earliest years as a politician: 'Those civil constitutions which promote industry [the first great instrument of national happiness and strength] are such as facilitate the acquisition, secure the holding, enable the fixing, and suffer the alienation, of property.' Now, in his *Thoughts and Details on Scarcity*, his comments on property, though they might seem outrageous statements of an archaic, aristocratic system, are the extension of that early position: the efficacy and justice of the principle of property lies simply in the possession, not in the 'equality' of its distribution. Indeed, the very inequality in property-holding is useful in creating a body (the great country landowners) powerful enough to defend it against invasion by government or by mobs – in its own interests, of course, but vicariously in the interests of everyone. So, Burke warns, 'When the poor rise against the rich, they act as wisely for their own purposes, as when they burn mills and throw corn into the river, to make cheap bread.'

Inheritance binds families together and discourages rash change

This principle of property applies universally, but may be seen functioning most clearly in the countryside. That is even more so with the third fundamental principle: the right and duties of trusteeship, by which property is secured. It is here where we apprehend the timeless significance of an hereditary interest. Again, the positive effects of acting in trust are not dependent upon the size of that trust, though great accumulations will provide its strongest defence. Families with the smallest inheritance will nevertheless be bound closer to each other (and less closely to the government) the more they feel their obligation to the past and to the future: 'The power of perpetuating our property in our families is one of the most valuable and interesting circumstances belonging to it, and that which tends the most to the perpetuation of society itself.' In every degree, trusteeship tempers our wilful impulses and the antagonisms of the hour pale before the needs of our children: on the wider stage, it raises the process of decision-making above the pressure of numbers and timetables. It also reminds us, in the unequal hand it deals, that the politics of arithmetic, with its concomitant antagonisms, is a moral fault in ourselves – work of 'the old evil counsellor envy' – and not a correction to the injustice of some primeval Establishment.

Two points should be noted about Burke's understanding of these fundamental principles. First, they are meditated in circumstances but are not dependent upon circumstances: when the landscape of political and social life changes, we are not wise to jettison them in favour of 'new' insights, but we should take care to bring them with us, to hold those changes in some sort of check, and to apply prudence in their application to new circumstances. It might not be hard to achieve this continuity in liberty and property in the transition from countryside to city; but, the principle of hereditary right is easier to lose. That it is most closely associated with an 'anachronistic' and 'undemocratic' pattern of tenure in the countryside increases the danger. For – the second point to note – these fundamental principles stand or fall as one. Some sort of liberty might survive without private property: the possessive instinct will not die with the hereditary instinct. But prudence and political wisdom will die without any one of them.

And House of Lords is broader national expression of the same principle

Here we come to the real importance of the constitutional reform of the House of Lords. Our constitution, Burke believed, must enshrine all three fundamental principles of political wisdom, not the transient circumstances of social fads and lifestyles: this is not undemocratic, but more deeply democratic, attending to the interests of the people, and not just to their wills. The hereditary interest in Parliament is not about numbers and economic influence, that is its whole point: it is about the preservation of a balance of political principles, essential for prudent government. For example, the greater disinterest which inheritance engenders, beyond the pull of electoral favours, and which the Lords has frequently displayed, moderates the partisan energy of the Commons, even if only as a brake. As Jim McCue has written: 'One test of a good constitution is that it be self-limiting, perhaps even self-thwarting.' The superficial form of trusteeship – the great estates of the countryside – is relevant to us in differing degrees, but trusteeship itself is essential, and its disappearance would be an incalculable loss to us all.

Burke's defence of aristocracy, then, rested not on its direct power, nor as a form of superior leadership ('I am no friend to aristocracy, in the sense at least in which that word is generally understood'), but on the need for an essential representation of the principles of private property and trusteeship. The personal attributes and deficiencies thrown up by heredity enrich this representation without hampering its execution. Indeed, Burke felt the 'sluggish, inert and timid' representatives of property needed special protection against the invasions of 'vigorous and active' ability: he was quick to appreciate the danger of creating an institution that based its authority on prevailing circumstances and majorities, and that, in the name of a liberty removed from property and trusteeship, took to itself a position pre-eminent and unrestrained in the constitutional process. He was, as he admitted, 'to well read in men not to know how often the desire and design of a tyrannic domination lurks in the claim of an extravagant liberty'.

Moves to scrap hereditary peers a continuation of Jacobin assault on ordered liberty

This threat presented itself to Burke as 'Jacobinism'. Jacobinism assaulted private property and heredity in the name of a new liberty bound to 'equality' and 'fraternity' – neither fundamental principles, not even genuine ones in the Jacobin plan, but a rallying cry, potent through envy and designed to undermine the prudence and wisdom that might restrain their ambitions. In this century, the same dangerous process has proceeded in fits and starts. In particular, the economic decline of the countryside has been used as the lever for finally obliterating the hereditary interest altogether.

In the debate over parliamentary reform in 1910-11, Balfour made a valiant effort to show that, 'it is folly for us as practical men simply to lay down the proposition that we have nothing to do with the hereditary principle'. By this he meant that the survival of a vital, if inconvenient, political principle should not be bound to outward forms of power; but he was doomed to failure at a time when the radicals had already established the politics of antagonism – 'Peers versus People', for example, after Lloyd George's scheme to increase the power of government under the name of the 'People's Budget'. (How depressingly familiar it all sounds!) Asquith revealed the intellectual shallowness of this enterprise by his justification of the assault on the Lords: 'What is the essence of democratic government? Surely it is…that the will of the people, by which we mean the will of the majority of the people for the time being, shall, both in legislation and policy, prevail.' Such a lack of political principle, masquerading as the highest of political principles, might just have brought a wry smile even to Burke's lips.

Hereditary peers more needed than ever as a voice for and of the countryside

But the situation is now well beyond a joke. Some adjustment in the mechanism by which the hereditary contributes to government might be appropriate: the destruction of that interest, as represented through our country estates, without its replacement by some body that may serve the principle of trusteeship in equal degree, is political madness. Far from recognising this situation – or perhaps because they do – the people's representatives are already pushing on beyond the hereditary peers, obliterating this salutary principle in any way they can: sneering at the rituals which reinforce their own power as a trust; trivialising our historical inheritance with their insatiable fetish for the 'new' (or 'the Future', for the New Conservatives); conspiring with the presumption that the royal succession is subject to opinion-poll findings. For powerful men in a rush, it is clear why the hereditary principle needs removing: at root, their assault is about nothing more elevated than numbers and deadlines. In 1770, Burke warned his countrymen: 'Any new powers exercised in the House of Lords, or in the House of Commons, or by the crown ought certainly to excite the vigilant and anxious jealousy of a free people.' The way of life of the countryside may be marginalised socially and economically, but its politics remains central to our country. In particular, amid prevailing trends and in the absence of any alternative, we need more than ever our hereditary peerage, with all its unearned estates, to perform its vital function in a healthy constitution.

29

'Not people like us': what modern Britons have against country people

Frank Furedi

Modern Britons have lost their old ideological certainties. What has taken their place? Dr Frank Furedi argues that the literature and art of modern Britons shows a misanthropic distrust of human potential. Everything human and man-made is seen as tainted, everything 'natural' as pure. When this sordid imagination is transposed onto decent, honest people pursuing their livelihoods in the countryside, the result is a travesty. So the farmer becomes the poisoner of food in much the same fictitious way as fourteenth-century illiterates believed that Jews were poisoning their wells. The fox hunter becomes a cruel sadist. If fox hunters could only write self-obsessed, self-hating, malodorous fiction about their pleasures modern Britons would perhaps have more time for them.

Farmers have become hate figures for modern Britons
The countryside has become a theme-park where Cool Britannia can work out its urban anxieties. Television images of irresponsible farmers secretly burying poisoned animal carcasses near rivers serve as potent symbols of anti-social behaviour. Callous hunters are now presented as the personification of moral depravity. Time and again the British public is informed that 'these people kill animals for pleasure!' A special issue of *The Sunday Times Magazine* in 1998, titled 'Who is Killing the Countryside?' pointed to the 'killing fields' of Cambridgeshire, where intensive farming methods 'are slowly stripping the landscapes of natural features and wildlife habitat'.[1]

Indeed the entire countryside now bears the stigma of evil. According to conventional wisdom, farmers have become parasites on the poor tax-paying public. Moreover, farmers are said to be using irresponsible methods which threaten to damage the food chain, with unknown consequences. A recent report by the National Consumer Council warned that intensive farming methods could lead to 'life-threatening illnesses', and noted that the 'risk to consumers is incalculable'.

The farmyard is increasingly depicted as a kind of rural concentration camp, where animals kept against their will are systematically subjected to the most barbaric practices. Farmers are not only indifferent to the fate of their animals, it seems they are also unconcerned about the devastating impact that their polluted food could have on the consumer. It appears that BSE is only the tip of the iceberg, as a variety of new infectious diseases creep out of the countryside to make our lives a misery. The clear message is that British food cannot be trusted – and nor can the farming communities that produce it.

Media image of the countryside in stark contrast to previous idealised images

Contemporary media images of the countryside stand in sharp contrast to the past representation of rural Britain as a site of pastoral harmony. Idyllic pictures like those produced by Constable in the nineteenth century helped nourish the nostalgia of generations of urban Britons. Not so long ago, the moral order of peaceful 'merrie England' was favourably contrasted with the decadent chaos of urban Britain. Urban myths about the countryside persist to this day. Indeed, if anything the worship of nature is probably more intense today than at any time this century. So it is something of a paradox to find that, precisely at a time when conserving the environment has become such a national cause, the countryside has acquired such a negative image. Or maybe there is a connection between the ascendancy of environmental consciousness and the deprecation of rural culture?

Today's 'idealised' countryside would not include people, as they are 'unnatural'

There can be little doubt that rural myths continue to excite the imagination of the British public. But it is a vision that is strikingly different from that evoked by Constable and his contemporaries. Today's environmental consciousness demands 'real nature'. Not, you understand, the real natural world where there is conflict and tension as well as harmony. Instead what is demanded today is a nature that is 'untouched' and 'unspoilt'. Environmental consciousness is now driven by the belief that nature must be saved or at least protected from human beings. So today's ideal countryside is one where there are fields and trees and hills, but no people. From this standpoint, rural people and their culture represent a negation of everything that is wholesome and pure about nature. That is why the application of 'unnatural' agricultural technology, especially biotechnology, is increasingly perceived as an act of sacrilege.

The debate about the countryside is often wrongly perceived as a simple clash between urban and rural values. However, there are more fundamental questions at stake, about the very meaning of right and wrong. When the relationship between people and nature is discussed today, it is always humanity that bears the mark of moral inferiority. The growing obsession with the environment expresses an indictment of the human condition. Romantics have always been critical of humanity's attempt to fashion the world in its own image. But whereas in the past the romantic world view contained a relatively benign view of people, today it is deeply suspicious of human motives. Faith in human nature now often gives way to the conviction that it threatens the integrity of 'real' nature. This shift in emphasis is clearly illustrated by the changing approach of the Royal Society for the Prevention of Cruelty to Animals.

Changes in RSPCA's values reflect wider denigration of human potential

Back in the nineteenth century, the RSPCA was set up to improve people's lives through the prevention of cruelty to animals. At the time it was widely believed that such cruelty diminished humanity. Cruelty to animals was rightly condemned because it degraded the human soul. In the uncertain 1990s, however, the philosophy of the RSPCA reflects a very different agenda. Recent RSPCA statements seem to promote a view of the world where animals are at least morally equivalent to human beings. Indeed the RSPCA's *Declaration of Animal Rights* appears to place a greater emphasis on the fate of animals than on people. Through eroding the line that separates the human species from animals, the RSPCA has redefined its traditional objective. Its goal is now not so much to improve the lives of people, as to prevent human predators from subjecting animals to their cruelty. The human species no longer has a special role to play in a viewpoint that regards a man and a gerbil as moral equivalents.

The RSPCA's abandonment of a human-centred conception of the world clearly expresses the temper of our times. Human action is invariably seen as problematic, and it therefore follows that the only moral course of action is to restrain people from inflicting more damage on nature. That is why discussions about farming are no longer restricted to economic or agronomic matters. Farming practices are increasingly evaluated from the standpoint of morality – although this morality is often expressed in the language of environmental consciousness. In this moral universe, good is on the side of the organic farmer. And those who interfere with nature, stand condemned for their evil ways.

Fear of GM foods shows how scared society has become of everything man-made

The preoccupation with the danger of interfering with nature assumes a pathological character when it comes to genetically-modified food. Even relatively intelligent observers believe that this technology represents a major danger to people and to nature. Fact-based arguments which point to the benign uses of genetically-modified food are invariably countered with the observation that 'nobody knows' what the ultimate result of using this technology might be. In a world where an outbreak of food poisoning tends be routinely interpreted as a prelude to a massive epidemic, anxieties about biotechnology are inevitable.

Anxieties, obsessions and panics cannot be countered by logic or other intellectual instruments. We fear the food we eat and the water we drink because we find it more difficult to trust each other. Fourteenth-century myths about malevolent people who, under the cover of darkness, poisoned village wells are today recycled in an inflated form. Today, it is not just the odd miscreant but the producers of our food who represent a threat to our lives. The fact that people have access to cheaper and more nourishing food than ever before is neither here or there. A society that is scared of its own creation, has no simple answer to the question 'how do you know what the consequences of that genetically-modified tomato will be for the children of your children?'

For modern Britons to be environmentalist or vegetarian means to be 'virtuous'

A loss of confidence in a human-centred moral order has led to a situation where, for many people, virtue is most likely to be found in the non-human. In a world where the person is increasingly characterised as a polluter, those who wish to appear virtuous often do so through a sad and dreary celebration of the environment. Many teachers, who find it difficult to inspire their students with a human-focused vision of what is right and what is wrong, opt for moral tales about protecting endangered species from people. Such pessimism about the human condition has led to a situation in Britain, where vegetarianism is increasingly endowed with moral virtues, while meat-eating is represented as the bad habit of morally inferior people.

In this climate, it is not surprising to find that more than 50 per cent of Britons are cutting their consumption of meat, while the market for vegetarian food is one the fastest growing sectors of the food industry. Sales of vegetarian burgers have increased by 139 per cent in the past five years. A simplistic morality, which claims that a virtuous life can be defined by what you don't eat is likely to attract more adherents in the period ahead.

Yet incest and abuse animate its art

The characteristic feature of the culture of Cool Britannia is its misanthropy. Mutilated bodies inspire its artists. Sculptors steal body parts and television producers celebrate 'Vile Bodies'. The theme of incest and abuse animate its writers and film makers. Unable to accept the ambiguities of human passion, Cool Britannia has become deeply suspicious of human nature itself. And the more that it seeks to deny the creative side of the human spirit the more it will be drawn to the fantasy of real nature.

Country people cannot adopt the myth of 'pure nature' versus 'human despoliation' – and are hence despised

The myth of real nature is less likely to inspire those whose lives are directly linked to the land. Food cannot be produced without interfering with the environment. By their very existence, people who live and work in the countryside are continually changing their environment. In this situation it is difficult for people to regard vermin and insects as their moral equals. Their culture and way of life must of necessity reflect a human-centred moral order. In contrast, advocates of Cool

Britannia, believe that the 'privileging' of human creativity is both arrogant and old-fashioned. That is why there is no place in Cool Britannia for the people and the culture of the countryside.

In the clash of values between Cool Britannia and Old Britain, the fox hunters are the easy targets. There has always been a legacy of populist resentment against the way of life of the rural gentry. But the real issues at stake cannot be reduced to fox hunting. Cool Britannia, which strives for a risk-free world, cannot comprehend the arrogance of those who believe humanity has the right to refashion the countryside in its own image. They must be evil or at the very least misguided people. As with all simplistic world views, Cool Britannia cannot resist the temptation to dictate to others about how they should live their lives. That is why advocates of Cool Britannia positively light up as the words 'Zero Tolerance' trip off their tongues.

A sad and anxious moral order by definition runs on zero tolerance. The stigmatization of the culture of the countryside represents not so much the affirmation of urban values but a desperate attempt by Cool Britannia to further rein in the scope for human action. The target is not just the fox hunter. Anyone who interferes with 'real' nature risks the opprobrium of a culture that finds it difficult to trust people. At the very least, such people must be made to understand that they are seriously in need of counselling.

30

Modern Britain's homogeneity versus the multicultural countryside

Aidan Rankin

Modernisers speak much of their commitment to 'multiculturalism' and diversity. But what they mean by this is extremely limited. It is approval of 'alternative lifestyle choices' and support for other cultures – however reactionary – so long as the culture is far away and can claim to be 'indigenous'. But the culture of modern Britain is in fact extremely homogeneous – the same mores, *the same bars, the same dinner parties. Dr Aidan Rankin argues that where diversity and 'multiculturalism' are really found is in the countryside. The way of life and concerns of a Welsh hill farmer are vastly different from those of a Norfolk publican. Yet modernisers lump them together – and then feel that country people are somehow backward. It is the modernisers who cannot abide values other than their own. Hence they seek to impose their own values upon others. It is ironic that it is 'progressive' opinion which cannot tolerate the lifestyles of others; 'old reactionaries' in the countryside do not seek to impose their values upon modern Britain.*

It is a well-known fact that the peoples of Germany never live in cities, and will not even have their houses set close together. They live apart, dotted here and there, where spring, plain, or grove has taken their fancy. Their villages are not laid out in Roman style, with buildings adjacent or interlocked. Every man leaves an open space round his house, perhaps as a precaution against the risk of fire, perhaps because they are such inexpert builders.

Tacitus, *Germania*, c.98 AD[1]

Sentimentalising of 'people of the soil' a far from modern phenomenon

This account of the rustic German tribes was not the kind of study that would appeal to a modern ethnologist. Many of the Roman historian's 'well-known facts' are untried suppositions, for his purpose was, in today's terms, journalistic. Tacitus did not intend to portray Middle Europe's primitives as they were, but as he would like them to be: a critical mirror held up to a decadent urban world, reflecting lost virtue. Theirs, to borrow a phrase from Burke, was a 'manly, moral, regulated liberty', a frugal warrior culture, based on respect for nature and the gods, where 'no one finds vice amusing, or calls it "up-to-date" to debauch or be debauched'.[2]

Such commentaries have obvious resonance to our society, as they have had in other periods of intense cultural change. Montesquieu used his *Lettres Persanes* to inveigh against the sophisticated strictures of enlightened France, whilst Rousseau invoked the rural cantons of Switzerland as repositories of republican purity. Today, the global village and the science of 'comparative politics' have between them put paid to this genre.

Progressive activists revere 'indigenous peoples', but would otherwise hate their values

To an extent, it survives in those parts of the ecological movement that revere the 'ancient wisdom' of tribal peoples, to the chagrin of those of us who work for the preservation of indigenous societies, · warts and all, for the sake of human diversity. Indigenous peoples, in turn, have mastered the art of green rhetoric. Their statements, politically incorrect on European lips, express the relationship between landscape and culture. One of the best examples of this form of eco-nationalism is the declaration by the Sioux, Navajo and Iroquois peoples in 1978, before most white liberals had even heard the phrase 'sustainable development':

> Our roots are deep in the lands where we live. We have a great love for our country, for our birthplace is here. The soil is rich from the bones of thousands of our generations. Each of us was created in these lands and it is our duty to take care of them, because from these lands will spring the future generations of our peoples. We will walk about with great respect for the Earth, for it is a very Sacred Place.

In a suburbanised Britain, few environmentalists bother to look to faraway societies of which they know little. Were they to do so, they might find that some of their other comfortable assumptions are challenged. When I was working for Survival International, I was assured by members of Bangladesh's Buddhist minority that they had fared better under colonial rule than 'independence'. Such ideological inconveniences are best left alone, and so our own countryside and its inhabitants become the focus of politicised sentimentalism.

Countryside has become focus for townies' *angst*

Country people, understandably, are starting to feel marginal to political debate. Yet there is a sense in which the countryside has moved centre-stage, as a focus of public concern, collective guilt, exasperation and an inchoate sense of something lost. Attitudes towards the countryside are marked by cultural confusion. At one level, it is seen as a sacred wilderness, to be preserved from development at all costs and to which all must have 'access'. At another, it is a semi-feudal backwater where uncivilised attitudes prevail. Far more interesting than formal politics (the bland leading the bland) has been the phenomenon of the 'eco-warriors', those dishevelled refuseniks who challenge the dominant ideologies of economic growth, with its attendant bypasses and supermarkets. When they lie down in front of bulldozers, their allies are more likely to be county ladies in tweed than the orthodox left. Newbury and Manchester Airport appear to be the only protests in recent times free from the drearily ubiquitous Socialist Worker banners. The same eco-warriors, to a man or woman almost, oppose country sports with an unquestioning zeal. Why?

Activists are latter-day puritans

There are, I believe, two answers. The first is the lingering spirit of puritanism that has dogged all reform movements in this country for the past 300 years. Eco-warriors interested in history identify themselves correctly with the Diggers, or True Levellers, of the English Civil War, who despised the 'Norman Yoke' and sought a return to simple Anglo-Saxon communalism. Yet the anti-hunt campaign extends well beyond radical greens to embrace the whole of 'progressive' opinion. One of my favourite quotations about hunting with dogs comes from Martin Linton, the otherwise intelligent and thoughtful Labour MP for Battersea. He opposes it, he says, because of his 'concern for the effects of hunting on the hunter'. Here, he has unwittingly grasped the nub of the issue: that the campaign is not really about animal welfare, but a 'civilising' mission to improve the backward country folk. There is a strand of continuity between the puritan officials who once banned 'heathen' dances round the Maypole, and the anti-hunt campaigners of today.

And sentimentalise nature

Secondly, there is in the green sensibility a wish to sentimentalise, rather than identify with, nature (and 'natural man'). Just as many Romans wanted to believe in Tacitus's primitive *Volksgemeinschaft*, so today's rebels against urban materialism want to think of the countryside as a rural idyll, a theme park peopled by placid yokels, where nothing is killed except behind firmly closed doors. This idealised view of the countryside probably offends country people more than anything else about 'progressive' townies who interfere in their lives. It is part of a pattern of cultural sentimentalism which includes the view that pagan Europe was inhabited by benign vegetarian moon-worshippers, and the refusal to believe that some tribal peoples practise slavery and blood sacrifice, or (worse still) might want access to the Internet. Confronted with reality, unstructured sentimentalism turns quickly into resentment and hate.

Contrary to perception countryside is multicultural, cities homogenising

Like indigenous peoples, country folk are simultaneously revered as 'people of the soil' and forced to conform to other people's ideas of 'progress'. They are placed in the centre of a cultural struggle between those who wish to turn their land into a vast heritage centre, and those who see it as real estate on which to build three-bedroomed homes for single executives. A clue to the dominant attitude is the way we speak of 'the countryside' as if it were a single entity. In a society obsessed to the point of mania with 'multiculturalism', there is an extraordinary refusal to recognise the cultural and ecological diversity of our rural regions. Reading the urban press, one might easily believe that Suffolk's Constable Country and the Yorkshire Dales were as one, that the Highlands and Brecon Beacons had identical interests. Cities are mixed, so the urban myth runs, whilst the countryside is homogeneous. There is in this view more than a hint of racism-in-reverse. In a recent conversation, a youth worker transferred from one of the northern cities to my part of Yorkshire told me that she hated the area because it was 'not ethnically mixed enough'. I told her that it was peopled by a mixture of Norse, Saxon and Celt, and that these ethnic differences were still reflected in speech patterns, place names and facial types. She then looked at me with a worried frown, as if I had proclaimed myself a supporter of, say, Colonel Qaddafi, and went on to complain about the weather.

Ethnic diversity, of course, is an enriching experience for all concerned. But the variety of dialects, customs, folk beliefs and histories that make up rural Britain should surely be the basis of our 'multiculturalism', not the cities and suburbs with their innate tendency towards the uniform. Members of ethnic minorities in country towns have told me that it is easier for them to preserve their cultures than it is for their urban counterparts. They are treated as individuals, they say, not made to wear a politically-correct label. Sometimes, they take part in field sports too, and face racist taunts from the hunt saboteurs.

Greens value biodiversity, but not human diversity

The multiculturalism of our countryside is one of the best arguments against the developers. Eco-warriors fight tooth and nail to preserve unusual plants and rare birds, but raise not a finger against the onrush of Estuary English, wiping out local idiosyncrasies of speech. They value biodiversity, but seem to care little for human diversity and regard attempts to connect the two as politically suspect. At a political level, this has cost Britain's Green Party dear. Once, it attracted ecologists of a conservative disposition and had the beginnings of a national base. Now, it is little more than an adjunct of the liberal-left, campaigns vociferously against country pursuits and polls highest in Islington North.

The Countryside Rally celebrated diversity; Gay Pride eulogised uniformity

In March, 1998, the Countryside Rally was hailed as a triumph for the new rural consciousness. One of the reasons for this was that it mustered the same numbers as the Gay Pride parade of the previous year. That the two events should be compared at all is interesting, for they represent polar opposites in our political culture. This is not to say, as Fidel Castro once did, that 'in the countryside, there are no homosexuals'. Gay Pride, however, epitomises urban liberalism's globalizing, homogenising spirit. In *bien-pensant* circles, one is expected to applaud at news of gay demonstrations in Asuncion and Ulan Bator, to rejoice on hearing of a Yakut shaman proclaiming himself 'out, loud and proud'. To the new missionaries of political correctness, these are among the most exhilarating examples of human progress. The Rally, by contrast, presented an opposing view of politics and culture. It was not an abstract, rights-based protest, but a patchwork of local demands and grievances, with field sports acting as a form of social cement. The marchers came from all regions of the country and across the spectrum of politics, yet theirs was a conservative message. They challenged, implicitly, the liberal assumption that history is a straight line, moving inexorably forwards and replacing local custom with universal principle. They reminded the compulsive modernisers of all parties that tradition can be as important as progress, if not even more so.

Politicians of all parties speak of the UK, and mean London

Baroness Buscombe, the Conservative Vice-Chairman with responsibility for women, wrote in 1998, 'If we want to win the next General Election we have to start resembling the country we live in'.[3] Reading this in the historic market town where I live, close to the Yorkshire-Lancashire border, I could not agree with her more. I look out at the early April snow shower and think of hill farmers, one of our most aggrieved and 'under-represented' minorities. I think of their wives, too, economists in the true sense, and the practical wisdom they might bring to Parliament. As I read on, I find that Baroness Buscombe is talking about women executives with shoulder pads, mobile phones and paid child-minders at home. The Tories, once the countryman's party, are now as urban and managerial as every one of the rest. Only electoral reform might allow an agrarian party to emerge.

Eco-warriors should naturally be allied with conservatives, not the progressive left

With this cheerful thought, I return to the eco-warriors. Their enthusiasm for saving the planet, and their corresponding interests in paganism, craftsmanship and non-materialistic living should be seen as a variant form of traditionalism. Falsely allied to the 'progressive' left, the protesters against roads belong more with the countryside marchers than with hunting's New Labour opponents. If conservative politics are to have a future, then the eco-warriors will need to be won over. Perhaps the Tories should try to persuade Swampy to be their leader.

31

Postscript: the myth of *The Archers* versus the truth about country folk

Anthony Rosen

For many townies their image of rural life, and especially farming life, comes from the radio soap The Archers. *At one point this offered a sympathetic and fairly accurate, if necessarily cursory, snapshot of the concerns and tribulations of the farmer. However since the late 1980s, argues Anthony Rosen, the programme has been seduced by fashionable townie prejudices. Its portrait of rural life has become unrecognisable to country folk.*

The four million listeners to the BBC's long running radio soap *The Archers* mistakenly believe the myth that this is truly, as the original sub-title suggests, 'an everyday story of country-folk'. The reality is that the three and three-quarter hours (including repeats) of weekly repartee of what purports to be a genuine reflection of what is happening in Britain's countryside is a parody.

The Archers from the 1950s to the 1980s – education for farmers and about farming

Soon after the Second World War ended an outstanding BBC radio producer, Godfrey Baseley, suggested to the Minister of Agriculture that if Britain, still burdened with food-rationing, were to feed its growing population then farmers needed to be encouraged to adopt modern farming methods. The famed pro-farmer Minister, Tom Williams, who instigated the farmer-friendly Agricultural Act of 1947, agreed with alacrity. It was this Minister's support for agriculture which encouraged farmers, until 1997, to vote Conservative but pray for a

Labour government.

Godfrey Baseley's idea was that a fifteen-minute daily radio programme could use radio drama to put across to farmers the necessity of increasing food production. The programme set out to be a true reflection of the social and economic life of the countryside.

Thus, in 1950, *The Archers* was born: at first it was indeed 'an everyday story of country-folk'. And for many years *The Archers* succeeded in its aim of encouraging the production of food, even at any price. The editor, the producers and the writers were all well-versed in the ways of rural life and for decades the series closely mirrored rural reality.

The Archers goes politically correct
In the late 1980s, *The Archers* changed. The politics and personalities behind the changes are not our concern, though the changes became more severe after the departure of long-standing and highly competent agricultural story editor, Anthony Parkin.

The programme began to remove itself from the realities of country life. Themes more associated with *Eastenders* or *Coronation Street* emerged. Extreme feminism, racism and homosexuality became 'issues' on *The Archers*. A heavy emphasis on non-sustainable 'organic' farming emerged. In other words *The Archers* lost its connection with rural life and became a reflection of how many urban people would like to see the British countryside evolve.

The males in the programme became ciphers, either stupid or wicked, or both. The females took over, becoming dominant, expecting their partners to acquiesce to the overt superiority of their betters.

Similarly racism and homosexuality were dragged into the plots, standing out as anachronistically as would a debate on sugar beet or milk quotas in the Rovers Return in *Coronation Street*.

No longer a recognisable sketch of rural life
In spite of the four farms in the series (Brookfield, Bridge, Grange and Home) being based on real life properties there is little in the programme which would be recognised by country-dwellers as bearing any resemblance to people who live and work in the country today.

The depiction of the landlord is reminiscent of Dickens with one fleeing the country after beating-up his girlfriend, the daughter of the yeoman farmer, Philip Archer. Another, the evil Brian Aldridge, is hell-bent on making an obscene profit from selling land for housing development at the same time carrying on with anything in a skirt. The two horse riding establishments and the pony club are run by non-hunting operators, which must be unique in rural Britain.

The tenants are the scrofulous Grundys who used to lie and cheat all and sundry until the controllers decided that the Grundys should recognise the error of their depraved ways and they are now depicted as being the true yeomen of England.

'The only good farmers are organic farmers'
In Britain, notwithstanding its Royal example, so-called 'organic' farming is responsible for less than 0.06 per cent of agriculture's annual output and therefore of little consequence. Put in financial terms this results in some £12 million worth of 'organic' products being produced compared with a total UK agricultural output in excess of £14 billion.

In spite of the virtual irrelevance of 'organic' farming to the future of British agriculture, the lopsided emphasis in the programme is on the wonders of 'organic' food and those who produce it. For those who have experienced the reality and vicissitudes of present-day farming, *The Archers* makes a mockery of all that they hold dear.

The Countryside March versus the Gay Pride March
Although the Gay Pride March figured little in farmers' – indeed many town people's – thoughts it received massive publicity in *The Archers*. In significant contrast the highly successful Countryside March of nearly 300,000 country-dwellers, plus a couple of politicians, to Hyde Park was treated only in passing in *The Archers*.

The only *Archers'* coverage of this massive overt support for the rural way of life by a wide range of concerned people consisted, almost insultingly, of minimalist interviews with two of the programme's most unlikely ruralists, Linda Snell and Mrs Antrobus. The fact that in real-life rural Britain the March had been a major point of discussion in every country pub and almost every farm for many months was certainly not reflected in *The Archers*, nor in any conversations in their fictitious Bull or Cat and Fiddle pubs.

The BBC has, from time to time, used judicious deaths in their soaps, either to draw attention from their competitors or to simply boost ratings. Was it a coincidence that one of *The Archers'* leading characters, Grace Archer, was killed, amidst much prior hyping, in a stable fire the same night as ITV was launched? Similarly did the death of John Archer under a crashing tractor happening to coincide with the Countryside March provide the editor with an excuse for her virtual exclusion of reference to the March, in startling contrast to her considerable coverage of the Gay Pride March earlier?

The Archers reflects urban prejudices about country folk

In fairness some of *The Archers'* characters are credible. There is the evil Brian Aldridge, the hen-pecked Neil Carter, the ever-suffering Mike Tucker and the odious self-obsessed David Archer with his well-deserved abominable shrew of a wife. But most of the rest are perverse caricatures and do little other than sound like actors.

The Archers reflects the countryside not as it is but as ignorant townies would prefer it to be. It serves a purpose however. For anyone who drives through Britain admiring the magnificent and beautifully cared for countryside while listening to *The Archers* can see just how wide has become the gap between urban myths and rural realities.

Notes and references

Chapter 3

1. George Allan England, *The Greatest Hunt in the World*, (1924) Montreal: Tundra, 1969, pp 40-324.
2. Quoted in Cynthia Lamson, *Bloody Decks and a Bumper Crop: The Rhetoric of Sealing Counter-protest*, St Johns: ISER, 1979, p 52.
3. Lamson, op cit, p 55.
4. Lamson, op cit, p 58.
5. Lamson, op cit, p 63.
6. See Vilfredo Pareto, 'Traite de Sociologie Generale', in *Ouevres Completes*, Tome 12, (1916) Geneva: Droz, 1968, pp 466-468.
7. Christie Davies, *Permissive Britain*, London: Pitman, 1975.
8. Ibid.
9. Pareto, op cit, pp 450-466.
10. Helmut Schoek, *Envy, a Theory of Social Behaviour*, London: Secker and Warburg, 1969.
11. Paul Mercer, *Peace of the Dead*, London: Policy Research Publications, 1986.
12. George Orwell, *The Collected Essays, Journalism, and Letters of George Orwell*, London: Secker and Warburg, 1968.
13. George Orwell, ibid, Vol 4, 'As I please', p 257.
14. Frank Parkin, *Middle Class Radicalism: The Social Basis of the British Campaign for Nuclear Disarmament*, Manchester: Manchester University Press, 1968.
15. Mercer, op cit.
16. See, Mark Neal, 'You Lucky Punters!' A Study of Gambling in Betting Shops', *Sociology* (Official Journal of the British Sociological Association), V 32, No 3, 1998, pp 581-600.

Chapter 6

1. I R Swingland, 'Commercialisation, structure and sustainability of biodiversity conservation', in M Walkey, I R Swingland and S Russell (eds), *Integrated Protected Area Management*, London: Chapman and Hall, 1998, p 394.

2. Cobham Resource Consultants, *Countryside Sports: their economic, social and conservation significance*, The Standing Conference on Countryside Sports, 1997, p 118.

Chapter 7

1. E O Wilson, *The Diversity of Life*, Harmondsworth: Penguin, 1992.
2. Council Directive on the Conservation of Natural Habitats of Wild Fauna and Flora, OJ L.206 22/7/92; Wildlife and Countryside Act, HMSO, 1981, c 69.
3. S Harrop, 'The Modern Battle on the Riverbank – Fisheries Predation and the Law, *Water Law*, Vol 8, Issue 1, 1997, pp 26-30.
4. Phelps, Allen and Harrop, *Report of a Review of Hunting With Hounds*, The Stationery Office, N0018449, 05/97.
5. Riordan and Cameron, 'The History and Contemporary Significance of the Precautionary Principle', Chapter 1 in Riordan and Cameron, *Interpreting the Precautionary Principle*, Cameron May, 1994.

Chapter 11

1. *Socialist Worker*, 28 February – 7 March, 1998.
2. *Hansard*, 28 November, 1997, Col 1216.
3. *Hansard*, 28 November, 1997, Col 1225.
4. *Hansard*, 28 November, 1997, Col 1210.

Chapter 13

1. Department of the Environment, Transport and the Regions (Welsh Office), *Access to the Open Countryside in England and Wales, a consultation paper*, p 28.
2. *Hansard*, 30 January, 1998, Col 696.
3. Dept of Environment, op cit, p 22.
    General references : *Access Campaign Bulletin*, Issue 9, March 1998; *Freedom to Roam Factsheet*, Ramblers' Association, 1997; 'Freedom with Responsibility', *Rambling Today*, Supplement, Spring 1996.

Chapter 17

1. *Combatting Drink-Driving – Next Steps*, http://www.detr.gov.uk/consult.htm
2. Written up in R F Borkenstein et al, 'The role of the drinking driver in traffic accidents', *Blutalkohol*, 11, 1994, Supplement, pp 1-132.
3. The DETR cites the analysis of Lund and Wolfe's results in P Zador, 'Alcohol-Related Relative Risk of Fatal Driver Injuries in Relation to Driver Age and Sex', *Journal of Studies on Alcohol*, 52, 4, 1991, pp 302-310.
4. *Combating Drink-Driving*, op cit.
5. Ibid.
6. *Road Accidents in Great Britain 1996 – the Casualty Report*, HMSO, 1997.
7. Ibid.
8. Rural Development Commission.

Chapter 21

1. M Pennington, 'Budgets, Bureaucrats and the Continent of Urban England', *Environmental Politics*, Vol 6, No 4, 1997, p 89.
2. J Cullingworth and V Nadin, *Town & Country Planning in Britain*, 11th edition, London: Routledge, 1994.
3. M Pennington, *Conservation and the Countryside: By Quango or Market?* London: Institute of Economic Affairs, 1996.
4. D J Reynolds, *Economics, Town Planning and Traffic*, London: Institute of Economic Affairs, 1966.
5. A W Evans, *No Room, No Room!* Occasional Paper 79, London: Institute of Economic Affairs, 1988, p 83.
6. P Hall et al, *The Continent of Urban England*, London: Allen & Unwin, 1973.
7. A W Evans, 'Rabbit Hutches on Postage Stamps', *Urban Studies*, Vol 28, No 6, 1991, pp 853-870.
8. J Herrington, *The Outer City*, London: Paul Chapman, 1984; DoE, *Green Belts*, London: HMSO, 1993; J Simmie, *Planning at the Crossroads*, London: UCL Press, 1993.
9. Pennington, 1996, op cit.

Chapter 22

1. Action with Communities in Rural England (ACRE).
2. NFU Electronic Publications *The Issues: Questions and Answers*.
3. NFU Electronic Publications *Environment*.
4. NFU Electronic Publications *The Issues: Questions and Answers*.
5. Ibid.
6. NFU Electronic Publications *Environment*.

Chapter 27

1. *The Daily Telegraph*, 7 April, 1998.
2. *Farming income* is the main official measure of income by MAFF. It is defined as 'the return to farmers and their spouses for their labour, management skills and own capital invested (excluding land) after providing for depreciation'.
3. A study by Bellerby found that the worldwide average ratio of farmers' 'incentive income' (roughly equivalent to entrepreneurial income) in agriculture to that outside was 55 per cent. J R Bellerby, *Agriculture and Industry: Relative Income*, London: Macmillan, 1956.
4. See for example, OECD, *Agricultural Polices, Markets and Trade: Monitoring and Outlook 1993*, Paris: OECD, 1993; World Bank, *World Development Report*, Oxford: OUP, 1986; R W Howarth, *Agricultural Support in Western Europe*, Research Monograph 25, London: Institute of Economic Affairs, 1971.
5. See for example, A E Buckwell et al, *The Cost of the Common Agricultural Policy*, London: Croom Helm, 1980; J K Bowers and P Cheshire, *Agriculture, the Countryside and Land Use*, London: Methuen, 1983; A Matthews, *The*

CAP and the Less Developed Countries, Dublin: Gill and Macmillan/Trocaire, 1985.

6. D R Harvey, *Farming Without the Government: What Would It Be Like?* Agricola Paper No 87/2, Wye College, University of London, 1987.

7. See J J North, 'Land Use for Food Production 2015', *Journal of the Royal Agricultural Society of England*, Vol 148, 1987.

8. D G Johnson, *World Agriculture in Disarray* (2nd edtn), London: Macmillan, 1991.

General references: B Hill, *Farm Incomes, Wealth and Agricultural Policy*, Aldershot: Avebury, 1989; R W Howarth, *Farming for Farmers? A Critique of Agricultural Support Policy* (2nd edtn), Hobart Paperback 20 (and hardback), London: Institute of Economic Affairs, 1990; R W Howarth, 'The Common Agricultural Policy', in P Minford (ed), *The Cost of Europe*, Manchester: Manchester University Press, 1992; MAFF, *Agriculture in the United Kingdom 1997* (and previous issues), London: The Stationery Office, 1998; MAFF, *Farm Incomes in the United Kingdom 1996* (and previous issues), London: HMSO, 1996.

Chapter 29

1. *Sunday Times Magazine*, 5 April, 1998.

Chapter 30

1. Tacitus, *The Agricola* and *The Germania*, translated by H Mattingly, Harmondsworth: Penguin Books, 1964, p 114.

2. Ibid, p 117.

3. Peta Buscombe, *The Reformer* (Journal of One Nation Conservatism), Spring 1998, p 5.

SOME PUBLICATIONS
FROM THE SOCIAL AFFAIRS UNIT

...on virtue and personal responsibility

THE LOSS OF VIRTUE
moral confusion and social disorder in Britain and America

edited by Digby Anderson

A NATIONAL REVIEW BOOK

ISBN 0 907631 50 9   £15.95

THIS WILL HURT
the restoration of virtue and civic order

edited by Digby Anderson

A NATIONAL REVIEW BOOK

ISBN 0 907631 63 0   £15.95

GENTILITY RECALLED
'mere' manners and the making of social order

edited by Digby Anderson

Published in co-operation with the
Acton Institute for the Study of Religion and Liberty

ISBN 0 907631 66 5   £15.95

LOYALTY MISPLACED
misdirected virtue and social disintegration

edited by Gerald Frost

ISBN 0 907631 70 3   £12.95

FAKING IT
the sentimentalisation of modern society

edited by Digby Anderson & Peter Mullen

ISBN 0 907631 75 4   £15.95

COME BACK MISS NIGHTINGALE
trends in professions today

edited by Digby Anderson

ISBN 0 907631 79 7   £11.95

On health and lifestyle...

A Code of Ethics for Health Promotion
Michael Kelly
RESEARCH REPORT 23
ISBN 0 907631 68 1 £5.00

The Death of Humane Medicine and the Rise of Coercive Healthism
Petr Skrabanek
ISBN 0 907631 59 2 £12.95

Take a Little Wine –or Beer or Whisky – for Your Stomach's Sake
Digby Anderson
ISBN 0 907631 60 6 £5.00

A New Diet of Reason: healthy eating and government policy 1985-1995
David Conning
ISBN 0 907631 64 9 £5.00

Health, Lifestyle and Environment: countering the Panic
Published in co-operation with the Manhattan Institute
ISBN 0 907631 44 4 £9.95

A Diet of Reason: sense and nonsense in the healthy eating debate
edited by Digby Anderson
Casebound:ISBN 0 907631 26 6 £9.95
Paperback:ISBN 0 907631 22 3 £5.95

Drinking to Your Health: the allegations and the evidence
edited by Digby Anderson
ISBN 0 907631 37 1 £14.95

On education and training...

A Ballon Waiting to be Burst? Pseudomanagement training
Stephen Williams
RESEARCH REPORT 22
ISBN 0 907631 67 3 £5.00

Educational Achievement in Japan: lessons for the west
Richard Lynn
Published in co-operation with the Macmillan Press
ISBN 0 333 44532 5 £8.95

The Wayward Curriculum: a cause for parents' concern?
edited by Dennis O'Keeffe
ISBN 0 907631 19 3 £9.95

Schooling for British Muslims: integrated, opted out or denominational?
Mervyn Hiskett
RESEARCH REPORT 12
ISBN 0 907631 33 9 £4.50

Trespassing? Businessmen's views on the education system
Michael Brophy et al
ISBN 0 907631 11 8 £2.95

Educated for employment?
Digby Anderson et al
ISBN 0 907631 03 7 £2.65

The Pied Pipers of Education
Antony Flew et al
ISBN 0 907631 02 9 £2.65

Detecting Bad Schools: a guide for normal parents
Digby Anderson
ISBN 0 907631 04 5 £1.00

On economic and corporate affairs...

When is a cat fat?
A critical examination of executive remuneration
Elaine Sternberg
RESEARCH REPORT 28
ISBN 0 907631 82 7   £5.00

Stakeholding:
betraying the corporation's objectives
Elaine Sternberg
RESEARCH REPORT 27
ISBN 0 907631 80 0   £6.00

Corporate Irresponsibility:
is business appeasing anti-business activists?
Robert Halfon
RESEARCH REPORT 26
ISBN 0 907631 78 9   £5.00

No Man Can Serve Two Masters:
shareholders versus stakeholders in the governance of companies
Joseph F Johnston
RESEARCH REPORT 25
ISBN 0 907631 76 2   £6.00

The Corporation Under Siege:
exposing the devices used by activists and regulators in the non-risk society
Mark Neal & Christie Davies
ISBN 0 907631 77 0   £9.95

The Secret of the Miracle Economy:
different national attitudes to competitiveness and money
Richard Lynn
ISBN 0 907631 41 X   £8.95

On consumer affairs...

What has 'Ethical Investment' to do with Ethics?
Digby Anderson et al
RESEARCH REPORT 21
ISBN 0 907631 65 7   £5.00

Keeping Cures from Patients:
the perverse effects of pharmaceutical regulations
Mark Neal
ISBN 0 907631 62 2   £5.00

False Economies:
the true cost of 'cheap' drugs
Diane B Fairweather & Ian Hindmarch
ISBN 0 907631 61 4   £5.00

Reaching for the counter. The new child consumers:
regulation or education?
Adrian Furnham
ISBN 0 907631 54 1   £7.50

Risk, Health and the Consumer
James McCormick & Digby Anderson
ISBN 0 907631 47 9   £3.50

Advertising Bans: administrative decisions or matters of principle?
John Gray
ISBN 0 907631 43 6   £4.00
Also available in Spanish translation

Advertising Bans:
consequences for consumers
Mark Bentley & Mai Fyfield
ISBN 0 907631 45 2   £4.00

Biotechnology Regulation:
the unacceptable costs of excessive caution
Henry I Miller
RISK CONTROVERSIES 8
ISBN 0 907631 69 X   £5.00

On the welfare state...

A Phantom Carnage:
the myth that low income kills
James Le Fanu
RESEARCH REPORT 17
ISBN 0 907631 51 7 £5.00

Magic in the Surgery. Counselling in the NHS:
a licensed state friendship service
Myles Harris
RESEARCH REPORT 20
ISBN 0 907631 56 8 £5.00

Popular Attitudes to State Welfare Services:
a growing demand for alternatives?
Peter Saunders & Colin Harris
RESEARCH REPORT 11
ISBN 0 907631 30 4 £3.00

Breaking the Spell of the Welfare State
Digby Anderson, June Lait & David Marsland
ISBN 0 907631 00 2 £2.65

The Megaphone Solution:
government attempts to cure social problems with mass media campaigns
Digby Anderson
RESEARCH REPORT 9
ISBN 0 907631 28 2 £3.00

On family matters...

Families in Dreamland:
challenging the new consensus for state childcare
Patricia Morgan
RESEARCH REPORT 15
ISBN 0 907631 48 7 £4.00

The Unmentionable Face of Poverty:
domestic incompetence, improvidence and male irresponsibility in low income families
Digby Anderson
ISBN 0 907631 42 8 £4.00

Finding Fault in Divorce
George Brown
MORAL ASPECTS OF SOCIAL PROBLEMS 2
ISBN 0 907631 35 5 £3.50

Full Circle: bringing up children in the post-permissive society
edited by Digby Anderson
ISBN 0 9076331 29 0 £8.95

Denying Homes to Black Children:
Britain's new race adoption policies
David Dale
RESEARCH REPORT 8
ISBN 0 907631 32 1 £3.50

On moral and social issues...

Why Social Policy Cannot be Morally Neutral:
the current confusion about pluralism
Basil Mitchell
ISBN 0 907631 35 5 £3.50

Self-Improvement and Social Action
Antony Flew
ISBN 0 907631 36 3 £3.50

The Kindness that Kills:
the churches' simplistic response to complex social issues
edited by Digby Anderson
Commissioned by the SAU
and published by SPCK
ISBN 0 281 04096 6 £3.95

Wealth and Poverty:
a Jewish analysis
Jonathan Sacks
ISBN 0 907631 15 0 £2.00

The Bible, Justice and the Culture of Poverty:
emotive calls to action versus rational analysis
Irving Hexham
ISBN 0 907631 16 9 £2.00

The Philosophy of Poverty:
Good Samaritans or Procrusteans?
Antony Flew
ISBN 0 907631 17 7 £2.00

The Christian Response to Poverty:
working with God's economic laws
James Sadowsky
ISBN 0 907621 18 5 £2.00

Do Animals Have Rights?
Tibor Machan
ISBN 0 907631 40 1 £3.50

On the environment and housing...

NonSense About Nature
Anthony O'Hear
RISK CONTROVERSIES 9
ISBN 0 907631 72 X £5.00

Environmental Alarums:
a medical audit of environmental damage to human health
James Le Fanu
RISK CONTROVERSIES 3
ISBN 0 907631 57 6 £5.00

After Government Failure?
D R Denman
ISBN 0 907631 24 X £2.50

Planning Fails the Inner Cities
R N Goodchild & D R Denman
ISBN 0 907631 25 8 £2.50

Caring for the Countryside:
public dependence on private interest
Barry Bracewell-Milnes
ISBN 0 907631 27 4 £2.50

Home Truths:
essays on housing
Barbara Robson et al
ISBN 0 907631 05 3 £2.95

Asian Housing in Britain
Jon Davies
RESEARCH REPORT 6
ISBN 0 907631 13 4 £2.00

On the United Nations...

Chattering International:
how Unicef fails the world's poorest
children
James Le Fanu
RESEARCH REPORT 19
ISBN 0 907631 53 3 £5.00

Who Benefits from WHO?
The decline of the World Health
Organization
Robert D Tollison & Richard E Wagner
RESEARCH REPORT 18
ISBN 0 907631 55 X £5.00

Who Needs WHO? Three views on
the World Health Organization's
dietary guidelines
*Petr Skrabanek, Mike Gibney & James
Le Fanu*
RESEARCH REPORT 16
ISBN 0 907631 49 £5.00

And...

Scot-Free:
how England would fare without
Scotland
*Simon Green, Robert Davies & Michael
Mosbacher*
RESEARCH REPORT 30
ISBN 0 907631 86 X £6.00

The British Woman Today:
A qualitative survey of the images
in women's magazines
*Edited by Digby Anderson & Michael
Mosbacher*
ISBN 0 907631 74 6 £7.50

The Silencing of Society:
the true cost of the lust for news
Kenneth Minogue
ISBN 0 907631 71 8 £7.50

The Case as yet Unheard:
hereditary peers and the hereditary
principle
Richard D North
RESEARCH REPORT 29
ISBN 0 907631 85 1 £6.00

Unwelcome Truths:
Edmund Burke on today's political
conceits
Ian Crowe
RESEARCH REPORT 24
ISBN 0 907631 71 1 £5.00

Extra Dry: columns in The Times
Digby Anderson
ISBN 0 907631 12 6 £2.95

The Social Affairs Unit

The SAU is an independent research and educational trust committed to the promotion of lively and wide-ranging debate on social affairs. Its authors — over 200 — have analyzed the factors which make for a free and orderly society in which enterprise can flourish. It is committed to international co-operation in ideas: eg *The Loss of Virtue* and *This Will Hurt* published as **National Review Books**, *Gentility Recalled* published in co-operation with the Acton Institute and joint Anglo-European projects on food and alcohol policy. Current areas of work include consumer affairs, the critical appraisal of welfare and public spending and problems of freedom and personal responsibility.

The Unit's impact and funding

The Times writes:
The Social Affairs Unit is famous for driving its coach and horses through the liberal consensus, scattering intellectual picket lines as it goes. It is equally famous for raising questions which strike most people most of the time as too dangerous or too difficult to think about.

To maintain its independence, the Unit is funded by a wide range of foundations and trusts, sales of its publications and corporate donations from highly diverse sectors. It has received support from over 100 sources. The SAU is registered as an educational charity, number 281530.

The Social Affairs Unit
Suite 5/6 1st Floor
Morley House
Regent Street
London W1R 5AB
www.socialaffairsunit.org.uk